D0926998

# THE HORSE IN VIRGINIA

# The Horse in Virginia

## AN ILLUSTRATED HISTORY

*Julie A. Campbell*

University of Virginia Press
CHARLOTTESVILLE AND LONDON

University of Virginia Press

Printed in China on acid-free paper

*First published 2010*

9 8 7 6 5 4 3 2 1

Library of Congress Cataloging-in-Publication Data

Campbell, Julie A., 1957–
The horse in Virginia : an illustrated history / Julie A. Campbell.
p. cm.
Includes bibliographical references and index.
ISBN 978-0-8139-2816-6 (cloth : alk. paper)
1. Horses—Virginia—History. I. Title.
SF284.U5C36 2009
636.1009755—dc22 2008050878

*Title spread:* Robert Llewellyn
Illustration credits, page 296

CONTENTS

To follow the history of the state's horses as they spread across the Old Dominion, it is helpful to know how the state looks on a map and how we refer to its parts. Virginia has five geographic regions. First comes the Tidewater, in the east, the coastal plain from the Atlantic Ocean to the fall line—the place where the rivers reveal a tumult of waterfalls and thus block watercraft from traveling any farther west. Four of the state's great rivers, going from north to south, are the Potomac, Rappahannock, York, and James. They flow roughly west to east, emptying into Chesapeake Bay. Virginians call the area of the Tidewater between the Rappahannock and the Potomac, the Northern Neck. The terms "Middle Peninsula" and "Middle Neck" refer to the region between the Rappahannock and York. The Peninsula is the area between the York and James; the Eastern Shore lies between Chesapeake Bay and the Atlantic Ocean.

From the fall line west to the Blue Ridge Mountains is the second region, a land of soft, rounded hills called the Piedmont. Beyond the third region, the Blue Ridge, lies the fourth, the great Valley of Virginia, which rolls down the western side of the state from Pennsylvania into Tennessee. The fifth region, the Allegheny Mountains, cradles the other side of the Valley, forming a rough and rocky border with West Virginia (which was part of Virginia until 1863).

Other named areas are the Southside, a chunk of territory east of the Blue Ridge, south of the James River, and north of the border with North Carolina. The term usually means the southernmost counties like Lunenburg, Mecklenburg, Brunswick, and so on, and those east of the city of Danville. Southwest Virginia is west of the Blue Ridge and south of the city of Roanoke. Northern Virginia means the communities curving around Washington, D.C., to the south and west. Over the centuries, horses would live in virtually every region, area, neighborhood, and community.

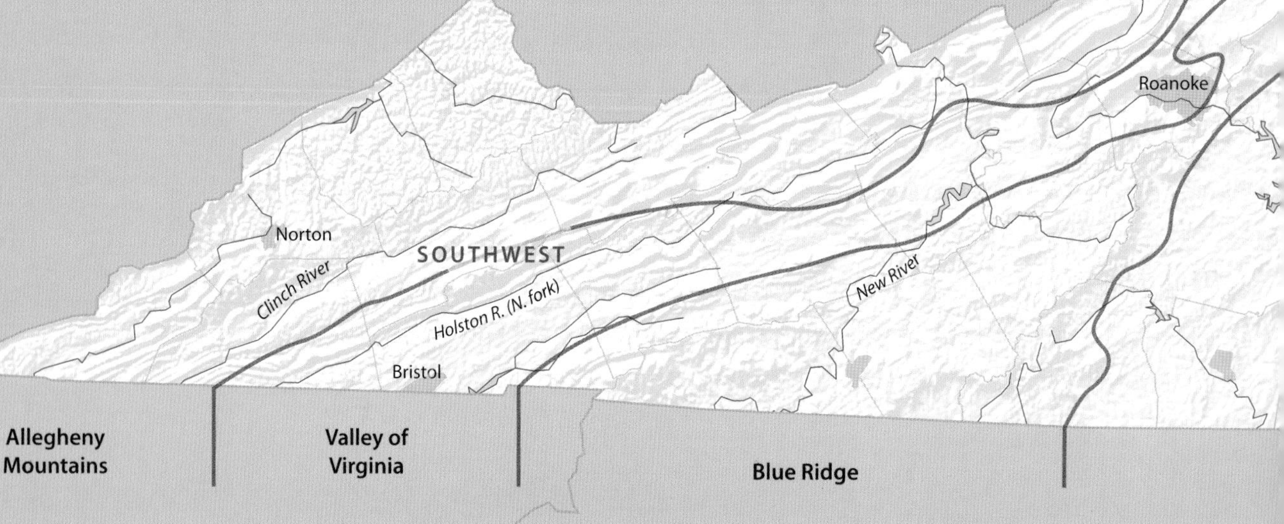

Winchester
SHENANDOAH VALLEY
NORTHERN VIRGINIA
Fairfax
Harrisonburg
Rapidan R.
Fredericksburg
Potomac R.
Assateague Island
Chincoteague
NORTHERN NECK
Rappahannock R.
Charlottesville
South Anna R.
MIDDLE NECK
Mattaponi R.
Pamunkey R.
EASTERN SHORE
THE PENINSULA
York R.
James R.
Richmond
Appomattox R.
Lynchburg
Petersburg
Blackwater R.
James R.
SOUTHSIDE
Roanoke R.
Nottoway R.
Norfolk
nville
Tidewater
Piedmont

# THE HORSE IN VIRGINIA

George Washington's
riding crop.

# 1607–1783

## THE ADMIRABLE LITTLE VIRGINIA HORSE

*That fondness for horses . . . was peculiar to the Virginians of all stations.*
—Thomas Anburey, 1779

To understand the horse's place in the heart and history of Virginia, there is no better way to begin than with George Washington, first president of the United States. At Washington's death in 1799, Henry "Light Horse Harry" Lee, a cavalryman of the Revolutionary War, hailed him as "first in war, first in peace, and first in the hearts of his countrymen." In 1814, Thomas Jefferson, the third president of the United States, added another superlative: "The most graceful figure that could be seen on horseback."[1]

Washington (1732–1799) grew up in the Northern Neck, the coastal plain between the Rappahannock and Potomac rivers. The first Virginia member of the Washington family had arrived from England in 1675, just sixty-eight years after the founding of Jamestown, the first English settlement. As an adult, George lived on his inherited plantation, Mount Vernon, near Alexandria. The plantation comprised five properties: River Farm, Muddy Hole Farm, Dogue Run, Union Farm, and the Mansion House at Mount Vernon. A military man and a politician, he served in the House of Burgesses and at the revolutionary conventions before taking the helm of the Continental Army during the Revolutionary War. In that role he oversaw the surrender of Lord Cornwallis, the British commander, at Yorktown. Washington ran the Constitutional Convention of 1787 and then served two terms as the first president of the United States, from 1789 to 1797.

Americans of the time knew the public side of Washington. Virginians knew the side that loved to spend hours cantering over his farm, bought books about equine diseases from England, hunted foxes with his own pack of hounds, and tried to save the life of a horse with a broken leg.[2]

Washington, like other young men of his time and station, grew up on horseback. A family story held that as a teenager, urged on by friends, he struggled to ride a wild, unmanageable horse, which fell over dead during the fracas. Aside from that unpleasant episode, all accounts point to a knowledgeable and humane horseman who broke and trained his own mounts.[3]

A horse-racing aficionado, Washington attended meets wherever his pursuits might take him—Annapolis, Philadelphia, Williamsburg—sometimes watching his own horses on the track. In 1762, he bred some of his mares, including an "English bay," to a Thoroughbred stallion named Ariel from the well-known Belair Stud in Maryland. Always on the lookout for a good horse, even while commanding the Continental Army, in 1781 he asked his cousin Lund Washington, who managed the plantation while he was away, to trade for a new horse that his wife, Martha, desired. The animal was brother to a carriage horse he already owned, so Washington advised his cousin to go ahead with the acquisition if it was "as handsome, and as fine a horse as represented, and the colour of the set she drives." Writing from the battlefield, he asked Lund for news of the equine population at Mount Vernon, and he quietly purchased rundown army mares (he preferred bays) to use as broodmares there. Washington expected his mares to work on the farm as well as to produce foals.[4]

Washington understood the harsh realities of war, but he still hated to watch the suffering of men or horses. He wanted the artillery horses to be used only for pulling cannon and to be well shod, and he threatened with punishment anyone using them otherwise. He ordered wagon masters to pay more attention to the care and feeding of horses, for many animals had foundered and died. "Any future negligence in this matter," he wrote, "will most assuredly produce examples of severity." In March 1778, he wrote of the desperate conditions at Valley Forge during the preceding winter, when the starving, bedraggled army had camped in Pennsylvania fields. "Could the poor Horses tell their tale, it would be in a strain still more lamentable, as numbers have actually died from pure want."[5]

During the war, Washington rode several mounts, including a chestnut horse, Nelson, a gift from Thomas Nelson Jr., governor of Virginia. In August 1778, he wrote the governor from the encampment at White Plains, New York: "With what propriety can I deprive you of a valuable, and favourite Horse? You have pressed me once, nay twice, to accept him as a gift; as a proof of my sincere attachment to, and friendship for you, I obey." Later that year he did some horse trading with Henry Lee, took a foundered horse off duty, and made plans to send two mares to Mount Vernon.

In September 1779, he asked Colonel Alexander Spotswood if he'd been able to scare up another mount for him, as none of his were currently of use. "Bleu-skin" (also spelled Blueskin), his dark gray horse who had come from the Dulany family, of Loudoun County, was out of service due to an injury; "the Sorrel"—presumably Nelson—also was ailing; and a mare was in foal. He asked for a bigger horse to carry his large frame and noted his preference for "a good bay." "I will take the horse . . . as Men take their Wives," he told Spotswood, "better for worse; and if he should prove a jade and go limping on; I must do as they are obliged to do, submit to the bargain." At Yorktown in 1781, a poised Washington sat on Nelson as he watched the British lay down their arms.[6]

When Washington returned to Mount Vernon after the war, Nelson and Blueskin in tow and ready for retirement, he found that the quality of horses had declined in his absence. To give his equine population a boost, he bought a five-year-old half-Arabian stallion named Magnolio (also spelled Magnolia) for £500 from the estate of his stepson, John Parke Custis, who had died in 1781. The sixteen-hand chestnut son of a stallion named Ranger (also known as Lindsay's Arabian) may have had special quarters his new owner planned for him near the greenhouse. He lived at Mount Vernon until 1788, when Washington exchanged him with Henry Lee for five thousand acres in Kentucky. Ever practical, Washington had decided that Magnolio's earnings from mating with other owners' mares did not offset the cost of his room and board.[7]

By 1785, Washington owned 130 horses for pulling, riding, and breeding. He may have supplemented the working stock of Mount Vernon with Conestoga horses, large, heavy draft animals of Dutch descent from

*The Surrender of Lord Cornwallis at Yorktown,* John Trumbull. George Washington and his mount are near the American flag *(center right, background).* Washington posed on horseback for the artist several years after the event. The painting hangs in the Rotunda of the U.S. Capitol.

Lancaster, Pennsylvania. He took good care of his own horses. When a prized wagon horse, Jolly, broke his right foreleg, Washington ordered him suspended in a sling to see if he would heal. As horses often do, Jolly struggled so much that he further injured himself, making recovery all but impossible. Washington had no choice but to order him put out of his misery.[8]

Combining his architectural and equine interests, Washington designed an innovative sixteen-sided treading barn. Wheat was usually threshed outside, with horses or people trampling it to separate out the grain. In his version, Washington included an area on the upper level of the barn so that horses could trample the wheat indoors, and the grain would fall through cracks onto the floor below, thus preserving the grain and making it easier to store and transport. (Mount Vernon has a replica of the barn today, and horses do the job in the exact same way that Washington's horses did more than two hundred years ago.)[9]

When he wasn't supervising livestock or inspecting crops, Washington reveled in the sport of foxhunting. He had his own kennel of hounds, and after the Revolution, the Marquis de Lafayette, the French nobleman who had fought with the Americans, gave him French hounds. Washington hunted at least three times a week, wearing a "true sporting costume, of blue coat, scarlet waistcoat, buckskin breeches, top boots, velvet cap," and often captured foxes alive in order to set them loose and try again. His slave William "Billy" Lee usually served as huntsman, riding a good jumper named Chinkling. One early December morning in 1785, Washington went "a hunting" with nephew George Augustine Washington, cousin Lund Washington, secretary William Shaw, and neighbor William Peake. They rode until midmorning before spotting a fox and sending eight hounds after it for an hour. "They put him up a fresh [a stream] and in about 50 minutes killed [him] up in an open field . . . every rider & every Dog being present at the death," Washington recorded in his diary. He sometimes rode Blueskin to the hounds, "a fine but fiery animal," according to his step-grandson Wash Custis. After the 1787 Constitutional Convention, however, Washington gave away his hounds and gave up foxhunting. The demands of the presidency and public life left him no time for the hunt.[10]

At the time of his death in 1799, Washington owned more than thirty horses, and twice that many mules and donkeys, at his five properties. The horses at the farms were work animals, but at the house lived coach horses, riding horses, one "steed" (a stallion, perhaps), and one brood-

Horses in the treading barn, re-created in the late twentieth century at Mount Vernon, George Washington's Virginia home.

mare. He gave the use of all the horses and other livestock to his wife but specified that some should be sold; in March 1800, a sale of eighteen horses and donkeys brought $1,514.83. In 1802, after Martha Washington's passing, the estate sold off other horses, including animals named Nancy, Poppett, Liberty, and Polly. Wash Custis bought his step-grandfather's riding horse.[11]

Long after Washington was gone, people remembered his way with a horse. A tall, athletic, well-dressed man, he liked a strong and able mount. He pronounced white horses his favorites in appearance, followed by dapple grey, dark bay, chestnut, and black. Whether on hunting field, battlefield, or wheat field, the handsome equestrian sat calmly astride a fine, blooded horse, conveying his wishes to his mount in a subtle manner. "He rode, as he did everything else, with ease, elegance, and with power," said Wash Custis. His "perfect and sinewy frame . . . gave him such a surpassing grip with his knees, that a horse might as soon disencumber itself of the saddle as of such a rider." The Marquis de Chastellux, another French officer, once rode a horse that Washington had trained himself. "I found the horse as good as he was handsome, but

Artists of subsequent centuries often depicted Washington on horseback: *Washington Receiving a Salute on the Field of Trenton,* engraving for the Kendall Bank Note Company, New York, ca. 1860 *(left); Washington Crossing the Delaware,* etching ca. 1833 *(right).*

above all, perfectly well broken and well trained, having a good mouth, easy in hand, and stopping short in gallop without bearing the bit." The marquis called Washington "a very excellent and bold horseman, leaping the highest fences, and going extremely quick, without standing upon his stirrups, bearing on the bridle, or letting his horse run wild."

Thomas Jefferson added to his 1814 accolade about George Washington one more: "The best horseman of his age."[12] From one Virginian to another, it was the supreme compliment.

Nearly two centuries separate the arrival of the first modern horses in Virginia from George Washington's death. As the life of that quintessential Virginian shows, the horse became an inextricable part of life and culture during the state's days as an English colony, as a new country in revolt against the parent civilization, and as a young republic. It still is. Men, women, Indian, black, white—all Virginians' lives have intertwined with the lives of horses, whether in the most immediate and personal way, say as an amateur owner or professional rider; or in the most remote and indirect manner, perhaps as a taxpayer who benefits from the money the horse business brings to the state. Owing to this vast history and to the overwhelming numbers of memorable horses and important horsewomen and horsemen that have graced Virginia, this book must, by necessity, look at only a relative handful.

For the more than four centuries of the state's existence, the horse's status has ebbed and flowed. Virginians' love of the horse, however, has stayed constant.

## BEARINGS

In 1609, the first Virginia horses trotted gratefully off the ship that had borne them across the Atlantic Ocean to Jamestown. Their owners, the English colonists of the Virginia Company, optimistically thought their new home encompassed much of the present-day United States, plus part of Canada. Wars and purchases and negotiations would change that claim, and Virginia's territory eventually came to resemble the 40,598-square-mile, lopsided triangle we know today.

At Jamestown's settlement in 1607, at least thirteen thousand native people occupied a territory of six thousand square miles in the Tidewater between the James and Potomac rivers. The population encompassed thirty groups, such as the Accomac, Chickahominy, and Pamunkey, who spoke the Algonquian language, pledged their fealty to a leader named Powhatan, and are remembered collectively by his name. Over in the Piedmont lived the Manahoac, Monacan, Occaneechi, Saponi, and Tutelo Indians, who spoke Siouan. The Meherrins and Nottoways, who spoke Iroquois, lived in Southside (their names would later be given to rivers and counties). At the time of the first permanent English settlements in the early 1600s, none of the tribes owned horses, at least as far as we know. The Powhatans, with whom the Jamestown colonists had the most dealings, certainly did not, or the English chroniclers would have written it down. It is possible, however, that the tribes from outside the Tidewater may have heard of horses, or may have even seen the strange new creatures during their travels. If so, the animals' owners came from another European country.[13]

## BEGINNINGS

Although Virginia can claim such significant American firsts as permanent English settlements and presidents, it must tip its hat to Spain when it comes to the first horses. By the early sixteenth century, when Spanish explorers arrived on the continent, the small prehistoric horses dubbed *Eohippus, Mesohippus, Miohippus,* and *Merychippus,* which ranged in height from fourteen to thirty inches, had been gone from North America for millions of years; the twelve-hand *Pliohippus* or *Equus caballus,* which we would easily recognize as a horse today, had made its departure thousands of years earlier.[14] (Horses' heights are measured at the top of their withers, or shoulders; one hand equals four inches, so a twelve-hand animal stands forty-eight inches, or four feet, at the shoulder.) Spain was intent on colonizing, exploring, finding riches, and spreading Christianity; to accomplish all of this, it needed horses.

In 1539, one of several expeditions arrived in Florida with 237 Spanish horses and the explorer Hernando de Soto, who also brought more than seven hundred people. They came as close to Virginia as western South Carolina and eastern Tennessee—maybe a Saponi Indian from southwestern Virginia spotted them—but, as far as is known, the horses never set a hoof in the Old Dominion. Four years later, de Soto was dead. He had lost more than half his people and all of his horses. Spanish settlements hung on in the Southeast and Southwest, however, and horses thrived in those parts of the continent.[15]

The Spanish animals comprised a small array of breeds: Andalusian, Asturian (or Asturçon), Galician, Garrano, Jennet, and Sorraia. Over the preceding centuries they had come to possess the blood of horses such as Arabians, Barbs (from North Africa), and Turks (from Turkey). The Andalusians and Jennets made especially good riding horses, as did the Asturians, small horses that ambled—a swift, four-beat walk in which the horse moved its lateral pairs of legs almost at the same time, making for a comfortable, flowing ride. Some of them also paced instead of trotted, moving their lateral pairs of legs at the same time, rather than their diagonal pairs. The conquistadors probably used the Galicians, Garranos, and Sorraias as pack animals. The Andalusians worked well around cattle.[16]

Most horsemen admired the Spanish horse because of its "quick, easy walk on springing pasterns, the cat-like adaptability to a broken terrain, and the impression of docile beauty and strength," wrote Fairfax Harrison, a renowned twentieth-century scholar of Virginia horses, as well as "the luminous intelligent eye, the sensitive mouth, the deep shoulder, the short head and the high crest." The southeastern tribes of Indians who lived near the Spanish settlements, the Cherokees and Chickasaws especially, warmed up to the new animals. Over the sixteenth century, they became expert breeders of the small (thirteen to fourteen hands), hardy, muscular horses.[17]

## HOBBY HORSES, GALLOWAYS, AND CHICKASAWS

While Spanish humans and horses traveled over a good portion of the modern United States, the English made their own plans for the New World. In 1607, the first permanent settlement took root at Jamestown. The first British horses, seven in all (probably six mares and one stallion), arrived in August 1609 aboard a ship called the *Blessing*, courtesy of the Virginia Company. The settlers intended to ride them, load them with supplies, and raise still more horses. Such basic intentions vanished in the snow and ice of the dreadful winter of 1609–10, when the colonists ran out of food. During what they later called the Starving Time, they ate their cats, dogs, and horses, right down to their hides. No horses, and few people, survived.[18]

Following the inauspicious debut of their unfortunate comrades, seventeen British horses arrived with Sir Thomas Dale in the spring of 1611. The Virginia Company encouraged their importation, for the settlers needed work animals. In the absence of horses or oxen, colonists tilled fields themselves, using hoes instead of plows. In 1613, Deputy Governor Samuel Argall raided French settlements in Nova Scotia and appropriated a number of trotting and pacing horses for use back in Virginia. Horses trickled in a handful or two at a time, as in 1620, when Major Daniel Gookin, of Newport News, imported twenty Irish mares. By 1649, approximately two hundred horses lived in Virginia, and by the end of the century, enough horses populated the colony to cause the authorities to prohibit further importation for the time being.[19]

Most of the imported British horses of the seventeenth century were Irish Hobbies and Scottish Galloways. At twelve or thirteen hands, both would be considered large ponies by today's standards. The Hobbies had developed from imported Spanish Asturians; called "palfreys," meaning a gentle saddle horse, they became favored mounts of women, who liked their small size and smooth gaits. The Irish named them the Hobby and made them into a breed. A typical specimen was "a prety fine Horse . . . tender mouthed, nimble, light, pleasant, and apt to be taught," wrote an observer named Thomas Blunderville in 1565, "and for the most part they be amblers, and therefore verie meete for the saddle." Their modern counterparts are Irish Connemara ponies. The Galloways, like the

Most horses naturally walk, trot, canter, and gallop, with several variations.

## GAITS

AMBLE—Peculiar to horses of the seventeenth and eighteenth centuries, a quick, four-beat walk in which the horse moved its lateral pairs of legs almost at the same time. Riders found it quite comfortable and easy.

CANTER—A slow, three-beat gait. A foreleg leads the motion of itself and the corresponding hind diagonal leg. When a horse is on the right lead, the right foreleg is out in front; left lead, left foreleg. The western version is a lope.

FOXTROT—A slow trot in which the diagonal hind foot hits the ground just before the diagonal forefoot. The horse's head nods as it goes.

The amble: Lewis Miller, an artist from Pennsylvania, depicted himself and his brother, the Reverend Charles A. Miller, of Christiansburg, on a ride through the Virginia countryside. The horses appear to be ambling—Miller depicts each animal's legs moving laterally.

GALLOP—A run. Fast, four beats, with each foot hitting the ground separately, and all four feet briefly in the air at the same time. As at the canter, a horse is on one lead or the other. Racehorses can change leads at top speed.

PACE—A version of the trot in which the pairs of legs on the same side move together.

RACK—A "fast, flashy, unnatural, four-beat gait," with each foot hitting the ground separately. "Easy on the rider but hard on the horse." Saddlebreds are famous for performing this gait.

RUNNING WALK—Slow, four beats, with the hind foot overstepping the front. Easy on horse and rider, this comfortable gait is exhibited by Tennessee Walkers, with the horse's head nodding and even its ears moving and teeth clicking. Some trainers of Tennessee Walkers encourage the animal to exaggerate the gait, occasionally using chains and irritating agents on the horses' feet.

STEPPING PACE, SLOW PACE—Four beats, with the four feet hitting the ground separately; hind and forefeet start off together but hind foot hits the ground first. A kind of walking pace for five-gaited horses.

TROT—Quick, two beats, with diagonal pairs of legs moving together; all four feet are briefly off the ground.

WALK—Slow, four beats, flat-footed.

*Source:* Ensminger, *Horses and Horsemanship,* 68–70.

*Top to bottom:* The canter; the gallop; and the rack as performed by a Saddlebred.

Many horses imported to colonial Virginia resembled these typical British workhorses of the late eighteenth century. *Haymaking,* from W. H. Pyne, *Microcosm: or, A picturesque delineation of the arts, agriculture, manufactures, & c. of Great Britain . . .*

Andalusians, possessed what Quarter Horse owners of the present call "cow sense," for their Scottish owners drove cattle with them; the Galloway's closest present descendant is the British Fell pony.[20]

They were the ideal horses for conditions in colonial Virginia. Both breeds were compact and muscular; they trundled easily along a road with a rider; and they withstood harsh weather and endured on what forage they could rustle up for themselves in field and forest. Contrary to English practice, few horses at the time could call a cozy stable home, let alone a corral with a leaf of hay tossed in now and then. "I do not believe there are better horses in the world," said a visitor to Virginia from France, Durand of Dauphiné, in 1686, "or worse treated."[21]

And they were fast. Durand of Dauphiné recorded an eigh-

teen-mile ride aboard a horse that covered the distance in two hours: "One has nothing to do but hold on." A Hobby could turn up its comfortable amble to a speedier version, and it could canter and gallop as well. Like many colonists, the wealthy Sir William Berkeley, the Virginia governor from 1642 to 1652 and from 1660 to 1677, admired the breed, and he imported Irish Hobby mares and a stallion to his Green Spring plantation near Jamestown.[22]

Toward the end of the 1600s, the distant Spanish cousins of these British horses made their way north into the Carolinas and Virginia. People called them Chickasaws for the Indians who bred and sold them. The animals also ran wild in herds and served as objects of trade, gaining renown as "handsome, active and hardy, but small; seldom exceeding thirteen hands and a half," according to an 1809 history of South Carolina. Many of these animals, including the Hobbies and Galloways, had lateral gaits and speed. From Rhode Island probably came a few Narragansett Pacers, another small, sturdy horse with a smooth, ambling gait. When all these animals met, the result was "the admirable little Virginia horse . . . not so much a degenerate descendant of the first horses imported from England as the native product of an unrecorded practice of crossing the English horse with a remote infusion of Andalusian blood, derived from the southern indians," wrote Fairfax Harrison. The cross produced "a native breed," as he called it, an animal "of spirit and small size." No matter where they came from, Virginia horses possessed a distinct set of characteristics that suited their home.[23]

## FAST TIMES IN OLD VIRGINIA

The English planters, who ruled the colony with their money and tobacco crops, brought a love of racing and fast horses from the home country. "They ride pretty sharply, a Planter's Pace is a Proverb," wrote John Clayton, a Jamestown parson, in 1688, "which is a good sharp hand gallop." A panoply of Virginians liked races too, everyone from African slaves to white indentured servants, rich men to working women, clergymen to children. Anyone could watch and cheer and wager, but only gentlemen—that is, white men with sufficient land and money—could race their own horses (and bet their own tobacco). In 1674, in fact, the officials of York County fined a tailor named James Bullocke one hundred pounds of tobacco for having the audacity to race his horse against one of his betters.[24]

The Chickasaw horse's nearly identical cousin is the Florida Cracker horse; there are few, if any, descendants of the original Chickasaw horses alive today. This modern Cracker stallion, Azeituno, has a Spanish appearance and a smooth gait that could be called an amble.

A match could be announced well ahead of time or decided on the spur of the moment, perhaps on court day or after church—or after the horses' owners had downed a tankard or two of ale in the local tavern. With the dense forests of the new land precluding long oval racetracks like those in England, the most convenient track held only two horses and stretched just a quarter of a mile on a path through the woods or down a main street.

The small, muscular Virginia horses, whether Hobby, Galloway, Chickasaw, or a mix, proved quite adept at quarter racing. Their strong hindquarters thrust them into a quick start and powered them down the straightaway in about twenty-six seconds. The competitors chose their paths by a novel colonial method—rather than flipping a coin, someone spit on a rock or a piece of wood, tossed it, and called "wet" or "dry" instead of "heads" or "tails." The jockeys circled together on their horses and gave a mutual signal to go, or a starter would shoot a gun, tap a drum, or blow a horn. Under ideal conditions, the horses made a clean start, stayed on their own paths, ran without interference, and one clearly triumphed. Ideal conditions were hard to come by, however. One jockey—the planter himself or one of his male slaves—would jump the gun; another might grab his opponent's arm or shove him off balance; a horse jostled the other or veered into the other's path; a dog could wander, accidentally or not, onto the racetrack and spook both horses; the judge at the finish line was known to claim the losing horse the winner. Under such conditions, disgruntled owners sprinted for the nearest courthouse and filed lawsuits to settle the question of the winner, the conditions, or the amounts of money or tobacco owed.[25]

## THE EIGHTEENTH CENTURY

By the eighteenth century, horse racing had an important place in Virginia. Races took place at tracks throughout the Northern Neck and the James River valley: in Henrico County at Bermuda Hundred, Malvern Hill, Varina, and Ware; in Northampton County at Smith's Field; in Northumberland County at Fairfield and Scotland; in Rappahannock County at Rappahannock Church; in Richmond County at Willoughby's Old Field; in Surry County at Devil's Field; and in Westmoreland County at Coan Race Course and Yeocomico. Most of the jockeys were enslaved African men and boys.[26]

When Virginia horses weren't pounding down a racetrack, the same versatile animals were pulling yeomen's plows and planters' fancy carriages, and ambling down a country road with silk-clad ladies or homespun housewives perched comfortably on their backs. The planters' "Saddle-Horses, though not very large, are hardy, strong, and fleet," wrote the Reverend Hugh Jones, a teacher of the time at William and Mary, "and will pace naturally and pleasantly at a prodigious rate." He also observed that Virginians "are such Lovers of Riding, that almost every ordinary Person keeps a Horse."[27]

Daniel Custis, far from ordinary as the head of a wealthy family, owned around forty horses at five properties: young and old workhorses, large and small bays, mares and colts, a stallion. Colonial women like Custis's widow, Martha Dandridge Custis Washington, relished and extolled the pleasures of riding—sidesaddle, of course, as was proper for ladies. "I was glad to hear that you had got the horse," she wrote her ailing sister, Anna Maria Dandridge Bassett, "and hope you have . . . found great benefit from riding everyday."[28]

Virginia's native tribes never developed the deep horse culture of the Plains Indians of the western United States, but not because they didn't desire horses. When the Pamunkeys (once part of the Powhatan confederation) of the 1670s allied with the English against other tribes, they were allowed to keep all plunder they obtained—*except* guns and horses, which suggests that both English and Indians valued such objects. Further, the colonists knew horses would give Indians more freedom of movement and therefore restricted their access. Nonetheless, the Pamunkeys eventually had horses, as did the upper class of the Powhatans.[29]

When William Byrd II, a prominent planter with a grand home, Westover, on the James River, surveyed the border with North Carolina in 1728, he encountered Indians who "laugh at the English, who can't stir to a next neighbor without a horse, and say that two legs are too much for such lazy people, who can't visit their next neighbor without six." Byrd and his party, however, did meet Saponis who rode horses. "The ladies bestrode their palfreys à la mode de France," he wrote (meaning astride), "but were so bashful about it that there was no persuading them to mount till they were quite out of our sight." Given the time and place, the women probably rode Chickasaw horses.[30]

A few draft horses joined the all-purpose Virginia animals hitched to plows and wagons but took their time catching on. In the 1760s, Thomas Mann Randolph (future father-in-law to one of Thomas Jefferson's daughters) had an imported Shire named Goliah—an appropriate name for a breed that can reach nineteen hands. In the 1770s, an ambitious breeder crossed a draft mare of some kind with a Thoroughbred stallion, producing a horse similar to the French Percheron, which would not arrive in Virginia for another several decades.[31]

Even the most elite Virginians would spend hours catching their horses, which roamed free in the forests, in order to ride just a few miles. Particularly skilled or adventuresome riders participated in a dubious sport called gander-pulling, in which participants galloped toward a live goose that had been hung upside down from a tree branch and attempted to grab its greased neck and decapitate it. Others used their horses to hunt foxes with hounds in an organized way, bringing yet another English equine tradition to Virginia shores.[32]

The sport took on a Virginia personality, of course. For one thing, the fox was just as likely to be the native gray, not the English red of foxhunting tradition. Marylanders reportedly had sixteen red foxes shipped to that colony from Britain in 1730; as legend has it, fifty or sixty years later their descendants scampered across a frozen Chesapeake Bay and slipped into Virginia. For a long time, Virginians used horses as transportation to follow the hounds; galloping across fields and jumping stone walls happened only now and then and were almost beside the point. One of the foremost foxhunters of the 1740s was Thomas, Sixth Lord

Fairfax, who owned millions of acres in the Northern Neck and lived in the Shenandoah Valley. When he moved to the colony from England, the hunting enthusiast arranged for his hounds to arrive before he did. Fairfax's friend, neighbor, and surveyor, George Washington, owned a pack of hounds before and after the Revolutionary War, and over in Albemarle County, Thomas Walker—a botanist, physician, and explorer—kept his Castle Hill hounds.[33]

The other desirable English tradition was horse racing, and by the early 1700s some Virginians had enough tobacco-funded resources to own horses for that purpose alone. They called on their ancestral homeland to help them crystallize the Virginia racehorse into an upper class of its own, and quarter-mile racing and its speedy horses became ever more popular and entrenched in the culture of the colony.

## RACING TO VIRGINIA

British racing fans had been cheering on their favorite horses long before any ship set sail for Virginia. Enthusiasts included the sixteenth-century monarch Henry VIII, who established facilities for his racehorses at Hampton Court, and seventeenth-century kings James I, Charles I, and Charles II, who patronized the great race meets at Newmarket and bestowed prizes called "plates" on the winners. Such royal endorsements led to racing's nickname: the Sport of Kings. The races usually consisted of two horses running three or four heats of two or four miles. Crowds streamed in from the surrounding cities, villages, and countryside, watching the excitement from the backs of their horses or the seats of their carriages.[34]

British racehorses derived their speed, stamina, and all-around quality from matings of the native Galloways and Hobbies (which already had Spanish blood) with imported horses from Spain (Andalusians and Jennets), northern Africa (Barbs), and Syria and Turkey (Turkmenes). The Hobbies moved with the comfortable lateral gaits, as did many of the Turks and Barbs, and therefore so did a good number of racehorses when they weren't in a flat-out run.[35]

Between 1690 and 1730, three outstanding stallions from exotic shores elevated the English racing type into a breed that came to dominate Virginia and much of the American horse world: the Thoroughbred. The first of the trio, the Byerley Turk, arrived in England around 1690. He was probably a breed called Akhal-Teke from Turkmenistan.

His owner, Robert Byerley, either captured the dark brown stallion during a battle or bought him from a Dutch officer who had seized the horse during the Siege of Vienna; he may have ridden him at the Battle of the Boyne in Ireland in 1690. However he fell into Byerley's hands, the stallion wound up in England, first in County Durham and then in Yorkshire, a center of racehorse breeding. His sons and grandsons sired fine horses that won lots of races and money and kept up the family name.

The second horse, the Darley Arabian, was bought by Thomas Darley in Syria in 1704. (Englishmen of the time used the term "Arabian" whether they meant Arabian, Moroccan, Persian, Syrian, Turkish, and so on.) Darley presented the horse to his brother, who put it to stud in Yorkshire. One of the Darley Arabian's mates was an English mare of Arabian breeding, Betty Leedes, and together they produced a great racehorse named Flying Childers, among other talented descendants.

The last horse was destined to star in a children's book. The Godolphin Arabian, also called the Godolphin Barb, was an Arabian or Barb horse from Morocco or Tunisia. In her 1948 novel *King of the Wind,* Marguerite Henry imagines that he was born to royalty but toiled as a carthorse in France before winding up in England. Whatever the facts of his journey, the animal did travel somehow to France, and then to England as the possession of Edward Coke. One variation of the story has him earning his keep as a teaser stallion, testing mares to see if they were ready for breeding to an English stallion. Another variation calls him a breeding stallion from the beginning. Regardless, the horse did mate with a fine English mare, Roxana, and their offspring, Lath and Cade, became winning racehorses, along with dozens more of his get. The Godolphin ended his years in the possession of Francis, the second Earl of Godolphin, in Cambridgeshire.[36]

This stellar trio of equines is remembered and revered three hundred years later because "all Thoroughbreds trace their lineage back through the generations from son to father to grandfather . . . directly to one of these three stallions, and to no other," according to Margaret Cabell Self, a Virginia-born horsewoman who published many books on the subject in the mid-twentieth century. "Even more remarkable," she continues, "each of the three original desert stallions had only one direct descendant, whose name appears in every pedigree of that line."

For the Byerley Turk, that descendant was Herod, a great-great-grandson born in 1758. The Darley Arabian also claims a great-great-grandson, Eclipse, foaled in 1767. The Godolphin's line flows through a grandson, Matchem, born in 1748.[37]

The foreign-bred stallions, the native-bred mares, and their growing families produced a new kind of English racehorse. The animals grew taller and stronger, ran faster, and became even better looking, with a dish face, arched neck, and high-set flourish of a tail. In fact, the early specimens looked more like today's Arabian horses than like today's Thoroughbreds. English breeders continued to mix and match the best animals, and by the end of the eighteenth century, the Jockey Club of England recognized the type as an official breed, the English Thoroughbred. Needless to say, discerning Virginian horsemen followed the exploits of the Byerley, Godolphin, and Darley stallions.[38]

While the Oriental horses were building the foundation of a new breed in England, Virginians continued their allegiance to their homebred quarter racers, or "short" horses. The scene at tracks all over the Northern Neck and the James River valley and spilling into the region south of the James was characterized by "the preliminary 'banter' by the owners, on shrewdly worded terms capable of more than one interpretation; the betting of whole crops of tobacco; the disguises, for purposes of

A scene from an eighteenth-century British horse race. *The Match between Driver and Aaron at Maidenhead, August 1754: Driver Winning the First Heat,* Richard Roper, ca. 1754.

carefully planned surprise, of already proven nags," wrote Fairfax Harrison. "The two parallel straight-away 'race paths,' lined throughout their brief length with neighbours, a true folk-moot; the signal of the smacked whip; the jockeying start by 'turn and lock'; the thrilling dash; the cheers of victory; and the spoiling of the Egyptians." Even a 1727 legal restriction of "excessive and deceitful" gambling failed to dampen Virginians' ardor for the races.[39]

Again following English fashion, in the 1730s Virginians began to enjoy the long races of four miles. Far from blotting out quarter racing, the establishment of mile-long oval courses only added another dimension to the sport. In 1737, John Pinkerton's Old Field in Hanover County hosted the first documented long race in Virginia, with twenty horses testing their mettle at the new length. Williamsburg had one of the new racetracks, and colonists scraped others out of fields in Alexandria, Gloucester, Port Royal, Richmond, and York. Enthusiasts formed jockey clubs to promote the sport in Dumfries, Fredericksburg, Petersburg, Portsmouth, Richmond, Warwick, and other venues. Churchgoers were as likely to discuss horses as they were other news of interest to the neighborhood, and at least one proud owner even brought a stallion to church so the owners of mares could look him over. The small, stocky, muscular, all-around Virginia horse added a mile to its repertoire. The English "long" horses soon joined them at the invitation of Virginia breeders who had the necessary enthusiasm, interest, and, especially, finances.[40]

Horse racing also advertised planters' elite status in colonial society. The mere possession of such valuable animals, which the planter bought for large sums in England and then spent equally large sums to import to and breed in Virginia, gave an approving nod to a man's wealth and virility (much as did an attractive wife with a substantial dowry who produced several heirs). Having one's horse win a race, especially a long one with several heats, only gilded the lily. With such high stakes all around, audiences enjoyed the spectacle of defeat just as much as the one of victory.[41]

The top importers of English horses bore such established Virginia names as Ambler, Baylor, Bland, Burwell, Byrd, Carter, Goode, Harrison, Hoomes, Lee, Ludwell, Spotswood, and Tayloe. A handful of them, working on their own and in partnership with other breeders, brought the finest English horses to the colony and introduced them to good native horses. "Such were the men who, before the Revolution, supported the Virginia turf for pure sport and without the suggestion of commercialism," wrote Harrison. Their efforts would eventually define two breeds, the Thoroughbred and the Quarter Horse.[42]

At the time, however, horsemen considered all Virginia racehorses with imported English breeding to be Thoroughbreds, whatever length they raced. Many of these first horses, in fact, carried such a quantity of Oriental blood in their veins that one could call them Arabian (encompassing animals from many countries in the region), the first of that breed in Virginia. Regardless of what anyone called them, however, "on occasion the same blood was responsible for creating the short horse and the long horse," as Robert Moorman Denhardt, an expert on Quarter Horses, wrote. From the 1730s until the Revolutionary War, races grew longer, more Thoroughbreds competed, and many horses still ambled or paced when they weren't running. As Thoroughbred blood came to predominate, however, the amble and the pace ever so gradually gave way to the trot.[43]

Breeders in the Rappahannock Valley and the Middle Peninsula (Gloucester and Northern Neck) handled most of the imports until 1754 and after 1763. Later in the 1760s, the center of racing and breeding traveled to the James River valley and the mouth of the Appomattox River as desirable stallions made their homes there. Williamsburg in the 1770s hosted race meets every fall and spring. Just before the Revolution, Fredericksburg was the racing center; after the Revolution, that honor went to Petersburg and Richmond. No matter where they lived, "Virginians, of all ranks and denominations, are excessively fond of horses," wrote John Ferdinand Dalziel Smyth, a British visitor to Virginia in 1769.[44]

A horse named Bulle Rock (a nickname meaning "boon companion") generally gets the nod as the first Thoroughbred to cross the ocean from England to Virginia. Possibly a son of the Darley Arabian, he raced in England before his importation between 1730 and 1740 by Samuel Gist, of Hanover County. Monkey, a bay grandson of the Byerley Turk, raced successfully in England before arriving in 1738 under the auspices of Nathaniel Harrison. He stood at Eagle's Nest, in Stafford County, and Brandon, on the James River, and then in 1748 moved to the Roanoke River valley in North Carolina, where he lived until his death in 1754. ("To stand at stud" or "to stand" means a stallion is available to breed with mares for a fee.) As the first Thoroughbred stallion in what became the prime quarter-racing region, along the border of Virginia and North Carolina, Monkey improved the local stock and left many foundation animals of the future Quarter Horse breed.[45]

Jolly Roger, a grandson of the Godolphin Barb, was another notable stallion of the time. The chestnut started his sojourn in Virginia in 1752, as the property of John Spotswood, of Spotsylvania County, and died around 1770 in Brunswick County. His get could run the long distances. One of his fillies was Poll Flaxen, a well-known racing mare and dam.[46]

If he had owned no other stallion but the imported Fearnought, John Baylor's place in the history of Virginia horses would be secure. A Middle Neck horseman, Baylor (1705–1772) was born in King and Queen County into a wealthy planter family. While at school in England, he doubtless spent time and money at Newmarket, for when he returned to Virginia and claimed his vast inheritance, he gave his Caroline County plantation the same name. Interested more in the fine points of breeding than the thrill of the race, Baylor concentrated on importing blooded horses from England to improve the Virginia equines. His operation housed at least one hundred well-bred horses, including Fearnought.[47]

In 1764, he paid one thousand guineas—a hefty sum—for the nine-year-old stallion. Born in England about 1755, a grandson or great-grandson of the Godolphin Barb, the bay horse raced for a few years before crossing the Atlantic to Virginia, where at 15.3 hands he towered over his new neighbors. Baylor bred his own mares to him, as did some of his peers in the horse world. Fearnought's offspring grew tall and won at either distance. After Baylor's death in 1772, his son John sold fifty horses, including Fearnought, to settle the estate. Southside resident William Edwards, of Hicksford in Brunswick County (now Emporia in Greensville County), bought the stallion, nearly twenty by then, and stood him for a couple of years before the horse's death in 1776. Fearnought gave "Virginia turf stock a standing equal to that of any running stock in the world," wrote Harrison, quoting a racing expert.[48]

Baylor's fellow horseman John Tayloe II (1721–1779) was born at his family's plantation, Mount Airy, in the Northern Neck. He became the head of the clan in 1747, when his father, John Tayloe, died, and around 1758 he built a house that would become as fine and well known as the Tayloe horses. Like Baylor, he attended school in England and indulged his love of racing and racehorses there and back home, where he imported, bred, bought, and sold horses that raced at either distance. The atmosphere at Mount Airy could be daunting for visitors whose interest in horses did not match Tayloe's. In 1774, a guest named Philip Vickers Fithian observed that the family's world revolved around horses right down to the décor of the dining room, which featured twenty-four drawings of "the most celebrated among the English Race-Horses, Drawn masterly, and set in elegant gilt Frames." Of his host, he reported that "we had some agreeable Conversation this morning; Horses seem to be the Colonels favourite topic."[49]

In 1761, Tayloe bought an outstanding racing mare named Selima, a fifteen-year-old daughter of the Godolphin Barb. Dr. Benjamin Tasker Jr., of Maryland, had imported her in 1750. In 1752, while under Tasker's ownership, the mare had soundly defeated horses belonging to the Virginians William Byrd III, Francis Thornton, and Tayloe. Selima produced several foals for Tayloe before she died at Mount Airy. (Her namesake race, the Selima Stakes, which matches two-year-old fillies, is run at Laurel Park, Maryland.) Tayloe also imported Childers, a great-grandson of that famed equine couple, the Darley Arabian and Betty Leedes. His main stallion, Yorick, was a homebred by a well-known imported stallion, Morton's Traveler, and out of Tayloe's own imported Betty Blazella. Yorick put together a good career on the track before retiring to stud. Yorick, a first-generation Virginia Thoroughbred, had speed and

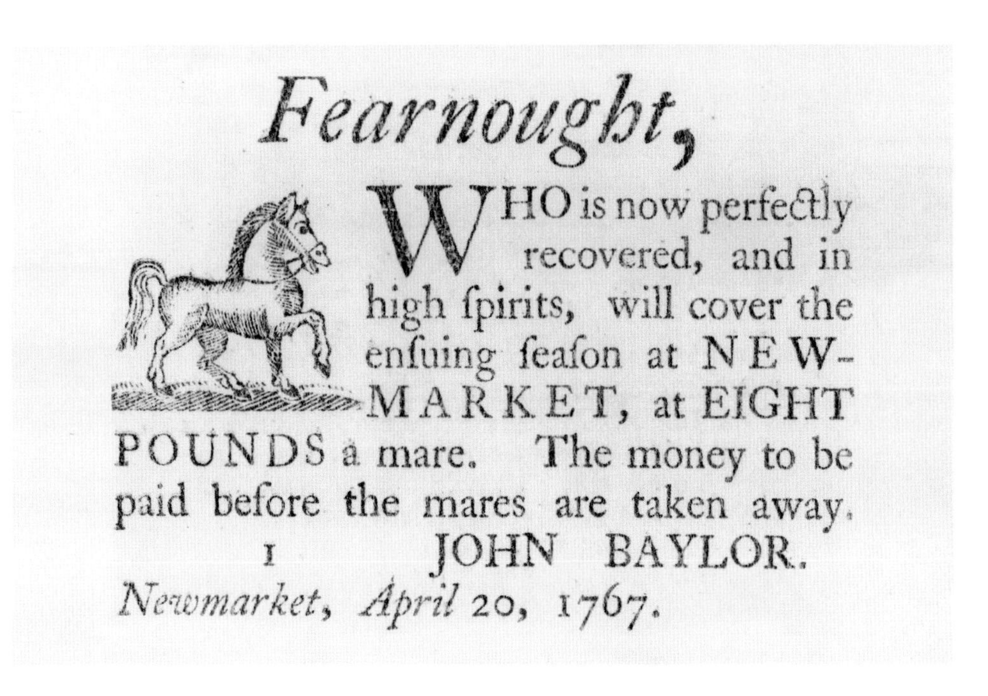


Owners advertised their stallions with broadsides, like this one for Fearnought.

*Childers,* James Seymour, 1773. The great-grandson of a famed equine couple, this stallion was imported from England by John Tayloe II.

strength: At age thirteen he returned to the track, carried a hefty 180 pounds comprising the jockey and additional weight, and won a five-mile race in 12:27. It was a hard life for a racehorse, though; after a five-miler in 1773, Yorick and the other horse, Gift, came up lame.[50]

Down in Southside Virginia, John Goode (1725–1783) presided over the racing world from his home at Cox's Creek, Mecklenburg County. The region (which encompassed part of North Carolina just over the border) became the nucleus of quarter racing and breeding as more English Thoroughbreds entered Virginia and long racing grew in popularity. Goode (nicknamed "Race Horse") was the proprietor of the Ridge Path Race Track (long) and Goode's Quarter Track (short). Wells's Race Paths and Lewis's Race Paths handled short races; when long races finally overtook the short contests, tracks at Elijah Graves's field, Christiansville, and Boydton flourished. Goode stood imported Thoroughbreds and bred and bought outstanding quarter horses such as Twigg, Babram, Pumpkin-Filly, and Paddy Whack. His brother Thomas (1730–1813), up in Chesterfield County on the Appomattox River, joined him in the family business, standing Shark, Diomed, and other imported Thoroughbreds.[51]

## JANUS

One of the best horses ever in John Goode's all-too-brief possession was Janus. A grandson of the Godolphin Barb on his sire's side and a great-grandson of the Darley Arabian on his dam's, he was born in England in 1746 to a sire also named Janus and a dam named Amoretta (or the "Little Hartley mare"). He also had other (less famous) Oriental blood, making him more than half Arab, Barb, or Turk. His coat was chestnut, a blaze decorated his face, and one or two socks or stockings splashed his hind legs. He topped out at 14.3 hands and boasted a substantial build, with large, muscular hindquarters. His concave face and plain neck showed the stamp of some Hobby relative.[52]

As a four-mile racehorse in England from 1750 to 1752, Janus went first by the name Stiff Dick (because of a leg tendon that troubled him all his life) and then by Little Janus. He compiled an unspectacular career as a long racehorse. Out of nine starts, he won twice, came in second three times, third twice, and sixth once, and withdrew once. He was a breeding stallion by 1757, when Mordecai Booth, a planter from Gloucester County, Virginia, bought him and shipped him to the colony. The eleven-year-old, who had long been out of training, promptly beat a Virginia horse, William Byrd III's renowned Valiant, in a four-mile race. Janus's reputation, however, did not rest on his career on the racetrack or on the number of long horses he sired.[53]

For what the horse Justin Morgan is to the modern Morgan breed of horse, Janus is to the modern Quarter Horse. When he met up with Chickasaw and other everyday Virginia mares, their foals looked like

OLD JANUS

IS now very fat, and as active as a Lamb, and ſtands at *Northampton* Courthouſe, *North Carolina*, in Order to cover Mares at forty Shillings a Leap, or four Pounds the Seaſon. The Paſturage, which is under a very good Fence, will be allowed gratis, but I will not be liable for any Mare that may be ſtolen or get away accidentally. Any Gentleman who thinks proper to ſend a Servant to ſee the Mares have Juſtice done in covering, and feeding with Corn at twelve Shillings and Sixpence a Barrel, ſhall be accommodated gratis. (1||) J. ATHERTON.

A newspaper ad for Janus's stud services.

him. They made good all-around horses for pulling and riding, many of them with lateral gaits, and they excelled in a quarter-mile sprint. Possibly because of his Hobby blood, Janus sired his best sprinters with mares of non-Thoroughbred ancestry. Of forty-three known quarter racehorses born between 1758 and 1783, he fathered twenty-eight; of the rest, one was probably by him, five were grandchildren, and five were descendants. The years between 1754 and 1763 were "a new and quite astonishing era of horse breeding . . . in Virginia," wrote Fairfax Harrison in *The Equine F.F.Vs.,* and Janus was one astonishing horse.[54]

During his twenty-three years on these shores, Janus managed to see a lot of Virginia, especially the Southside and even part of North Carolina, the cross-state region where short racing ruled. The compact chestnut stallion zigzagged from owners to leaseholders, from Gloucester County southwest to Brunswick, Powhatan, and Amelia Counties, back to Brunswick, then down to North Carolina, then up to Chesterfield County, and back to North Carolina. "Janus produced just the kind of colt that the horsemen of Virginia and North Carolina wanted," said Robert Moorman Denhardt, "and so they never let him leave." John Goode owned him from 1775 to 1776 and then sold him to James Barnes, of Halifax County, North Carolina. Goode so valued the horse (or at least the income he provided in stud fees) that in 1780 he bought back the thirty-four-year-old stallion (ancient for a horse) for £150 sterling. Janus was headed to Virginia when he died in Warren County, North Carolina.[55]

When restless Virginians left the Old Dominion for Kentucky and Tennessee, they took with them their rugged quarter racehorses, most of which carried Janus blood. Not only did the animals provide sport, they also provided a broad back to ride on and strong legs to pull a wagon. One of Janus's probable grandsons, Printer, was bred in Virginia, but his dam was stolen and wound up in Kentucky, where Printer debuted in 1795. Although he was a dark bay, he was otherwise the spitting image of his grandsire in conformation, speed, and his ability to transmit those qualities to his own descendants. However, the Quarter Horse as a recognized breed, rather than the quarter horse as a type, was still at least a century in the future. Before that could happen, another Virginia horse, Sir Archy, had to take his turn. And before that happened, a war would intervene.[56]

## THE REVOLUTION

The upheaval of the Revolutionary War from 1776 to 1783 called a halt to horse racing in Virginia. The sport was a luxury, too close to British tastes for comfort, and therefore far from patriotic for liberty-loving Virginians. English horses, like English tea, were something they were just going to have to forego. Further, time spent on horse racing meant time away from productive pursuits and community involvement. Planters of wealth and farmers of modest means had to pull together if the Revolution was to succeed. If the absence of racing had been the worst wartime equine hardship, the residents of the colony would have been lucky. But the Continental Army and the local militias needed horses. And when British forces invaded in 1781, they brought an expert and formidable cavalry. The enemy stole Virginia horses for their own use and sometimes even killed them to demoralize, punish, and impoverish the patriots.[57]

Henry "Light-Horse Harry" Lee, famed cavalry officer, father of Robert E. Lee.

The American cavalry of the 1770s was a far cry from such future incarnations as the organized fighting units of the Civil War and the Indian Wars. In fact, most of the Revolution's military horses hauled supplies and wagons, not riders. Officers, however, needed horses so they could move quickly behind the lines and see battlefields from better vantage points. On or off horseback, Virginians fought in New Jersey, New York, Pennsylvania, and South Carolina, and endured the grueling winter of 1777–78 with George Washington at Valley Forge. Cavalry became more active in the latter years of the war, with Virginians, as expert horsemen, composing most of the mounted troops.[58]

One of Virginia's stars on horseback was Henry Lee, a member of a prominent Virginia family. He joined the army when he was only nineteen and soon became such a skilled cavalryman that he earned a lieutenant colonelcy and the nickname "Light-Horse Harry." "The fire of cavalry is at best innocent, especially in quick motion," he explained in his memoirs. "The strength and activity of the horse, the precision and celerity of evolution, the adroitness of the rider, boot-top to boot-top, and the keen edge of the sabre, with fitness of ground and skill in the leader, constitute their vast power so often decisive in the day of battle." One of his eight children would encounter even greater fame in a war more than eighty years in the future—Robert E. Lee.[59]

Lieutenant Colonel George Baylor, a son of John Baylor, of Caroline County, received a horse from Congress for his exemplary service at the Battle of Trenton and commanded the Third Continental Dragoons, a regiment of light horse. One of his duties was to obtain Virginia horses for the cavalry. The desired animals came from a cross of native animals and imported Thoroughbreds that were "wonderful in their endurance of hunger, thirst, and fatigue," wrote John Stuart Skinner, editor of the *American Farmer,* and "respectable cavalry remount[s]," wrote Fairfax Harrison.[60]

In late 1775, fighting occurred around Norfolk, and in January 1776, both British and American troops burned the city. In 1779, the British navy seized Portsmouth and Suffolk. Nevertheless, Virginia largely escaped destruction and disruption until January 1781, when General Benedict Arnold, the traitorous American who now fought for the redcoats, sailed up the James and burned warehouses and public buildings in Richmond.[61]

In May, another enemy leader, Lieutenant General Charles, Lord Cornwallis, arrived from North Carolina. After further harassing Rich-

Tarleton's enemy horsemen clashed with the legendary Peter Francisco, a Virginia hero of the Revolution, who single-handedly captured several of the British mounts—which the British may have stolen from Virginians. *Peter Francisco's Gallant Action with Nine of Tarleton's Cavalry in Sight of a Troop of Four Hundred Men,* ca. 1831.

mond and forcing Governor Thomas Jefferson and the General Assembly to flee to Charlottesville, Cornwallis unleashed Lieutenant Colonel Banastre Tarleton. The ruthless British cavalry leader had a well-deserved nickname: Bloody Tarleton. Facing him were the Marquis de Lafayette, a young Frenchman who fought for the Americans, and his three thousand Virginia militia, who feared Tarleton's "Immense and excellent Body of Horse . . . like they would be So Many wild Beasts," as Lafayette wrote General Washington.

The marquis had only fifty mounted men and recognized all too well "the Enemy's great superiority in Horse, giving them such advantage over us, that they have it almost in their power to over run the County," as one of his aides wrote Jefferson. The governor and the House of Delegates encouraged county officials to hide local horses from the invaders, and allowed Lafayette to impress horses where he could find them. For the most part, the enemy beat him to the punch. "Cavalry is everything in Virginia," Lafayette lamented.[62]

While Cornwallis headed west, bound for the James River and Jefferson's property there, Tarleton and his cavalry charged ahead on a parallel path a few miles to the north. Tarleton's target: Governor Jefferson himself and the General Assembly. On the evening of June 3, they stopped for a break at the tavern at Cuckoo, a crossroads in Louisa County. Jack Jouett, a captain of the Virginia militia, happened to be there too. He figured out the identity and purpose of the newcomers and managed to sneak away on his Thoroughbred mare, Sallie. Avoiding the main road to Charlottesville, Jouett and Sallie sped off on the rugged Mountain Road to warn Jefferson. After several hours of dodging tree limbs and struggling through briars in the dark, Jouett and his trusty steed made it to Monticello, Jefferson's home near Charlottesville, before dawn. His alarm allowed Jefferson, the Speakers of the Senate and House, and other members of the General Assembly to escape. He downed a glass of wine and rode on to Charlottesville to continue his successful mission.

Tarleton succeeded in frightening the residents of the area and destroying supplies, but he failed to capture Jefferson. In a few days, the British officer joined Cornwallis at Elk Hill, where the redcoats stole the governor's usable horses and brutally killed the young ones by cutting their throats. In July, Tarleton made a swing through Southside, wearing out many horses and replenishing his equine supplies by stealing some of the area's blooded horses.[63]

Some breeders, like John Tayloe II, had sent their fine horses to remote areas of the colony for the duration of the conflict to hide and protect the animals. Sometimes this tactic worked, sometimes it didn't. Fearnought, for example, did not leave a strong male line, as many of his get served in the war and either died, left the state, or fell into British possession. (A Fearnought filly, however, carried Baron Friedrich von Steuben, a member of the Continental Army.) Romulus, an Arabian stallion from Mecklenburg County, was appropriated by the Continental Army and died during the war, leaving his owner David Dardin, not a particularly wealthy man to begin with, impoverished in another sense. At Yorktown, the British deliberately drowned many fine horses, including Little Bacchus, Red Bacchus, and Nancy Wake, all quarter racers with Janus blood belonging to Colonel John Dickinson, a staunch patriot.[64]

The war, and the passing during those years of such fine imported stallions as Janus and Fearnought, meant the end of what Harrison called "the heroic age of horse breeding in Virginia." With the disruption of imports, racing, and breeding, the overall quality of horses declined for a time after peace finally settled over the state. Except for Tarleton's quick depredations, however, Southside Virginia had escaped the worst of it and held on to its importance as a breeding region.[65] Overall, the Revolutionary War did not ravage the horse population of Virginia with anywhere near the ferocity of the Civil War that loomed eight decades down the road.

## THE MAN ON THE HIGHBRED HORSE: THOMAS JEFFERSON

Thomas Jefferson liked the finer things in life—good books, vintage wine, French cooking, classical architecture. Perhaps unsurprisingly, he also "was passionately fond of a good horse."[66]

Jefferson (1743–1826) was born and died in Albemarle County. During this Virginian's distinguished career of public service, he served in the legislatures of both colony and state, as governor, as U.S. minister to France, as secretary of state, and as vice president and two-term president of the United States, from 1801 to 1809. In addition, he found time to write the Virginia Statute for Religious Freedom and the Declaration of Independence, establish the University of Virginia, and design Virginia's Capitol in Richmond as well as his own homes at Monticello, in Albemarle County, and Poplar Forest, in Bedford County.

Like his well-to-do horse-owning friends and contemporaries of the late 1700s and early 1800s, he bred and purchased blooded horses of imported English lines. The sire of his horse The General was Janus; another one, Sprightly, had Janus breeding as well. Caractacus was Fearnought's grandson; Jefferson stood him at stud, charging varying amounts for "a leap of Caractacus." The roan Tarquin, a former racehorse, carried Monkey bloodlines. Diomede was a son of the famous Diomed, and Peacemaker was a grandson. The Eagle, the riding horse of his last years, had Fearnought in his pedigree. In 1801, Jefferson purchased Wildair from Diomed's importer, John Waller Hoomes. Jefferson was "extremely pleased with him, & attached to him as a riding horse," he wrote Hoomes, "& am thankful to you for having thought of me . . . & furnished the opportunity of procuring so fine a creature."[67]

Despite the racing blood in many of his horses, Jefferson had no interest in sending them to the track. He "never had nothing to do with horse racing," said Isaac Jefferson, a slave. "Bought two race horses once, but not in their racing day." However, possessing "the partiality of a Virginian for this sport," as Henry S. Randall, an early biographer, put it, Jefferson enjoyed watching many a horse race, including the Washington Jockey Club's meets when he was president. He had other plans for his horses, however, and he did not thrill to the foxhunt like his fellow president George Washington.[68]

In 1808, he explained his feelings about the matters to a grandson. In his youth, he "was often thrown into the society of horseracers, cardplayers, Foxhunters, scientific and professional men, and of dignified men," he wrote Thomas Jefferson Randolph. "And many a time have I asked myself, in the enthusiastic moment of the death of a fox, the victory of a favorite horse, the issue of a question eloquently argued at the bar or in the great Council of the nation, well, which of these kinds of reputation should I prefer? That of a horse jockey? A foxhunter? An Orator? Or the honest advocate of my country's rights?" He approved of breeding racehorses as a means of improving horses in general, and he thought gambling over a race was less risky than games of cards or dice. After all, one card game could relieve a man of all his money, but it would take more than one race to wipe out his savings, which might give him pause.[69]

Since they weren't winning (or losing) money for their owner, Jefferson's blooded horses had to pull a coach and carry a rider. Even with their fancy breeding, Diomede and Brimmer, another former racehorse, pulled a carriage, along with Tecumseh, Wellington, and Eagle, all bays. "He would not ride or drive anything but a highbred horse," said Edmund Bacon, overseer of Monticello. For everyday farmwork, though, he used mules as well as Chickasaw horses, still a Virginia breed in the early 1800s despite the growing prevalence of Thoroughbreds and early Quarter Horses.[70]

For such fine animals in his fields and stables, Jefferson insisted on expert care and a good appearance. If a saddle horse "did not shine as faultlessly as a mirror," wrote Randall, he would swipe it with a white handkerchief and scold the groom if any dirt appeared. Sometimes he drove the phaeton (a light carriage pulled by two horses) himself. When he rode in the more formal coach, pulled by four horses, his slaves Jupiter and John accompanied him, one driving the coach and one riding postilion. The stallion Caractacus, one of his favorite riding horses, often pulled the coach, along with Gustavus, Otter, Remus, Romulus, and Senegore.[71]

Thomas Jefferson, though a notable horseman, did not appear in equestrian portraits as did his contemporaries like George Washington. Jefferson's home and personal effects, however, demonstrate his appreciation of horses. *Top,* the stables at his home, Monticello, as they appear today; *left,* his riding boots.

One can easily imagine that the well-read Jefferson enjoyed his horses' classical, historical, mythical, and popular names, many of which he bestowed himself. They boasted such appellations as Alfred, after the English king; Blucher, a German general; Odin, a Norse god; Peggy Waffington (actually Woffington), an English actress of the time; Polly Peachum, one of Woffington's stage roles; and Zanga, a character in a 1721 novel. Less lofty names included The Grey, Stella, and Turncoat; Bremo apparently was named for the home of John Hartwell Cocke, a friend of Jefferson's.[72]

Observers considered Jefferson "a bold and fearless rider" and "master of his horse," as his grandson Thomas Jefferson Randolph remembered. A slave, Wormley Hughes, once watched Jefferson arrive at Monticello from Washington, D.C., with a new horse named Arcturus. When the animal reared and shied at a protruding rock on the road up the mountain, Jefferson applied spur and whip until Arcturus was "glad to put his fore feet on the rock and stand still." (His harsh methods were not unusual for the time.) Bacon called him "an uncommonly fine rider—sat easily upon his horse and always had him in the most perfect control."[73]

Of the many horses in Jefferson's pastures and writings, two favorites make frequent appearances. Caractacus, the homebred, named for a British chieftain, once sent the thirty-eight-year-old Jefferson tumbling off, breaking his arm. (The British had just chased him and his family out of Monticello, stolen his broodmares, and killed the young horses at Elk Hill; it was a calamitous time for the then-governor.) Eagle, "fleet, fiery, but gentle-tempered," with reported Diomed breeding, was the horse of his old age. Overseer Bacon had bought the sixteen-hand bay with white hind socks and a white star from John Graves, of nearby Louisa County. During one outing, Eagle stumbled and fell while crossing a river, upsetting his elderly rider. Man and horse recovered, but the accident exacerbated an earlier injury to Jefferson's wrist, adding to the aches and pains of a man in his early eighties.[74]

That he was still riding near the end of his life is a testimony to Jefferson's lifelong enjoyment of the pastime. In his mid-forties, however, he had expressed his doubts. A vigorous man who ate a near-vegetarian diet, he echoed the thoughts of the Indians that William Byrd had encountered nearly sixty years earlier: "I doubt whether we have not lost more than we have gained by the use of this animal [the horse]. No one has occasioned so much the degeneracy of the human body." Around the same time, he pronounced, "of all the exercises walking is best. A horse gives but a kind of half exercise, and a carriage is no better than a cradle." Over time, Jefferson changed his habits and his thinking, riding nearly every day to look over his property or just to be alone with his thoughts. At age seventy-five, he called his horse "the most sovereign of all Doctors." At eighty-one, he testified that "to old age the daily ride is among the most cheering of comforts." Only the illness of his last three weeks kept him from a ride on Eagle.[75]

In 1793, Jefferson needed a new horse. He was in his final year as secretary of state and preparing to leave Philadelphia, then the nation's capital. "I think it will be better to get a good one . . . in Virginia," he wrote his son-in-law Thomas Mann Randolph Jr., "than to buy an indifferent one here." It comes as no surprise that he would have considered a Pennsylvania horse unsuitable. It seems inconceivable that Thomas Jefferson, one of Virginia's greatest thinkers, leaders, and promoters, would have considered buying a horse from anywhere but his beloved home.[76]

# 1784–1865

## ALL THE FINE HORSES OF THE STATE

*He has an unconquerable Love for Horses; he often tells me that he should have been a skillfull, & useful Groom; that he should be more fond & careful of a favourite Horse than of a Wife.*—Philip Vickers Fithian, writing of eighteen-year-old Benjamin Carter, *Journal and Letters*, 1774

For five or six decades after the Revolutionary War, thousands of people and horses would leave the Old Dominion for Tennessee and Kentucky. Two of those emigrants, one of each species, gave a preview of things to come in the Virginia horse world. Abraham Buford, of Culpeper County, had been an officer in the Continental Army during the Revolution and survived an encounter with Banastre Tarleton, an enemy cavalryman. Around 1800, Buford claimed his reward of land in Kentucky (which had been part of Virginia until 1792), moved there, and began importing Virginia racehorses. In 1805, the Virginia-born horse Truxton made his name as a racehorse not in his native state but in Tennessee, as the property of Andrew Jackson, future U.S. president and lifelong horseman. Truxton successfully campaigned on the track and at stud. Buford the man and Truxton the horse embodied the shift of the centers of racing and Thoroughbred breeding away from Virginia and into Tennessee and Kentucky over the next half century.[1]

Six horses of varying builds pulled this Conestoga wagon, a common sight on the Great Wagon Road of the Shenandoah Valley in the mid-eighteenth century. This particular wagon was still in use more than a century later, when this photo was taken.

It took a lot of horses to get Virginians where they were going, whether they were headed to Kentucky or to Richmond. In 1791, when George Washington was president, he toured the South with a chariot pulled by four horses; a baggage wagon with two horses; four saddle mounts; and an extra horse that someone led. Two slaves, a coachman (who drove the team), and a postilion (who rode a member of the team) accompanied the entourage. When John Randolph of Roanoke, a prominent antebellum politician and horse breeder, traveled out of state, he did so with three blooded horses. He rode one and his servant the other, and the third horse carried the luggage on its back. After ten or twelve miles, the little party would stop to switch packs, saddles, and riders to keep the horses fresh.[2]

Ordinary folk with fewer horses and a less lofty social station could ride in horse-drawn stagecoaches, such as the one that ran between Richmond and Charlottesville once a week in the 1820s (five dollars for a one-way fare), ride their own saddle horse (as Thomas Jefferson often did), or even travel via shank's mare—on foot. A party headed overland might contain wives riding double with their husbands on pillions

(cushions attached behind the saddle) or everyone piled into a Conestoga wagon with the driver on a horse next to the left front wheel. Pulling the wagons, carrying riders, or walking behind on a lead rope, horses of all kinds left Virginia for new territory—racehorses long and short, work animals of high and low breeding.[3]

## "A RACE IS A VIRGINIAN'S PLEASURE"

Racing didn't leave the state just yet. After the Revolutionary War and into the early nineteenth century, wealthy breeders pursued their interests because they just plain enjoyed it and could afford to indulge that pleasure. After all, no one really *needed* a racehorse. A typical operation consisted of a planter with a few Virginia mares and an imported English stallion or two. Less prosperous breeders enjoyed the pastime too, but their broodmares had to work on the farm as well as produce young horses. Professional horsemen dealt in racehorses to make money, not necessarily for the craft and delight to be found in breeding and bloodlines.[4]

The Virginia races greatly amused a British actor named John Bernard, who traveled around the former colonies from 1797 to 1811. At a long race, he was astonished when the horse he called a "low, long-backed, shaggy plebeian" with "a monstrous head set upon a short, straight neck" beat "the sleek, proud, well-trained, elegant-limbed English racer, just imported." The quarter racers amused him even more. He called them "cattle" and thought them a "peculiar breed," describing them as "somewhat larger than ponies, shaggy as bears, but frisky as lambs." The unlikely steeds ran the quarter mile so fast "that the affair was over before you imagined it begun."[5]

By the 1820s, short and long racing had flowed down into Southside and spilled over into North Carolina, particularly Brunswick and Mecklenburg Counties in Virginia and Granville, Halifax, Northampton, and Warren Counties in North Carolina. A good-natured cross-state rivalry developed. In 1825, the *American Farmer* magazine (a must-read for Virginia horsemen) opined that the nation's "cotton, our tobacco, and our race horses, are called by the name Virginia; while our ague and fever, our bad roads, and our bars and shoals, are admitted, even by the Virginians themselves, to belong to North Carolina."[6]

Active in the first half of the 1800s, the Richmond Jockey Club tied its racing calendar to the social season. Race fans had three nearby ven-

Sir Archy's bloodlines were well represented at this 1830 meet at Tree Hill.

**THIRD DAY'S RACE,**
**OVER THE**
***Tree-Hill Course.***

***Jockey Club Purse, $1000....Four Mile Heats.***
***ENTRIES.***

**William R. Johnson enters ch. h. Havoc, by Sir Charles, 4 years old, weight 100 lbs. Dress, blue jacket and blue cap.**
**John M. Botts enters br. m. Mischief, by Virginian, 4 years old, weight 97 lbs. Dress, orange jacket and black cap.**
**William Wynn enters b. m. Kate Kearney, by Sir Archie, 5 years old, weight 107 lbs. Dress, red jacket and red cap.**
**Hector Davis enters b. m. Sally Hornet, by Sir Charles, 4 years old, weight 97 lbs. Dress, yellow jacket and blue cap.**

**J. M. SELDEN,**
***Proprietor.***

***Thursday, April 29th, 1830.***

ues to choose from: the old one at Fairfield, in Henrico County on the Mechanicsville Turnpike; Broad Rock, in Chesterfield County; and Tree Hill, also in Henrico County, run by Miles Selden. Petersburg, with the New Market track nearby, also had a jockey club. Dues ran about twenty-five dollars per year for such amenities as Tree Hill's dining room, clubhouse, and seating for women. When Thomas Jefferson was in the market for a new horse, he decided to wait for the 1809 Petersburg spring meet and its "collection of all the fine horses of the state." Spring and fall races brought well-dressed women and men in shiny coaches and on shiny horses for several days of visiting, dancing, and courting. In the Albemarle County of the 1820s, the Birdwood Jockey Club held meets featuring three days of races, one- and two-mile heats, with purses ranging from $100 to $250. No doubt the social scene resembled that of Richmond.[7]

Other parts of the state hosted the sport too. In the 1830s in Lewis County, south of Clarksburg (now in West Virginia), a man named Cummins Jackson raced horses and maintained a four-mile track. His favorite jockey was his nephew, a youngster named Thomas Jackson, who perched on short stirrups and leaned over so far that his torso and head practically paralleled his horse's neck. Thirty years later, the grown-up boy would exhibit the same odd style, albeit with longer stirrups. By then he was better known as General Stonewall Jackson of the Confederate army.[8]

Anne Ritson, of Norfolk, spoke for many a resident of the Old Dominion when she wrote in 1809:

> A race is a Virginian's pleasure,
> For which they can always find leisure;
> For that, they leave their farm and home,
> From ev'ry quarter they can come;
> With gentle, simple, rich and poor,
> The race-ground soon is cover'd o'er;
> Negroes the gaming spirit take,
> And bet and wager ev'ry stake;
> Males, females, all, both black and white
> Together at this sport unite.[9]

When Ritson claimed that racing united black and white Virginians, she had a point. The first African Americans had arrived in Jamestown in 1619. Over the years, both enslaved and free blacks had learned to work with horses on every level—cleaning stables, plowing fields, riding races—and many experts arose. In the racehorse business, they groomed, trained, and rode the animals. Austin Curtis, an enslaved man from North Carolina who belonged to a horseman named Willie Jones, was a famous jockey in the Virginia–North Carolina area in the 1770s. After Jones freed him in 1791, Curtis continued in the horse business in Virginia.[10]

In the antebellum era, an enslaved man named Charles Stewart gained renown and a measure of freedom through his partnership with his owner, the famed racehorse expert William Ransom Johnson. Stewart was born around 1800 in a community named Pocahontas, near Petersburg, the son of a free black man and an enslaved woman. When Stewart was ten or eleven, Johnson bought him and, sensing a budding horseman, sent the boy to his training stables at New Market. As "Johnson's Charles," he rode his first race at age thirteen.

He shuttled between Virginia and North Carolina, training and riding Johnson's horses. He even traveled as far as New York, where he witnessed the famous 1822 match race between Sir Charles, a Virginia horse, and American Eclipse. Johnson set up the twenty-year-old Stewart at a training stable near New Market, where Stewart supervised several slaves and a couple of white employees and worked with the

Charles Stewart, a slave, gained renown and a measure of freedom through his ability as a horse trainer. Here he shows Medley, a well-known stallion of the day.

imported Medley, among other well-known horses of the time. "How I did love them horses!" Stewart told *Harper's Magazine* in 1884. "It appeared like they loved me too, and when they turned their rainbow necks, all slick and shining, around searching for me to come and give them their gallops, whew-e-e! How we did spin along that old New Market course, right after sunrise in the cool summer mornings!" He later moved to Kentucky, where he trained horses and supervised grooms and jockeys. At Stewart's request, Johnson sold him to a judge from Louisiana, where he continued his career, enjoying a good deal of autonomy while still technically a slave.[11]

## ANTEBELLUM BREEDERS

The top breeders of the time slapped each other's backs at the races and exchanged money, horses, and hospitality on a regular basis. John Waller Hoomes (1755–1805), a Caroline County neighbor of the Baylor family, called his place Bowling Green. He was such a racing enthusiast that he watched the activity on his training track from his dining room and porch. He bred and raced his own horses, and beginning in 1790 brought to Virginia nineteen English stallions and thirteen English mares. Along with John Tayloe III, Hoomes ran the stagecoach line between Richmond and Alexandria. If the horses did not perform up to snuff on the racetrack, then they earned their keep in harness.[12]

One of Hoomes's most famous horses, Diomed, didn't have to pull a coach to earn his keep. He arrived in Virginia in 1798 after a profitable racing career in England that included the Derby Stakes at Epsom. He was a chestnut, 15.3 hands, with an elegant head and neck, a white star, and some white on his legs. Hoomes and John Tayloe III bought him from their English agent, James Weatherby. Getting on in years—he was twenty-one—he descended through his grandfather Herod from the Byerley Turk. English experts called Diomed a "proved bad foal getter." The old stallion spent the rest of his life proving them wrong. Tayloe sent mares to him while he stood at Bowling Green, and then Hoomes sold him to Miles Selden and Thomas Goode, who stood him at Selden's Tree Hill, near Petersburg, and Goode's Chesterfield County farm. (In 1805 one of Goode's Diomed colts, Truxton, became the Tennessee racehorse that belonged to President Jackson.) Diomed wound up with Nathaniel Rives in Greensville County by 1807 and died the next year at

A four-horse stagecoach negotiated a rutted road near Lynchburg, ca. 1870.

Diomed's fine head and arched neck showed his Byerley Turk heritage.

Bowling Green, once again as the property of Hoomes. During his decade in Virginia, Diomed had sired so many excellent racehorses that Rives could unblushingly advertise that "the great size, figure and performance on the turf, added to the high price which his colts command, give him a decided superiority over any stallion in America."[13]

John Hoomes's friend and business partner, John Tayloe III (1771–1828), presided over Mount Airy, in Richmond County, continuing his father's equine traditions. His son, Benjamin Ogle Tayloe (1796–1868), later wrote about his father's career as one of the nation's best breeders of racehorses, and compiled but never published material for a studbook. Between 1792 and 1805, John Tayloe imported seven stallions and eight mares from England. Between 1791 and 1806, his horses won 80 percent of their races. Any breeder would be proud to claim such a record.[14]

John Randolph of Roanoke (1773–1833) served Virginia as a congressman and senator from Charlotte County and as a member of the Virginia Constitutional Convention of 1829–30. One of Virginia's great eccentrics, he was tall, thin, sharply intelligent, and orated in an unusu-

Fanny, a descendant of Diomed and American Eclipse, was a successful racehorse herself. She belonged to William Ransom Johnson.

ally high voice. He once dueled with Henry Clay and ran for office against Patrick Henry. And he loved horses. In his youth he was a jockey; as an adult, raising horses at Roanoke Plantation, he favored stock of Janus, Diomed, and Sir Archy blood. He bred Thoroughbreds but asserted, in an 1832 advertisement for his stallion Rinaldo, that "the true, serviceable horse is the quarter horse," it being "active, sure-footed, speedy and capable of breaking down the fashionable stock in a hard ride." He owned a good-sized library about equine matters and, like Benjamin Ogle Tayloe, worked on, but never finished, a studbook of Virginia horses. On his deathbed, he had his friend John Stuart Skinner, the editor of the *American Farmer*, read to him a list of his horses' pedigrees and names. Randolph was a true Virginia horseman from birth to death.[15]

William Ransom Johnson (1782–1849), called the "Napoleon of the Turf," was born in North Carolina but in 1817 moved to his father-in-law's plantation, Oakland, near Petersburg, in Chesterfield County. His career as one of the top racing figures of the time covered the border region of Virginia and North Carolina. Johnson seemed to be everywhere that good horses raced and bred, extending his reach even into the Shenandoah Valley, standing two horses at Martinsburg (now in West Virginia) in 1830. Charles Stewart, his jockey and trainer, called him "the picture of a fine old gentleman . . . with thick white hair, and eyes that just snapped fire at you." One of the finest horses ever to grace Johnson's stables came from a thoughtful mating engineered by John Tayloe and another well-known breeder, Archibald Randolph.[16]

## "THE BEST COLT THAT IS ANYWHERE": SIR ARCHY

In 1799, John Tayloe III imported an English filly, Castianira. She came complete with a trainer named Thomas Larkin. She went blind at a young age but had a long career as a broodmare. Tayloe and Archibald Randolph partnered to breed Castianira, sending her in 1804 to the stallion Diomed, then standing at Tree Hill near Petersburg.[17]

In the spring of 1805, a dark bay colt, the offspring of the two English horses, arrived. His dam was in residence at Randolph's place, Ben Lomond plantation, along the James River in Goochland County. Randolph named the colt Robert Burns, after the Scottish poet. Little Robert Burns and Castianira made a long trek to the Shenandoah Valley, bound for Randolph's Carter Hall in Frederick County (now Clarke County).[18]

There the youngster underwent training with Thomas Larkin for his intended career as a racehorse. The rigorous regimen involved four-mile walks twice a day, while blanketed; two meals a day of oats and corn; two opportunities for water each day, but only forty swallows each; baths with castile soap and rubdowns with straw; and morning gallops of two miles.[19]

In 1807, Randolph sold his share of Robert Burns to Ralph Wormeley IV and sent the colt to half-owner Tayloe at Mount Airy. Randolph thought the horse was "the best colt that is anywhere," but Tayloe nonetheless traded his half-share to Wormeley for four hundred dollars and the mare Selima. Before the colt left Mount Airy, however, Tayloe changed his name to Sir Archy in honor of Archibald Randolph.[20]

At Wormeley's nearby plantation, Rosegill, Sir Archy continued his training with Larkin. Even though Wormeley put the young horse and others up for sale, he scheduled Sir Archy for his first race: the October 1808 sweepstakes at the Fairfield course near Richmond. Before he could make his debut, the colt came down with distemper, a life-threatening disease, so Wormeley had to scratch him. With the help of a diet of egg whites and wine, the young horse recovered and raced in Washington, D.C., with John Randolph of Roanoke (and possibly President Thomas Jefferson) cheering him on. Despite his dramatic recovery and glittering audience, it was an inauspicious debut, for Sir Archy lost there and at Fairfield a little later.[21]

William Ransom Johnson also saw him race. "If he just only walked by a horse to look at it," said Charles Stewart of Johnson, "he could tell you just how far that horse could run." Johnson must have thought that Sir Archy could run a fair distance, for he bought the horse for $1,500 and packed him off to Warrenton, North Carolina, where Sir Archy continued his education under Arthur Taylor, a twenty-year-old Englishman. In 1809, he repaid Johnson's confidence by winning at Fairfield and other tracks. At New Market, he tied in the first heat with Wrangler, a half brother via Diomed that Selden owned, but Wrangler's trainer withdrew him from the rest of the heats, as neither horse was running at his best. The colt went lame but recovered before his next meet, where he won the first heat so decisively that he was declared the overall winner. He turned the same trick the next week at New Market. In another victory, he ran four miles, the first two in 3:46. At his last race, in North Carolina, he beat a horse named Blank in the first four-mile heat by more than a length at 7:52. He won the second heat in 8:00.[22]

In 1809, the four-year-old changed hands again, making Johnson a tidy profit. His new owner was William R. Davie, a Revolutionary War hero and prominent North Carolinian who lived at New Hope, in Halifax County, North Carolina. He bought him from Johnson for five thousand dollars. Johnson told Davie that Sir Archy was the best horse he'd ever seen and that he'd bet five thousand dollars on him anytime, anywhere. Davie promptly gave the colt to his son, Allan Jones Davie, who advertised him at stud for forty dollars for the season. In his prime, the bay horse, who had a white sock on his right hind foot, stood at least sixteen hands high and sported the kind of sleek, strong, muscular conformation that won races. Sir Archy the racehorse, the Virginia-born son of two imported English Thoroughbreds, was now Sir Archy the breeding stallion. Davie hoped he would pass those sterling qualities down to his offspring. He did.[23]

As Sir Archy's sons and daughters began to win race after race, owners of mares demanded his services, and his fees went up. Davie leased him out to other breeders now and then, so Sir Archy found himself back

*Sir Archy by Diomed out of Castianira,* Alvan Fisher, ca. 1823–1825. This portrait shows the stallion's powerful build, well-shaped head, and alert demeanor. The handler's elegant clothing suits the occasion.

Sir Charles, one of Sir Archy's illustrious offspring.

in Virginia, first with Johnson in 1811, then with William Edward Broadnax, of Brunswick County, and later with Edmund Irby, of Nottoway County. The mares came from Virginia and North Carolina to wherever Sir Archy set up camp. In 1816, Davie, who had gotten himself in debt, sold him to one of his creditors, William Amis, of Mowfield plantation, Northampton County, North Carolina. This time the horse stayed put and lived out the rest of his days at Mowfield, covering hundreds of mares, including his own daughters and sisters, a common practice of the time. When Amis died in 1824, he willed the stallion to his son John. By 1830, the younger Amis was charging seventy-five dollars for a season, saying that the horse's "blood, great size, performance on the turf, and celebrity as a foal getter are sufficient recommendations."[24]

As often happens with famous figures, rumor tainted Sir Archy's glory years. The instigator was John Randolph of Roanoke. He had sent mares to Sir Archy but for some reason speculated that perhaps the illustrious Diomed had not sired Sir Archy, that instead a teaser stallion named Gabriel was Sir Archy's true father. After all, Randolph pondered, Sir Archy was a bay, like Gabriel, but Diomed was a chestnut. If this was true, then breeders and buyers who thought they were getting the prized Diomed blood had been cheated. The ludicrous story spread despite the accounts of witnesses to the 1804 mating of Diomed and Castianira—and despite the knowledge that Gabriel had died *before* Sir Archy's conception.[25]

Sir Archy outlasted the scandal and kept on doing his job until John Amis retired him in 1832. He enjoyed the well-deserved good life in a comfortable stall that was left open so he could come and go as he pleased. In his late twenties, the once-strapping, handsome stallion was now hairy and bony, "the worst looking and would be the last taken for the most celebrated horse of his age." The great horse died on June 7, 1833, at age twenty-eight. Before he was buried at Mowfield in an unmarked grave, a couple of his hooves were reportedly removed as souvenirs.[26]

Virginia could claim Sir Archy's birthplace without a doubt, so it wanted to claim his final resting place as well. Since at least 1911, some residents of Goochland County have believed that Sir Archy's remains lie at his place of birth, Archibald Randolph's Ben Lomond, along with those of his groom and a dog (presumably buried later, not sacrificed at graveside). In 1970, twenty explorers dismantled a stone wall at Ben Lomond, took a backhoe to the earth inside, and found a human skull along with bones they thought might be those of a dog and a horse. In 1973, the Deep Run Hunt Club dedicated a marker to Sir Archy at the location, and the Goochland Historical Society dedicated the restored stone wall. If this story is true, then either Sir Archy died in Goochland County (which the historical record does not support), or in 1833 someone spent several days transporting a dead horse about one hundred miles in the heat of summer, or they waited until the carcass had decomposed and delivered a bundle of bones at a later date. Whatever the truth may be, Virginians do feel strongly about their horses.[27]

Long before they wondered about Sir Archy's grave, Virginians had no doubt about his remarkable ability to produce colts and fillies of astounding and consistent speed. In 1819, for example, his get won more than forty races; in 1823, they triumphed in forty-five contests. He sired horses that won at four miles and horses that won at a quarter mile. No wonder breeders kept him busy into his old age. One of his sons, Copperbottom, moved to Texas and there became a foundation sire of the Quarter Horse.[28]

Another son, Sir Charles, became the leading American sire of Thor-

Boston, a Sir Archy grandson. His genes influenced racehorses that won at the gallop and the trot. He was as well known for his bad temper as he was for his speed.

oughbreds for five years in the 1830s. He was foaled in Virginia in 1816 at Diamond Grove, in Brunswick County, owned by James J. Harrison. He racked up an excellent record on the racecourse before losing a match race in 1822 to the northern horse American Eclipse. William Ransom Johnson and his son George stood him at stud, as did John Charles Craig. Along with other sons of Sir Archy like Rattler and Tariff, he stood a season or two in the Shenandoah Valley. Sir Charles died on the same day as his sire, June 7, 1833.[29]

One of Sir Archy's grandsons, Boston, seemed destined for greatness, with Diomed on both sides of his family. Born in 1833 at the Henrico County plantation of John Wickham, a prominent Richmonder, he belonged to Nathaniel Rives after Wickham lost the horse in a card game. Boston had a foul temper, but he also had a twenty-six-foot stride and won forty of forty-five races from Virginia to New York, New Jersey to Maryland. In many of those races, his jockey was Cornelius, one of William Ransom Johnson's slaves. For a few years in the 1840s, he stood in Hanover County, but he wound up in Kentucky, as did many a Virginia-bred horse of the time. Some of his descendants were good trotting horses. A sixteen-time leading sire of American racehorses, Boston died in 1850.[30]

Eight times between 1800 and 1860, in fact, a Virginia horse was the leading stallion in America. The top tier included Diomed, the imported Sir Harry (who also stood in Maryland), Sir Archy (although living in

North Carolina by then), Sir Charles (five times), and Revenue. (Before 1776, it had been Fearnought, and from 1776 to 1800 the two leading stallions were Medley and Shark, both imports.)[31]

By the late 1850s, when another branch of the Sir Archy family tree appeared on the scene, racing had taken on an unsavory cast. Respectable ladies and gentlemen stayed away from crowds that now came solely to gamble professionally, not to appreciate the fine horses and socialize with other elite folk while also casting a genteel bet. Planet, born in 1855, restored some of the sport's luster before the Civil War halted four-mile contests in the United States. He was bred by Thomas Doswell (1824–1890), of Bullfield Stud—also known as the Red Stable—in Hanover County. Planet had Sir Archy as a great-great-grandsire twice over, Sir Charles as a great-grandsire, and Boston as a grandsire. With that pedigree, he trotted about as fast as he could gallop, raced best at four miles, and won twenty-seven of thirty-one races—not to mention a great deal of money. In 1858 and 1859, he won the Great Post Stake at New Orleans, an important race of the era. The war interfered with his breeding career, but he eventually left many fine descendants. In 1868, a Kentucky breeder bought Planet, and the Virginia horse lived out his life at Woodburn Farm in Kentucky.[32]

Planet, born at Bullfield Stud in Hanover County, was transplanted to Kentucky from Virginia shortly after the Civil War.

Whether in Virginia, Tennessee, or Kentucky, the American Thoroughbred was growing strong and true as a breed, becoming distinct from the English Thoroughbred thanks to Diomed and Sir Archy.[33] At the same time, the quarter horses were steadily moving west of Virginia and still developing into a recognized breed.[34] Their far-flung travels followed an established Virginia pattern: fast horses and enterprising owners roaming around the state in search of races, money, and mares. Their get galloped all over Virginia and south into North Carolina. Quarter racers of the time went down in the studbooks as "Celebrated American Quarter Running Horses" or "Famous American Running Horses" or "Running Mares."[35] Thoroughbred stallions, on the other hand, generally stayed put, with owners sending mares to them, and their offspring often staying in the neighborhood.[36]

## PAPER HORSES

In the days before photography, Virginians turned to painters to immortalize their favorite horses. One of the best, and most sought-after, artists was Edward Troye (1808–1874). Born Edouard de Troy in Switzerland, he immigrated to the United States in 1831 from the West Indies. He won his first commissions to paint horses the next year. Among his many equine subjects all over the eastern United States, he depicted the stallion Medley, who belonged to William Ransom Johnson, in 1832, along with Johnson's trusted trainer, Charles Stewart. Troye lived at Johnson's Oakland while working on paintings. In the course of his long career, Troye also received commissions in 1858 from Major Thomas Doswell, of Bullfield, and from General John Hartwell Cocke, of Bremo. Alexander Mackay-Smith called the Troye portrait of Cocke's horse Roebuck "probably the best representation we have today of what a Virginia colonial Quarter Horse looked like." Troye died in Kentucky, leaving a rich artistic legacy in the form of paintings (now in museums and private hands) and of widely published engravings of some of the best-known horses of his time.[37]

Other Virginians of the nineteenth century used words to depict the equine world. Patrick Nisbett Edgar (ca. 1785–1857) came to the United States from Ireland around 1808. He lived in the famed racehorse region of Southside Virginia and northern North Carolina. In 1833, he published *The American Race-Turf Register, Sportsman's Herald, and General Stud Book . . .*, which remains an important reference.

James Junkin Harrison (ca. 1780–1851) lived at Diamond Grove, along the Meherrin River in Brunswick County. A prominent racing figure from 1814 to 1830, he owned offspring of Sir Archy, including Sir Charles. Harrison thought the United States needed a studbook like the English volume, so he, Edgar, and Theophilus Feild (president of the Richmond Jockey Club and an owner of the New Market racetrack near Petersburg), and others collected pedigrees, which Edgar used in compiling his book.

Virginian, a stallion belonging to James J. Harrison. The Brunswick County breeder of racehorses also owned Sir Charles.

Richard Mason, of Surry County, published *The Gentleman's New Pocket Companion,* which ran to twenty-two editions from 1814 to 1883. Virginia horsemen called it *Mason's Farrier* or the *New Pocket Farrier* and would not be caught without this essential reference.[38]

John Stuart Skinner, of Baltimore, founded and edited the weekly *American Farmer* (published from 1819 to 1829). He also wrote about Virginia horses and pedigrees in a weekly magazine and in the monthly *American Turf Register and Sporting Magazine.* Skinner published the *American Turf Register* from 1829 to 1835, then sold it to James W. Pegram of Petersburg, son-in-law of William Ransom Johnson. Items he published in

*Tobacconist, with Botts' Manuel and Botts' Ben,* Edward Troye, 1833 (detail). Tobacconist, a grandson of Sir Archy, belonged to John Minor Botts, of Half Sink Plantation. The horse won the New Market Plate at the Virginia course of the same name, which was owned in partnership by Botts's brother, Alexander. The jockey and the trainer exemplify the many skilled horsemen of the era who practiced their trade within the constraints of slavery.

the *Petersburg Intelligencer* in the 1820s were collected and published as a supplement to Mason's *New Pocket Farrier*, with contributors including John Randolph of Roanoke and Allen Jones Davie.[39]

## STEEPLECHASES, SHOWS, AND SPANISH HORSES

Flat racing was the most popular horse sport in Virginia but hardly the only one. Riders enjoyed yet another British import, steeplechasing, a long gallop of a race over the countryside with solid jumps thrown in for good measure. The name and sport came about in 1752 in Ireland, when two foxhunters raced from one village to another, using church steeples as their landmarks. Enthusiasts pursued it in the 1830s at the National Race Course (now Rock Creek Park) in Washington, D.C., and in the 1840s near Warrenton, among other places. John Bernard, the British actor, turned his piquant gaze on the hunt as well. Of hunting foxes and deer, he thought it "curious" that "the slave states alone were decidedly English in their public amusements" and wondered if it was "generally beneficial to so young a country." However, he thought, "the planters had wealth and leisure, two incentives to enjoyment, besides a greater [incentive] than either—a warm climate." Hunting was "a healthy recreation" but in Virginia "was a far different thing from its English original." It was the Virginia way—bending an English custom to its own environment.[40]

Virginians refined their version of foxhunting in the first half of the nineteenth century, with plantation owners offering their private packs of hounds to invited guests. An 1833 hunt near Alexandria featured fine horses descended from Diomed and Sir Archy: "They were not large, but compact," said attendee James Norris, "and possessed unusual portions of speed, strength and endurance." John Marshall, the chief justice of the Supreme Court, rode to the hounds, and in 1840, twenty-year-old Richard Henry Dulany, of Welbourne, in Loudoun County, established the Piedmont Hunt, which is still in existence.[41]

Many Virginia women of the early republic and antebellum years enjoyed their own time on horseback. In 1794, Eleanor "Nelly" Custis, the teenage granddaughter of Martha Washington and step-granddaughter

Foxhunting in Fairfax, Virginia.

*The End of the Hunt,* unknown artist, ca. 1800. This painting of a foxhunt on the Powhatan County property of Bartholomew Truehart reportedly depicts Truehart in the center, aboard a horse named Shylock.

of George Washington, learned to ride on a horse named Rozinante. She pronounced herself "very much delighted." Even when she fell off after an encounter with a tree branch, she immediately remounted and "never felt the least inconvenience." Her worried mother, Eleanor Calvert Custis, and concerned grandmother kept her out of the saddle for a time, but "at last I persuaded them my neck was not to be broken yet awhile. . . . It has given me more courage, & more caution also." She rode another mount, a four-year-old gray, "gentle, goes well except starting—called Sir Andrew Pellew," when she and her brother, George Washington Parke Custis, had an exhilarating adventure during a recreational ride from their home at Mount Vernon to Alexandria. A violent rainstorm overtook the pair en route, so they had to gallop all the way to town. Nelly Custis loved every minute. Despite her fondness for riding, though, she endured horse races only for the social benefits, when attendance was still a wholesome activity.[42]

A couple of other Virginia girls from horse-loving families also relished the freedom and excitement that horses could

provide. In the 1840s, Elizabeth Ashby, who hailed from a family of riders, liked nothing more than a good gallop across her home county of Fauquier. In 1855, Flora Cooke, living on the Kansas frontier with her army officer father, Phillip St. George Cooke, impressed a new officer with her skillful handling of a big, high-strung horse. The young man, a fellow Virginian named James Ewell Brown Stuart, fantasized about saving Flora if her horse ran away, but she made it clear that she needed no help. The two young equestriennes proved good matches for the men in their lives—Elizabeth's brother Turner Ashby and Flora's future husband, Jeb Stuart. Both men went on to earn fame with the Confederate cavalry during the Civil War.[43]

Just as not all horse enthusiasts were men, not all horse enthusiasts of the time agreed on the superiority of the Thoroughbred. Some breeders missed the easy-riding gaited mounts and so imported Spanish horses to keep up the supply. General John Hartwell Cocke, of Bremo, in Fluvanna County, was well known for his antislavery views, service in the War of 1812, and agricultural interests. He bred saddle horses and preferred a half–quarter horse stallion named Roebuck for his own mount. He liked the bloodlines of Janus, Mark Anthony, Fearnought, Jolly Roger, and other stallions of an earlier time, feeling that their compact, quarter-horse-type descendants were superior to the tall, wiry Thoroughbreds of the early 1800s. In 1818, he and fellow members of the Agricultural Society of Albemarle (which included Thomas Jefferson and Jefferson's son-in-law Thomas Mann Randolph Jr.) undertook the importation of an Andalusian stallion from Spain. After dealing with international red tape, the society appointed John Stuart Skinner, the editor of *American Farmer*, to choose the animal. One of the horses on the society's radar was "of Arabian & Andalusian blood" and could "rack [amble] 14 or 15 miles an hour," wrote Skinner. "That is a quality in the saddle horse of which our country people are very fond." The project eventually fell apart, and this particular organization, at least, did not bring Spanish horses to Virginia.[44]

Thomas Jefferson, always looking to improve any Virginia crop, thought Arabians would suit the state and vice versa. "A good foundation is laid for their propagation here by our possessing already great numbers of horses of that blood," he wrote, meaning the English Thoroughbreds, "and by a decided taste and preference for them established among the people." He admired their "patience of heat without injury" and "superior wind," which "fit them better . . . even for the drudger-

## HORSE-DRAWN VEHICLES

George Cole Scott taking his four-in-hand for a spin in Richmond.

BARGES—Horses on the banks of riverside canals pulled these watergoing vessels.

BROUGHAM—Four-wheeled closed carriage with the driver's seat outside.

BUCKBOARD—A type of open four-wheeled wagon.

CARRIAGE—Four-wheeled light passenger vehicle. More for show than for practical use.

CART—Either a small two-wheeled vehicle or a light, open four-wheeled vehicle. One or two horses pulled it.

COACH—Large, covered four-wheeled passenger vehicle, with the driver's seat outside and on top. Often used for long-distance travel. Passengers found it more comfortable due to its size and suspension. Wealthier Virginians often had their own. Stagecoaches transported paying passengers between towns; hansom cabs operated in cities like New York. An omnibus was a horse-drawn bus. In England, Cleveland Bays pulled coaches; in Virginia, Thoroughbreds, such as Thomas Jefferson's, initially performed the task.

GIG—Light two-wheeled vehicle with an open top. Pulled by one horse.

PHAETON—Light four-wheeled vehicle with a folding top.

PLOW—Wheel-less implement with a sharp leading edge used to work fields. Horses (or mules or oxen) pulled it with a human guiding from behind with handles. Other field vehicles included mowers, hay wagons, and rakes.

SLEIGH—Light vehicle with runners instead of wheels, for use on snow.

SURREY—Four-wheeled light passenger carriage with a top (not enclosed like a coach).

TROLLEY—Horses pulled these passenger vehicles that followed a track.

WAGON—Open four-wheeled vehicle used for hauling freight and passengers. One to six horses pulled them. The large, heavy Pennsylvania Conestoga wagon of the mid-eighteenth century is a famous example; it was a common sight on the Great Wagon Road down the Shenandoah Valley from Pennsylvania, through Virginia, and into the Carolinas.

*Sources:* Lay, *Ways of the World,* 23–25, 32–33, 122–26; www.buggy.com; www.morvenpark.org/carriage.htm; www.horsecenter.org/view.asp?id=workhorse.

Two scenes from turn-of-the-century Richmond. *Top left:* Mary Wortham Thomas and an unknown attendant on Gamble's Hill. *Right*: A patient pony in mufti as a reindeer at Capital Square, 1917. *Bottom:* W. P. Hulbert used a coach to convey his party guests to the 1926 Middleburg Hunt Cup.

ies of the plough and waggon." As president, Jefferson received three Barbs from a foreign leader. He auctioned off two, with the proceeds going to the U.S. treasury. His son-in-law John Wayles Eppes bought one of them, a mare, and used her as a broodmare of racehorses. In 1824, a purebred Arabian made it to Petersburg and into the hands of Colonel Robert Bolling, of Centre Hill. The stallion, an eight-year-old chestnut named Syphax, stood in the usual racehorse area of North Carolina and Southside Virginia, and as far west as Staunton in the Valley and Monroe County (now in West Virginia). Syphax's descendants brought the horses of that part of the state up to a new level.[45]

In 1853, Richard Henry Dulany began a long-lasting tradition, the Upperville Colt and Horse Show. A lifelong horseman (his family had given George Washington one of his favorite hunters, Blueskin) who had traveled abroad and imported European horses, he decided that his county friends and neighbors had to brush up on their horse husbandry and to raise better animals. One method was to offer good stallions for free breeding to good mares, so in the 1850s he brought two stallions to the area, a Morgan named Black Hawk and a Cleveland Bay named Scrivington. (The Morgan was a fairly new breed, from Vermont; small and muscular, it could reel off a lively trot as easily as it could pull a wagonload of lumber. The Cleveland Bay was a light draft horse from England, stylish and strong while pulling a carriage.)

The other method was a horse show. The first one took place in June 1853 at Dulany's Number Six farm. Fillies showed in one class, colts in the other, and the impressive silver trophies came from New York's Louis Tiffany. Enthusiastic horsemen formed the Upperville Union Club, made Dulany its president, and added divisions for "quick" (light) draft, heavy draft, and riding animals, with three age groups in each: one-, two-, and three-year-olds. The event was soon going strong as the Upperville Union Club Colt Show.[46]

Another kind of horse show, the tournament, entertained Virginians in the 1840s and 1850s. Yet another British pastime, it had migrated to colonial America and eventually faded out everywhere but the South, where the popularity of the Scottish author Sir Walter Scott and his historical novels and poems of knights and chivalry like *Ivanhoe, Waverly,* and "Rokeby" assured their existence. Tournaments (also called ring tournaments or jousts) featured mounted contestants holding a lance, galloping along a line of vertical posts with attached rings, and trying to snatch up the rings on the tip of the lance. In addition to its identity as a test of skill, the event took on the trappings of medieval competition when the competitors, all men, dressed up as knights and gave themselves names like the Knight of the Black Steed or the Knight of Ivanhoe. The winners then awarded their favorite women, watching from the sidelines, such titles as Queen of Love and Beauty and Maid Royal. The events were enormously popular, with an 1856 contest in Fredericksburg drawing five thousand spectators. Tournaments wrapped up chivalry, horsemanship, and soldierly qualities in one big, pretty package.[47]

The antebellum years saw the horse's already important place in Virginia society become further entrenched. To be sure, the animals served as ordinary livestock, but they also served as symbols of tradition, wealth, and prestige throughout the South. The cultural divide between North and South was complex and expressed itself in many ways; the culture of the horse was one. By 1861, quality descendants of the highbred Sir Archy and humble descendants of the sturdy Chickasaw horses all had new roles to play, and the pretend knights of the tournaments became real soldiers in a war that dimmed the glow of chivalry.

## THE CIVIL WAR

In 1861, the Civil War erupted, and Virginia seceded from the Union and joined the Confederacy. Richmond became the capital. Over the next four years, twenty-six major battles and more than four hundred other fights raged across the state, from the Tidewater to the Shenandoah Valley.[48] Men and boys left their homes for a few years if they were lucky, forever if they were not. Part of the state returned to the Union and became a new state, West Virginia. The Confederate quartermaster and the Union raider alike stripped the rich farmlands of crops and livestock and emptied the pastures of thousands of horses. The Old Dominion suffered the hardships and horrors of war as did no other Confederate state—and so did its horses.

In 1861, as the war heated up, the state's reputation as a producer of good horses made it a vital supplier. The army needed horses and mules to pull supply wagons and artillery, and to transport officers and cavalrymen. A four-horse team could pull 2,800 pounds under good conditions, and mules had five times the endurance of horses. The army simply could not function without the animals, which were critical for bringing supplies of food, clothing, and ammunition to the troops. The quartermaster had to find the necessary work animals as well as food to keep them go-

"Capt. Perkins' 'Sesesh' horse captured at Cornwallis' Cave, Yorktown, Va." The Confederate who had owned this horse no doubt regretted the loss.

ing. In the beginning, the Confederate army bought most of its equines from Virginia's Shenandoah Valley, which had a large helping of draft animals; the southwest part of the state; and Fauquier and Loudoun Counties. It also sought animals in North Carolina, Kentucky, and Tennessee. The supply held out until the summer of 1862, when parts of the Confederacy became off-limits, and horses in and out of the army grew worn and hungry.[49]

The mounted branch of the service, the cavalry, fought battles both mounted and on foot, but most of its contributions came away from the battlefield. In the mountains, valleys, creekbeds, roads, and trails of Virginia and other states, the cavalry provided reconnaissance, screened the Confederate army, scouted ahead, and watched the enemy.[50] The cavalry demanded and got the best from its men and horses.

The Virginian cavalrymen, after all, had grown up on horseback, leaping stone walls in pursuit of foxes, competing for glory and honor in tournaments, drilling with the local militias. They had sturdy quarter horses and blooded Thoroughbreds to carry them into battle. When it came to the Union cavalry, there was no comparison—at first. Virginians did not hold back with critiques of the enemy's equestrian abilities. "The riding of the Yankee cavalry is absurd," thought Laura Lee, of Winchester, in the Shenandoah Valley. Her neighbor Kate Sperry called them "very poor horsemen." By the summer of 1863, however, the Yankees had become better riders, seasoned, battle-hardened, with a supply of good horses that was quickly replenished from the North. The situation leaned more and more in their favor as Confederates found it harder to care for the horses they did have and to replace the ones that died or fell out of service.[51]

Confederate cavalrymen and officers had to provide their own horses and tack, which presented no problem at first. The government paid cavalrymen forty cents a day for the use of their mounts and reimbursed them for horses killed in action. Although this system worked while there were plenty of horses to replace the ones lost in battle, and while the Confederate dollar held its value, neither situation lasted long. Death, injury, illness, and lack of fodder meant there weren't enough horses to go around, and the devaluation of Confederate currency meant most men couldn't afford to buy one anyway. To make things worse, when men had to leave the front to find a new horse, they could be gone for several weeks and therefore deprive the army of soldiers.[52]

All the militia drills and ring tournaments in the world could not have prepared horses and riders for actual combat. At first, the pageantry stirred the blood and morale, providing "a grand spectacle to see these gallant horsemen coming toward us out of the gloom of night into the glare of the fires," said Alexander Boteler, an aide to Jeb Stuart, "making . . . the earth to tremble beneath their horses hoofs." On the battlefield, spectacle turned to tragedy. Henry Kyd Douglas, an aide to Stonewall Jackson, watched a cavalry charge on a line of riflemen: "A deadly volley stopped their wild career. Some in front, unhurt, galloped off, on their way, but just behind them horses and riders went down in a tangled heap. The rear, unable to check themselves, plunged on, in, over, upon the bleeding pile, a roaring, shrieking, struggling mass of men and horses, crushed, wounded and dying. It was a sickening sight." During another fight, the two cavalries galloped toward each other, faster and faster, until they crashed into each other. "So sudden and violent was the collision," wrote William E. Miller, a Union officer, "that many of the horses were turned end over end and crushed their riders beneath them."[53]

The carnage spared neither the cavalry chargers nor the mules and horses that pulled the artillery and wagons. What better way to impede the enemy's progress than to kill its artillery horses and thereby halt the movement of its cannons? Why not throw a cavalryman to the ground for killing or capture by shooting his horse? At the battle of Fredericks-

*A Stormy March—(Artillery)—Spotsylvania Court House,* Edwin Forbes. An artist's rendering of the harsh conditions under which artillery horses labored.

burg in 1862, Prospect Hill, studded with Confederate artillery, gained a new name: Dead Horse Hill. Battlefields everywhere revealed gruesome sights: here a cavalry horse, running in a panic, its intestines trailing behind; there an artillery horse, its hind legs torn and paralyzed from a shell, trying to stand and looking for help. In the aftermath of a battle, soldiers sometimes found the cries of wounded horses harder to listen to than those of humans. Freezing rain and snow hardened roads, killing and crippling animals as they struggled to pull heavy loads. Horses and mules slipping on ice, sinking in mud, broke their legs and had to be put out of their misery. Too often they died before that mercy came.[54]

If they could not express their own feelings of horror in words, horses could be eloquent in other ways. At the battle of Antietam in September 1862, Douglas made a nighttime ride over a battlefield strewn with dead and dying men, "a dreadful scene, a veritable field of blood." His horse "trembled under me in terror, looking down at the ground, sniffing the scent of blood, stepping falteringly as a horse will over or by the side of

Casualties of war: dead Confederate artillery horses at Fredericksburg, May 3, 1863.

human flesh; afraid to stand still, hesitating to go on, his animal instinct shuddering at this cruel human mystery."[55] The people had created this fight; the horses had no choice.

Hazard came from all quarters. One Virginia cavalryman loaded his animal down with so much plunder from a captured Union wagon train—blankets, jugs of wine, even a new saddle—that the poor horse fell to the ground. Jeb Stuart once sent a courier ahead on a horse to draw fire and thus see where the enemy was. The resulting gunfire wounded the courier's horse in the muzzle; the animal walked right up to Stuart and rubbed his bloody nose all over him, as if in protest.[56]

In June 1863, the battle of Brandy Station, Virginia, embodied everything about the Confederate cavalry that was great and stirring, and everything about the Union cavalry that prophesied the outcome of the war. On June 5, Jeb Stuart, the flamboyant commander of cavalry, hosted a grand review of his troops at Brandy Station. Visiting friends, family, men, and women streamed into the area. Three bands played stirring music, the artillery fired blanks, and the cavalry performed a mock charge that produced goose bumps and tears in every spectator. A pair of festive balls bracketed the event. Two days later, the irrepressible Stuart ordered another review for General Robert E. Lee, the commander of the Army of Northern Virginia. Stuart had garlanded his horse and saddle with flowers for the occasion, prompting Lee to issue a mild barb comparing him to John Pope, a Union general who had lost the second battle of Manassas/Bull Run. Before dawn the next day, Union troops surprised the Confederates and initiated a daylong battle, with the horsemen the main combatants in the biggest cavalry fight of the entire war. The Confederate army won, but they had met their match at last in the Union cavalry. "Up to that time confessedly inferior to the Southern horsemen," wrote Major Henry B. McClellan, a member of Stuart's staff, "they gained on this day that confidence in themselves and in their commanders which enabled them to contest so fiercely the subsequent battle-fields."[57] Like Gettysburg and other events of 1863, the battle of Brandy Station proved a tipping point in the war.

After a year or two of fighting, hope and abundance dwindled. As Douglas Southall Freeman put it, "The final exhaustion of the horse supply, which was destined to cripple the army in the winter of 1864–65, was ominously forecast as early as the autumn of 1862." Lee tried his best, for he cared deeply about the well-being of both man and horse. In fact, he checked on the horses so often that a teamster who didn't recognize him exclaimed, "Who *is* that durned old fool? He's always a-pokin' round my hosses as if he meant to steal one of 'em." But neither one man nor one army could cope with widespread equine ailments such as "sore tongue," "greased heel," "soft hoof," and glanders, a highly infectious respiratory disease. By the spring of 1863, only three-fourths of Jeb Stuart's cavalry had mounts. When the Union general Philip Sheridan burned fields and barns of corn in the Shenandoah Valley, he destroyed morale along with desperately needed food for the Confederate and Virginia horses. When the Confederate army impressed their draft horses, Virginia farmers couldn't keep growing corn and other fodder. And when they couldn't grow enough feed, the army horses starved.[58]

Lee tried to cope with shortages in the winter, when the armies were in camp and fighting was suspended, by sending horses to the James River, the lower Rappahannock, and the Shenandoah Valley. Nonetheless, the winter of 1862–63 claimed the lives of hundreds of horses. Lee coped by cutting back on the numbers of supply wagons and by refusing requests to increase the artillery. However, in 1863, the Union cavalry had grown better and Union horse supplies bigger, quite the opposite from the Confederate situation. "The destruction of horses in the army is so great that I fear it will be impossible to supply our wants," said Lee. "There are not enough in the country."[59]

To remedy things, the Confederate secretary of war proposed buying horses from Texas and Mexico, but nothing came of the plan. Lee also suggested going behind enemy lines to trade tobacco and cotton for horses. In May 1863, a raid captured 1,200 to 1,500 Union horses, which helped, but not enough. During the summer campaign that year, which took Confederates into Pennsylvania, they appropriated many local draft horses, but the rigors of battle and travel wore all the animals down. In August 1863, a desperate and grimly realistic Lee said, "Nothing prevents my advancing now but the fear of killing our artillery horses. They are much reduced, and the hot weather and scarce forage keeps them so." Lacking even horseshoes, Confederates would cut the hooves off dead horses in order to salvage the shoes. Toward the end, Henry Kyd Douglas, for one, was so hungry that he stole corn from his starving horse.[60]

During the first half of the war, the care of ill and injured animals was left to the quartermaster and his agents, who turned them out to pasture to fend for themselves. Needless to say, many animals died from the lack of treatment. In fall 1863, the Confederacy established horse infirmaries, with Virginia's in Lynchburg. It was a mixed success. Most horses did not arrive until they were too far gone, and diseases swept through the herds. During the fifteen months of the infirmary's existence, it admitted nearly seven thousand horses but returned only about one thousand to service. Nearly three thousand died, and the rest were lost, stolen, sold, or out of commission.[61]

Constant exposure to the deaths of men and horses usually inured cavalrymen to the deaths of their own mounts. For some men, however, the experience deepened their emotions. At the battle of Cedar Creek, Douglas's mount received a wound first in the leg, then in the jaw. Thrashing his head in pain, spraying blood everywhere, he still carried his rider across rocky terrain in the dark to escape the enemy. He collapsed, "lifted up his head in pain and tried to rub it against me in mute appeal for help," Douglas remembered. There was nothing he could do; the horse contracted tetanus and died two days later. When a Virginia officer named George Baylor lost a mare in battle, he knelt beside her,

*War Horse,* by Tessa Pullan, at the Virginia Historical Society, in Richmond. This statue of a wearied, riderless horse memorializes the estimated 1.5 million horses and mules killed or injured in the Civil War.

threw his arms around her neck, and sobbed into her mane until she died.[62]

At the surrender at Appomattox on April 9, 1865, Lee found a bright moment in the gloom of the day when Ulysses S. Grant, commander of the Union army, accepted his tactful suggestion that the surrendered men be allowed to keep their horses. Although the surrender's terms forbade nonofficers from taking their mounts, Grant tweaked them, understanding that the soldiers needed horses to start their lives over. "This will have the best possible effect upon the men," Lee told Grant. Those men were lucky to have an animal at all, for the war had decimated the population of horses and mules all over the South, and especially in Virginia. When the drummer boy William West returned home to Alleghany County, he found that "horses to work were something great. Only the rich could buy them!"[63]

The Civil War killed or wounded an estimated 1.5 million horses and mules. By comparison, 970,000 men died or suffered an injury. In 1997, the Virginia philanthropist and horseman Paul Mellon commissioned a statue from the British sculptor Tessa Pullan honoring those animals. It stands at the U.S. Cavalry Museum at Fort Riley, Kansas; in the driveway of the National Sporting Library, in Middleburg; and, in a slightly larger version, in front of the Virginia Historical Society, in Richmond. Rather than the usual military statue of a vigorous, prancing mount, it depicts a thin, tired horse, no rider in sight, its head drooping to the ground as if pressed by an unbearable weight.[64]

## THE CAVALRYMEN

James Ewell Brown "Jeb" Stuart (1833–1864) was born at Laurel Hill, in Patrick County, south of present-day Roanoke and near the border with North Carolina. As a boy he loved horses and became a good rider. He became an even better one as a cadet at West Point, class of 1854. With a Virginian's pride in his equestrian skills, he made fun of the fellow students he called "Yankees . . . on horseback." He and seven other cadets received the honorary title of "cavalry officer" because of their extraordinary performance in the saddle. His informal title at West Point was "Beauty."[65]

After West Point, as a young army officer, Stuart served in Kansas on the Indian-fighting frontier. There, in 1857, he chased a group of Cheyennes across the plains, wearing out one horse in the process and appropriating another man's animal to complete the chase. During his antebellum army career, he designed tack and weaponry for the military's use. In 1861, like so many other southerners, he resigned from the U.S. Army to fight with the Confederate States of America. His initial commission assigned him to the infantry, but he soon moved to the cavalry because of his experience in that area. Another Virginian, Turner Ashby, had rounded up a volunteer cavalry of Virginians, and he begrudged General Stonewall Jackson's decision to place the cavalry under Stuart. Jackson neatly solved the problem by giving each man a regiment of cavalry.[66] Stuart's final promotion made him a major general of cavalry in the Army of Northern Virginia, under Robert E. Lee.

Jeb Stuart loved his job. He relished the pageantry of rowdy soldiers and hot-blooded horses and surrounded himself with jaunty music and lively companions. And he certainly dressed the part of dashing cavalry leader: “a short gray jacket covered with buttons and braid, a gray cavalry cape over his shoulder, a broad hat looped with a gold star and adorned with a plume, high jack boots and gold spurs, an ornate and tasseled yellow sash, gauntlets that climbed almost to his elbows.” Even the name of one of his horses reflected his philosophy: Skylark. He rode another horse aptly named Virginia. Altogether, with his impressive beard, eye-catching clothing, and fine horsemanship, Stuart “looked like an equestrian statue,” said one of his aides, Alexander Boteler.[67]

“A good man on a good horse can never be caught,” Stuart told his men. “Another thing: cavalry can *trot* away from anything. . . . We gallop toward the enemy, and trot away, always.” Stuart and his troops galloped toward the enemy at the first Battle of Bull Run, Chancellorsville, Gettysburg, the great cavalry battle of Brandy Station, the Wilderness, and Spotsylvania. His legend sprouted in June 1862, when the audacious Stuart rode all the way around the Union army, which was moving on Richmond from the east. First he sent ahead Lieutenant John Singleton Mosby, another cavalryman, to see what George McClellan, the Union commander, was up to. After Mosby’s favorable report, Stuart obtained Lee’s permission to proceed in hopes of gaining information about the enemy’s plans and to interfere with their supplies and communications.

Jeb Stuart *(above)* in his signature plumed hat, as depicted by the *London Illustrated News* in 1862.

Jeb Stuart's saddle, with a detail showing his name tooled into the leather.

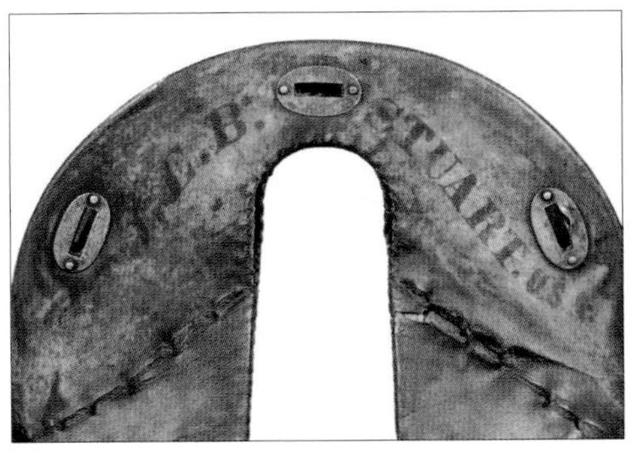


Stuart also saw another benefit to the plan: his father-in-law, fellow Virginian Phillip St. George Cooke, had kept his allegiance to the Union and was out there with McClellan. Stuart was eager to outfox him.[68]

From June 12 to June 15, Stuart and 1,200 cavalry and artillery swooped one hundred miles in all, starting just north of Richmond, riding in an eastward arc that ended in triumph in the capital city. Mosby and a few of his men joined the party as scouts. Stuart suffered only one casualty, Capt. William Latané, who was riding a half-Arabian horse named The Colonel when he was shot and killed during hand-to-hand fighting. The expedition captured 260 much-needed horses and mules (plus food and liquor). They clashed a few times with the Union army, and even built a bridge in three hours to cross the Chickahominy River. As soon as the last rider exited the bridge, they burned it; ten minutes later, a handful of Union soldiers rode up on the opposite bank. Before erecting the bridge, one of Stuart's men, Rooney Lee, son of Robert E. Lee, had swum across the swollen river to see if it was safe to ford. Some accounts later claimed that Stuart, not Lee, had crossed the river, and on horseback. Stuart did little to quash the story. Such exploits led even his enemies to dub Jeb Stuart "the greatest cavalryman ever foaled in America."[69]

During his three years' service, Stuart had four horses shot from under him. Virginia, who once jumped a wide, deep stream in tandem with another horse and rider while escaping from enemy pursuers, died of distemper, as did a mount named Star of the West. His other horses died in combat, were captured, or, like his horse Chancellor, died of a wound. Stuart's record with horses was nothing unusual for Virginia cavalrymen; it was hard to keep a horse sound and alive what with scarce feed, harsh weather, and whizzing bullets.[70]

Stuart died on May 11, 1864, while defending Richmond from a Union advance. He was shot at Yellow Tavern, to the north of the Confederate capital. He died the next day in Richmond after giving away his possessions, including two horses. His wife, Flora, arrived too late for a good-bye. She had first caught his eye nine years earlier as she rode a spirited horse.[71]

Turner Ashby (1828–1862) could not have been anything but a cavalryman. He was born in Fauquier County into a family renowned for its horsemanship. In 1755, his great-uncle Jack Ashby had ridden three hundred miles in three days to deliver a message from George Washington to the House of Burgesses. With similar élan, Turner Ashby reportedly once rode his horse into a resort ballroom via the stairs. The residents of Fauquier County loved to watch ring tournaments, and Ashby loved to compete. In one thrilling display, he rode bareback, dressed as an Indian, whooping and hollering as he galloped into the arena, hooked the ring, jumped a stone wall, and disappeared into the distance.[72]

Fulfilling his birthright, Ashby formed a company of militia cavalry, the Mountain Rangers, after John Brown's 1859 raid on Harpers Ferry. In the Civil War, the group became part of the Seventh Virginia Cavalry, and he fought in the Shenandoah Valley as one of Jackson's cavalry commanders. "To romantic Southerners he looked as if he had stepped out of a Waverley novel," wrote Douglas Southall Freeman. "With fierce mustachios and a beard that a brigand would have envied, he was of middle height and of a frame not apparently robust, though wiry and of astonishing strength. His eyes were dark, deep-set, sad and earnest." On a horse, Ashby only grew in stature and charisma.[73]

"Riding his black stallion, he looked like a knight of the olden time," wrote Henry Kyd Douglas. "Galloping over the field on his favorite war horse, his white one, eager, watchful, he was fascinating, inspiring. Alto-

The Virginia cavalryman Turner Ashby, probably astride his famed horse Tom Telegraph, from a carte-de-visite.

gether he was the most picturesque horseman ever seen in the Shenandoah Valley."[74]

The black horse, called Black Charger, died during a fight at Kelly's Island in 1861, whinnying to Ashby as he lay dying and bringing the cavalryman to the brink of tears. The white horse was the Fauquier County–bred Tom Telegraph, also known as the White Charger. He was thought capable of "the most wonderful feats. He will drop to the ground in a flash, at the wish of his rider, and rise again as suddenly, bound through the woods like a deer, avoiding trees and branches, clearing every obstacle, jumping fences or ditches with perfect ease." Tom Telegraph died in combat in 1862 after carrying his rider to safety from a fight. "The big-hearted Cavalier bent over him, stroked his mane, stooped down and gazed affectionately into his eyes," wrote Douglas. "Thus the most splendid horseman I ever knew lost the most beautiful war-horse I ever saw."[75]

Friends and foes thought Ashby was invincible when he was on a horse and considered him the South's premier equestrian. He could break the wildest horse and jump the highest fence. For many Confederate soldiers, Ashby, with his fine horsemanship and gentlemanly behavior, also represented what they felt they were fighting for, ideals of home and state.[76]

Perhaps he was invincible on horseback. On foot, things changed. In

John Singleton Mosby, at right on the white horse, as painted by Edouard Armand-Dumeresq, *Mosby Returning from a Raid.*

a battle on June 6, 1862, near Harrisonburg, he was riding a bay horse, the replacement for Black Charger. The horse was shot and killed, throwing Ashby to the ground. Ashby then died while leading a charge.[77]

Ashby's body was buried; the bodies of his horses met different fates. Their manes and tails found their way to people who saved the hairs as precious souvenirs. One woman even braided her hank of horsehair and sent it to Ashby's mother. People carved the teeth and bones of the bay horse he had ridden in his last battle into jewelry with "Ashby" etched into the surface. Today Ashby's saddle and one of Tom Telegraph's bones and teeth are displayed at the Stonewall Jackson Headquarters Museum in Winchester. In life, and especially after death, Turner Ashby was "as perfect a specimen of modern chivalry as the South has produced," wrote a Richmond newspaper editor.[78]

Jeb Stuart's occasional scout, John Singleton Mosby (1833–1916), was born at Edgemont, in Powhatan County. After a sickly childhood in which he took more than his share of bullying, he became a daredevil. At the University of Virginia in the early 1850s, he disturbed the peace by galloping his horse through Charlottesville; even worse, he wounded another student and spent time in jail for the crime.[79] He enlisted as a private in the First Virginia Cavalry, was commissioned a first lieutenant in 1862, and organized the Partisan Rangers in January 1863. His organization waged guerrilla warfare in Loudoun Valley and other areas of Virginia, harrying Union troops and diverting supplies.

Like Ashby, Mosby was small and unprepossessing on foot but became a charismatic leader on horseback. "Gaunt, thin-lipped," wrote Freeman, "with his satirical smile, his stooped neck and his strange, roving eyes," Mosby sometimes wore a gray, red-lined cape and embellished his hat with an ostrich plume. He led charges at a fast gallop right into enemy lines, a pistol in each hand. One time he even led a cavalry charge on foot. He and the Partisan Rangers, skilled riders all, wore snappy uniforms, liked to jump fences and walls, and could somehow ride as quietly as if their horses trod on feather beds, a skill with which they often surprised Union soldiers.[80]

Mosby's Rangers snatched up approximately 3,500 horses and mules during the war. Confederate policy dictated that the government would pay them for the animals. Mosby, however, would distribute the best horses to the men who'd shown the most impressive performance during the raid, and then divide up the rest by lottery so the rangers could sell the extra horses to the quartermaster. His men, eager for a good fight and a good horse, would sometimes pick out a fine-looking Union animal before they entered battle, hoping it would soon be theirs. In the wake of one successful raid, Mosby's men used the captured money he had given them to buy him a horse, Coquette.[81]

Mosby survived the war. Unwilling to surrender along with everyone else in April 1865, he disbanded the rangers soon after Appomattox. Thirty years later, in Boston, Mosby met a former Union chaplain, Charles A. Humphreys, who had once escaped from him on a swift roan horse. Mosby didn't remember the man, but he did remember the horse.[82]

## STONEWALL JACKSON AND LITTLE SORREL

In appearance, style, and breeding, there could not be two horses—or owners—more different than Traveller and Little Sorrel, and Robert E. Lee and Thomas J. "Stonewall" Jackson. But when it came to the qualities that produced great warhorses and great military leaders, there was scarcely any difference.

Thomas Jonathan "Stonewall" Jackson (1824–1863) was born into poverty in what is now West Virginia, lost both parents as a child, and struggled through West Point. After proving his worth as a soldier in the Mexican War, he resigned from the U.S. Army and took up the teaching profession at Virginia Military Institute, in Lexington. Known to everyone as a devout Presbyterian, Jackson joined the Confederate Army and earned his nickname at the first Battle of Bull Run for his steadfastness. He reached the rank of lieutenant general in October 1862. His Stonewall Brigade fought hard all the way through the war, and General Lee himself called their leader his right arm.

Jackson met his equine soul mate in the spring of 1861, when Confederate troops captured a Union supply train containing a car packed with horses. The quartermaster helped him pick out two animals: a tall, flighty sorrel gelding with a rough gait, and its opposite in everything but color: "a plebian-looking little beast, not a chestnut; he was stocky and well-made, round-barreled, close coupled, good shoulder, excellent legs and feet, not fourteen hands high, of boundless endurance, good appetite, good but heavy head and neck, a natural pacer with little action and no style." Jackson dubbed the smaller horse Fancy and called him that the rest of his days. Everyone else called him Little Sorrel.[83]

His owner rode with none of the dash of Jeb Stuart or the quiet authority of Robert E. Lee. Instead, hearkening back to his days as a teenage jockey, Jackson perched in the stirrups and leaned out far over his mount's neck. He "rode boldly and well, but not with grace or ease," said his aide Henry Kyd Douglas, "and 'Little Sorrel' was as little like a Pegasus as he was like an Apollo." Stuart and Jackson, standing together with their mounts, made a fascinating contrast. Stuart wore a gray uniform, shiny boots, and a yellow sash, and rode a big stallion. Jackson wore his usual ratty-looking suit and his "old dingy" Virginia Military Institute (VMI) cap and sat atop his short, scruffy mount.[84]

"It would have been impossible to have found another horse that would have suited his new owner so exactly," thought Douglas. "He was made for him." Jackson could ride along with a slack rein, deep in thought or catching a few minutes of sleep, and Little Sorrel would march along, his smooth gait cosseting his master's needs. Perhaps he was a Morgan; many of the hardy, Vermont-bred animals served in the Union cavalry, and he had arrived in Virginia on board a train from the North.[85] With his often-mentioned amble and pace, he may have had Narragansett Pacer blood, or some traces of the old Hobby and Galloway blood that had made Virginia horses so desired.

As Jackson's wartime reputation grew, so did Little Sorrel's. On one occasion, admirers clustered around Jackson and began snipping Little Sorrel's mane and tail for souvenirs. The event so disconcerted Jackson that he and his staff departed town in a hurry. Such events taught Little Sorrel that Jackson disliked displays of emotion, so when soldiers would start to huzzah for their leader, he would pick up a gallop and carry Jackson away.[86]

In late August 1862, Little Sorrel went missing, causing his master great concern. In his absence, Jackson tried to ride a gray mare, a gift from a Maryland farmer. Instead of a small, willing horse, he now had a large, heavy animal that reared and fell with him. In the same period, an aide's horse kicked Jackson's foot as they rode alongside. Fortunately, Little Sorrel somehow returned a few weeks later.[87]

On May 2, 1863, during the battle of Chancellorsville, Jackson was riding Little Sorrel when he was accidentally shot by Confederate troops. For the first and only time in their partnership, the reliable horse bolted in a panic, running Jackson into a tree limb before aides could catch him. After Jackson dismounted, Little Sorrel ran straight toward the enemy and disappeared in the dark. On May 10, word of Little Sorrel's recovery by Private Thomas R. Yeatman, a member of Stuart's horse artil-

Little Sorrel in his golden years at the Virginia Military Institute, ca. 1880s.

lery, was dispatched to the home where Jackson lay dying of pneumonia following the amputation of his left arm. The historical record does not say if Jackson understood or acknowledged the news. The general died that afternoon.[88]

For the next twenty years, Little Sorrel lived in North Carolina with Anna Jackson, the general's widow, earning his keep under saddle and in harness. Around 1883, Anna Jackson sent him to VMI. He appeared at the state fair in Richmond, with VMI cadets warding off souvenir hunters in search of mane and tail. With the rise of the Lost Cause, the southern enshrinement of the Civil War, the horse also traveled to New Orleans for the 1885 World's Fair, where he went on display as a living reminder of the South's experience. After that grand trip, he ended up in Richmond at the Confederate Home for Veterans. Despite his many years away from the battlefield, he would prick up his ears and trot in the direction of gunfire when the residents plinked away at birds. The veterans, some of them former soldiers of Stonewall Jackson's, cared for the elderly horse, even doing him the dubious kindness of hoisting him up in a sling for visitors when he could no longer stand. The animal died in 1886, at around thirty-six years old.[89]

The taxidermist Frederick Webster, of Washington, D.C., set to work stuffing Little Sorrel's carcass. His payment: the skeleton. The stuffed horse wound up back at VMI, where students would pet him for luck. Years of such affectionate attention wore the hair off his skin, so Little Sorrel underwent at least a couple of renovations and today resides in the VMI Museum, safely out of petting range. At the museum's

Little Sorrel is remembered at VMI in different ways. *Top:* Maintenance being performed on the stuffed hide of the horse. *Right:* The grave holding his bones, on the parade ground in front of a statue of his master, Stonewall Jackson.

gift shop, one can buy postcards, magnets, and stuffed toys depicting the little horse.[90]

His bones have made an equally colorful journey. They ended up back at VMI in the 1940s, where they were displayed in a biology classroom until 1989, when they went into storage. In 1997, they were cremated and buried at the base of the statue of Stonewall Jackson on the VMI parade ground. Civil War reenactors fired a volley, a band played "Dixie," the United Daughters of the Confederacy provided dirt from all the battlefields Little Sorrel had trod, and the school's flags flew at half-mast. "Old Jack and Little Sorrel were more than a man and his mount," said eulogist James I. Robertson Jr., a professor of history at Virginia Tech and author of a 1997 biography of Jackson. "They were, for a time, the inspiring symbol of a nation's hopes. Man and horse imparted to each other great care, service, and dependability." VMI officials thought Jackson would have approved of the ceremony.[91]

## ROBERT E. LEE AND TRAVELLER

When visitors to Washington and Lee University stroll by the president's house, better known as Lee House, they see almost the same thing as visitors did in the 1860s. The handsome brick house has an appendage, a brick structure with just enough room for two cars—or two horses. The most famous resident of the house was Robert E. Lee, commander of the Confederate army during the Civil War and president of Washington and Lee (then Washington College) from 1865 to 1870. The stable's most illustrious inhabitant was Lee's warhorse, Traveller.

Born in 1857 in Greenbrier County, Virginia (now West Virginia), Traveller wasn't registered as a member of any breed, or at least no records give that information. Fairfax Harrison, Virginia's equine genealogist, called him "bred" and thought it was "reasonably certain" that "he was infused with as good horse blood as there was in Virginia," possibly that of Diomed and Sir Archy. His owner, Andrew Johnston, named him Jeff Davis, showed him with success at county fairs, and then gave him to his son, J. W. Johnston. Lee got his first glimpse of the horse in 1861, when J. W. Johnston rode him in the Confederate army.[92]

Lee liked the animal, which he jokingly called "my colt," so much that he kept track of him even when Johnston sold him to Joseph M. and Thomas L. Broun. Joseph Broun was riding the horse, then named Greenbrier, when he reported for duty in Charleston, South Carolina, where Lee also was serving. In 1862, Broun offered him as a gift, but Lee insisted on buying him for two hundred dollars. He bestowed on the horse his third and last name: Traveller.[93]

Before Traveller, Robert E. Lee (1807–1870) had ridden and cared for many horses. A son of Ann Carter and Henry "Light-Horse Harry" Lee, the Revolutionary War hero, he was born in the Northern Neck, at Stratford Hall in Westmoreland County. Both sides of his prominent family had lived in Virginia for generations. He graduated from West Point, entered the U.S. Army, served in the Mexican War from 1846 to 1848 and in the Southwest, and oversaw West Point from 1852 to 1855. He was married to a great-granddaughter of Martha Washington, Mary Custis Lee, and with her raised several children at Arlington, the Custis family home near Washington, D.C. In 1861, the army offered him command of

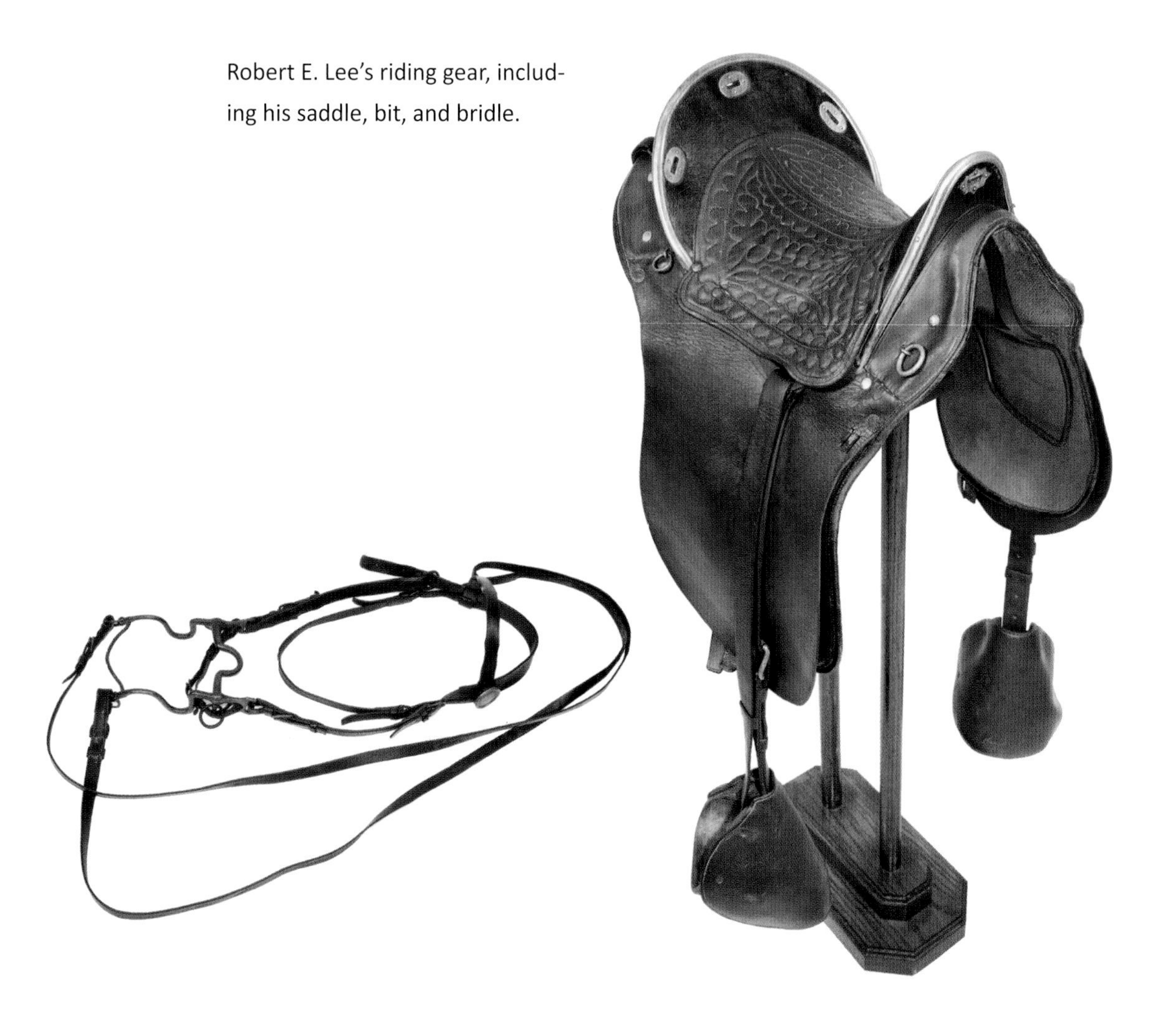

Robert E. Lee's riding gear, including his saddle, bit, and bridle.

Lee's boots, with a detail showing his spurs.

the Union forces, but he resigned and joined the Confederate army, unable to bring himself to fight against his native state. In June 1862, he took over the entire command of the Army of Northern Virginia.

During the Mexican War, Lee had Creole, a small dun mare from New Orleans; a sorrel mare from Mexico; and a bay horse, Jim, from San Antonio. In 1861, someone gave him a bay stallion named Richmond, who was high-strung and noisy. He died during the war. Lee bought a horse he called The Roan or the Brown-Roan in western Virginia; the horse went blind, and Lee retired him to a farm. Jeb Stuart gave him a mare named Lucy Long. Lee alternated between her and Traveller until she disappeared sometime during the war. A fourth horse, Ajax, was a tall sorrel. It was quite a collection of horseflesh, but Traveller was his favorite.[94]

"The horse was somewhat nervous, had a fast, springy walk, but preferred a 'short, high trot,' which was hard on riders who had a less good seat than Lee," wrote Douglas Southall Freeman. Lee lovingly described "his fine proportions, muscular figure, deep chest, short back, strong haunches, flat legs, small head, broad forehead, delicate ears, quick eye, small feet and black mane and tail. Such a picture would inspire a poet." If his trot was less than comfortable, his walk and canter were strong and smooth, and he could keep them up for miles. Lee repaid his mount's service, fussing with his shoeing and tack and making sure he had plenty of rest.[95]

Traveller and his master in Rockbridge County, Virginia, during Lee's term as president of Washington College (now Washington and Lee University).

The nearest Traveller came to letting his owner down was the day that a dismounted Lee reached for the reins when the startled horse reared. Lee tripped and injured his hands, which left him unable to ride for several weeks. The horse made up for it at the battle of Spotsylvania, when he again reared, this time with his rider in the saddle. As he pawed at the air, a cannonball shot underneath them. This time, Traveller's fractiousness saved both of their lives.[96]

On April 9, 1865, Lee rode Traveller to Appomattox to surrender his army to Ulysses S. Grant, the commander of the Union forces. After the negotiations concluded, an emotional Lee found a moment of solace in easing his mount's forelock from under the bridle before riding off to tell his men the war was over. Lee and Traveller rode through the crowds of cheering, sobbing men, the horse tossing his head as soldiers reached out to caress horse and rider.[97] The general made his way on Traveller back to Richmond, where he was reunited with his family.

The partners again hit the road in September, when Lee headed for

Lexington and a new posting—as president of Washington College. They arrived at the Lexington Hotel with no fanfare, just a man on his horse, his saddlebags packed with clothes. When his identity dawned on nearby men who happened to be veterans of his army, they reverted immediately to military procedure, saluting their former leader before gripping Traveller's stirrup and bridle so Lee could dismount. Nearly every day, President Lee took time from his duties to revel in a long, relaxing ride on his "beloved steed," as his wife called Traveller. Like Thomas Jefferson, he preferred to ride alone, but sometimes a companion tagged along. "Traveller moved as if proud of the burden he bore," said the student W. H. Tayloe, Alabama kin of the Mount Airy Tayloes. "To me the horse was beautiful and majestic." When not carrying Lee through the Rockbridge County countryside, Traveller roamed the campus, as did other horses belonging to the faculty, and extended his range even into the Lees' yard, where he would nod his head in greeting when Lee came for a visit, a ride, or just to bestow a lump of sugar. In 1869, the Lees' new brick home had a stable joined to the house by a covered passageway. Lee loved having his horse under the same roof.[98]

Traveller's stablemate in the new structure was the long-lost Lucy Long. After her disappearance during the war, she had ended up in the possession of a former soldier, who sold her to William Campbell, of Essex County, for $125. A friend of Campbell's recognized her as Lee's mare, so Campbell contacted Lee, offering to give him the animal. Lee's son Fitzhugh confirmed her identity and paid Campbell $125 at his father's insistence. She lived with the Lees until her death in 1891. Ajax, the other wartime mount, lived in Lexington until he died in a strange incident by accidentally impaling himself on a gate latch.[99]

In September 1870, Lee and Traveller continued their traditional afternoon rides. One day they had companions, two young girls aboard their swaybacked old horse. One of the girls was just getting over the mumps, and Lee, who loved the company of children, teased her about giving Traveller the ailment. The last ride of horse and master occurred sometime before September 28, when a cold rain and a business meeting at Grace Church kept Lee out of the saddle. That evening he fell ill, probably having suffered a stroke, and immediately took to his bed. During the next several days, his doctor tried to boost his spirits by reminding him that Traveller needed a ride. Lee died on October 12. The horse's next duty for his master came when he walked behind the hearse in the funeral procession.[100]

Traveller's resting place, at Washington and Lee University.

A few months later, in June 1871, Traveller stepped on a piece of metal and came down with tetanus. The disease took him quickly. When he could no longer stand, the family even placed a featherbed in the stable for his comfort. His cries of agony kept everyone awake until he finally died. He was only fourteen. Eight mourners—Lee's son Custis, three men who transported the body and dug the grave, and four local girls—attended his burial in Wood's Creek behind the college. Custis Lee, with "tender grimness," covered Traveller with the horse's blanket before the grave was filled in.

As with his possible ancestor Sir Archy and his fellow warhorse Little Sorrel, the remains of Traveller met a curious fate. Around 1875, someone dug up his bones and sent them to Henry A. Ward, a "museologist" in Rochester, New York, for some kind of preservation treatment. Ward didn't finish, and the bones spent thirty years in an unknown location. In 1907, they made their way back to Lexington and the institution now called Washington and Lee University in honor of Traveller's owner. Joseph Bryan, a Richmond newspaper owner, paid for the mounting of the skeleton, which went on display in a campus museum. While VMI students patted Little Sorrel for luck, W&L students felt compelled to leave their initials on Traveller's bones. After the skeleton of either a goat, colt, or pony was placed next to Traveller's, guides would joke to visitors that the small frame was Traveller as a colt, and the large one was Traveller as an adult. In 1929, the skeleton was moved to a museum in Lee Chapel. In 1940, clever students perpetuated the Lexington rumor that the bones were not Traveller's at all, embellishing the story to claim that they were actually those of General Grant's horse. (The students certainly knew how to stir up Virginians.) In the 1960s, the horse found yet another resting place—storage. He finally received his due in 1971, a century after his passing. Traveller's mortal remains were buried for the second and last time, outside Lee Chapel and the crypt containing the remains of the Lee family.[101]

Traveller's many visitors leave flowers, coins, apples, and other tokens of affection at his grave. A plaque on the outside of his stable, now also a garage for the president's cars, further commemorates the great horse. In a final tribute, the doors to the stable are always open, so that the spirit of Traveller may come and go as he pleases, just as he did in life when he strolled over the campus of Washington College, waiting for a gallop across the Virginia countryside with his owner.[102]

North side of the 700 block of High Street at Green Street, Portsmouth, 1930s.

# 1866–1945

## HORSE AT A CROSSROADS

*The horse is not just a fancy of the people, it's a tradition . . . an inseparable part of the heritage of old Virginny.—Eastern Breeder,* March 1941

After four years of war, Virginia had nothing but mourning families, heaps of ashes, and bittersweet relief. Approximately thirty thousand Virginians had died, as had many more thousands of horses and mules. Soldiers counted themselves fortunate to return home with an equine, no matter its age or breeding or condition, for at least they had a way to plant crops and get around. Horse racing had all but disappeared, along with foxhunting, steeplechasing, horse shows, and all other pleasurable and profitable equine pastimes. Before long, however, breeders and farmers began to reconstitute the horse population of the Old Dominion. Owners who had sent their fine horses out of state to escape the danger brought the animals back. As the state entered a new century, Virginia horses kept on doing what they had for hundreds of years. They also took on new roles.

For the rest of the 1800s, the horse ruled the road, with its only competitor the train. In country and city, horses pulled plows, wagons, passenger trolleys, fire engines, hearses, buggies, and carts. They carried riders bound for church, market, court, school, and home. In fact, the heavy workload they bore in Richmond, Virginia's largest city, prompted the Society for the Prevention of Cruelty to Animals to pay a visit in 1893 to investigate conditions. In New York City in 1900, for example, horses lasted on the job only about five years, and twenty working animals might die in the city in any one day. Even in smaller communities such as Virginia's, horses' waste filled the streets and assaulted the human nose and eye. The noise of their iron-shod feet clattering on pavement, pulling rumbling wagons, assaulted the ear as well.[1]

From 1890 through about 1919, purchasers bought their horses everywhere from the Great Southern Horse Bazaar in Richmond to the horse market in Rockbridge County. In 1908, the Smyth Brothers and McCleary-McClellan Company of Norfolk moved their horse-trading business to Richmond, where they conducted a sale of one thousand mules and horses consigned from states all over the South and Midwest. In 1893, W. H. Harbaugh, a Richmond veterinarian, bought a team of draft horses from the West to pull his horse ambulance. In the 1930s, men like Tom Hand, of Culpeper County, traded horses and mules, but not the blooded animals or half-bred hunters for which the region was known. Rather, Hand bought old horses and resold them to glue factories. For some practical sorts, the romance of the Virginia horse had its limits.[2]

Whether Virginians of the late nineteenth and early twentieth centuries owned a vast plantation or a patch of land, they needed horses to work their farms. Farmers of the 1870s also used oxen and mules, but horses held their ground; sixty years later, it was hard to find a farm

William Patterson "Pat" Davis; his horse, Old John; and his grandsons J. Robert and Oscar Leon Davis, in Burke's Garden, Tazewell County, 1912. During the Civil War, Davis reportedly hid his horses in a cave to protect them from Union troops. The enemy soldiers, however, still managed to steal one of Davis's horses but left a mare in its place. Old John was the son of that mare.

Horses at work in Richmond. *Clockwise from top left:* Dairy wagons deliver the day's milk; fire horses race to a blaze; a three-horse hitch provides public transportation before the advent of streetcars and buses.

with oxen, but equines were still very much in use. Around 1900, when John and Josephine Wright, a young couple with three children, moved to a rented farm in Craig County, they had the bare necessities when it came to livestock: one cow, one horse. Over in Alleghany County around the same time, John Ernest Bess Sr. lost two of his three animals. "It's a poor go on a farm with only one horse," he said. Bess remembered Chub, another "grand horse [that] lived to be twenty-seven years old and gave no one any trouble. . . . My youngest brother had to plow corn with Chub for a few days one summer without having corn to feed, just pasture, and it was almost more than he could stand. He said he would rather not eat than to hitch up old Chub without feeding him."[3] Horses continued as the draft animal of choice for several decades.

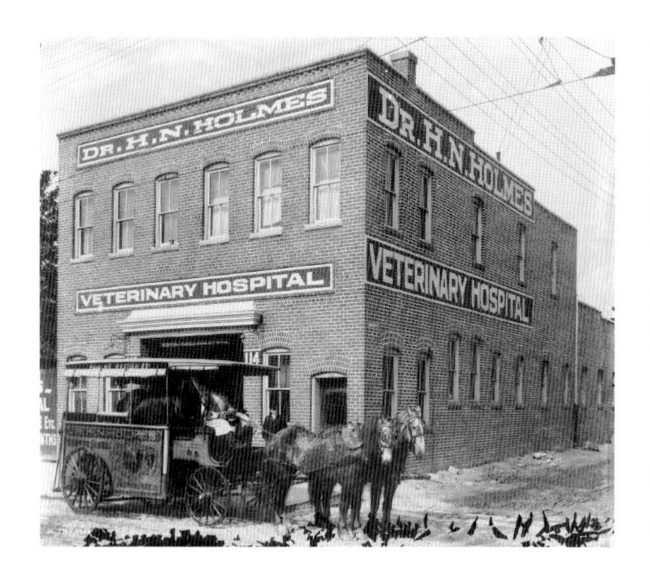

Horses were part of the everyday fabric of life in towns and cities all across Virginia. *Top,* a veterinary ambulance in Norfolk; *top right,* a street scene in Staunton; *right,* businesses like this one in Norfolk, ca. 1900, boarded horses as well as selling and exchanging them.

Virginia equines first met the competition in 1888, when Richmond added electric streetcars to its stable of horse-drawn vehicles. The electric versions took over completely by 1900, putting horses out of business in that area of transportation. Norfolk hosted the state's first automobile in 1899, but Henry Ford's Model T didn't motor down the roads in any significant numbers until 1913, with around two hundred cars in Richmond alone. Tractors started to plow their way into farms after the mid-

Virginians used horses for work and pleasure. *Left:* Out for a ride in Albemarle County, 1918; note the horse's docked tail. *Bottom left:* Two residents of Nicholson Hollow, in the Blue Ridge Mountains. Arthur Rothstein, a U.S. government photographer, was documenting the controversial removal of the area's residents to form Shenandoah National Park in the 1930s. *Bottom right:* A draft horse and farmer, Fairfax County, 1938.

1920s. By the 1930s, horsepower in the form of a paint job and four tires was steadily overtaking a sleek coat and four legs.[4]

Mechanization did not deter some horse lovers. Between 1910 and about 1930, a handful of Richmonders, at least, shunned cars for horses and buggies and continued to traverse the city in style, including Mr. and Mrs. Archer Anderson (he was head of the Tredegar Ironworks) and Charles E. Bolling, the city engineer. There were "all those who,

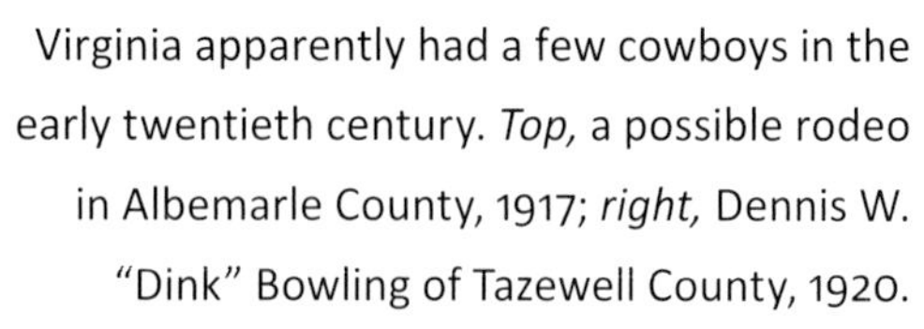

Virginia apparently had a few cowboys in the early twentieth century. *Top,* a possible rodeo in Albemarle County, 1917; *right,* Dennis W. "Dink" Bowling of Tazewell County, 1920.

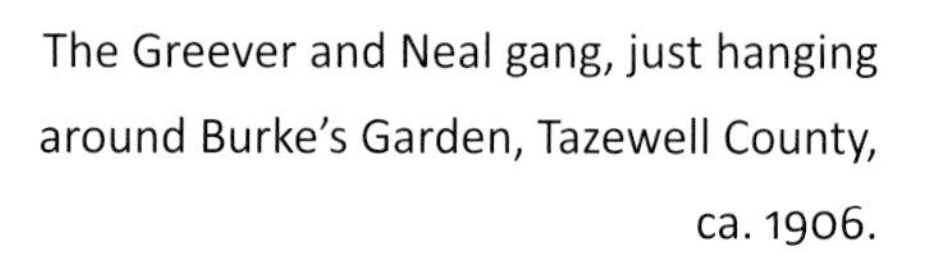

The Greever and Neal gang, just hanging around Burke's Garden, Tazewell County, ca. 1906.

Children of Amelia County on their way to school.

despite the convenience of the motor car and the civilizing labours of the State Highway Commission," wrote Fairfax Harrison in 1928, "still use and cherish the Virginia bred horse, whether they ride steeplechases or merely practise hill topping to hark to the sweet music of a pack of hounds in full cry."[5]

In rural Virginia of the 1920s and 1930s, even with cars plentiful and somewhat affordable, children rode ponies to school or drove a horse and buggy, and so did their principals and teachers. Many schoolyards had barns and stalls for the horses' shelter during the school day. Farm wives drove the horse and buggy to town for shopping, and even country children who might ordinarily ride to school in their parents' cars still turned to horses when bad weather made the roads impassable. Horses as reliable transportation were not quite obsolete.[6]

## RACING

The Civil War had wiped out racehorses and breeding stables all over the South. For Virginia, with its Thoroughbred business already diminished by the earlier shift to Kentucky as a breeding center and with professional gamblers taking over the grandstands, the war and its aftermath hastened the end of the sport as a thriving, respectable way of life. "The general tone of the Virginia turf in the eighteen fifties was lower than that of the [eighteen] twenties," as Fairfax Harrison put it, and in the 1870s and 1880s, "it descended lower still . . . [and] reached a nadir of disrepute in Virginia." Albemarle County enthusiasts of the 1880s

Racehorse Robert Waddell with jockey Wesley Walker and trainer Hezekiah Seaton. The two men probably came from formerly enslaved families in the area of Charles City County, clans that produced expert horsemen.

refused to give up, with jockey clubs, the Albemarle Racing Association, and the James River Valley Fair hosting steeplechases and flat races at William Garth's Ivy Creek and in Scottsville. By then, racing in multiple heats of two or four miles had changed to racing as we know it today, with horses racing shorter distances only once.

The quarter-mile races, too, belonged to the past. By now, the Quarter Horse as a distinct breed was percolating not in Virginia but in Texas, where the cow sense it had inherited from Spanish and Scottish forebears, and the all-around versatility it had developed in Virginia, were coming in handy to manage the vast herds of cattle that roamed the ranches and prairies.

In the 1880s, a surge of religious feelings across the South led to the legal restriction of horse racing and its associate, gambling. In 1891, a new law effectively ended both pursuits in the state, thus closing "a pleasant and characteristic chapter of Virginia history," wrote Harrison, and putting them on hiatus for nearly a century.[7]

The Civil War had brought good change, however, for one group of Virginia horsemen—African American jockeys. Free to pursue their careers on their own terms, they competed in large numbers on U.S.

racetracks, with black jockeys winning thirteen Kentucky Derbies between 1875 and 1902. By 1913, with the imposition of laws segregating the races, they were largely gone from the sport, all but ending a long Virginia tradition that had begun during slavery with skilled men like Charles Stewart. Many black men, however, found employment as grooms and trainers, sometimes with racing stables, sometimes on their own. Alexander McDaniel, of Doswell, born in the 1850s, had started as an exercise rider and then become a trainer, and raised a son who was a jockey. Around the turn of the century, Essic Hairston Sr. was a well-known trainer and breeder in Pittsylvania County.[8]

In the larger horse-racing world of the 1890s, one of the best starters in the business hailed from Virginia: James Rowe, of Fredericksburg. Born about 1850 in Richmond, he started his racing career as an exercise rider in New Jersey. In the 1870s, he worked his way through the ranks in the usual way (as a stable boy, jockey, and trainer) and in unusual ways (as a circus rider and "comic opera proprietor") before settling in as a starter at New York tracks. For his efforts, he received a Tiffany's silver table service from grateful horsemen and the honor of judging classes at the New York Horse Show. Some of Virginia's traditional ardor for the track must have influenced him as a boy, for Rowe became a trainer for national racing luminaries such as James R. Keene and Harry Payne Whitney, reaching prominence from 1913 to 1927.[9]

Despite the gloomy state of the sport, not all Virginia racehorses ran out of the money. In 1901, a horse named Robert Waddell, owned by Robert "Virginia" Bradley (1835–1907), of Charles City County, won the American Derby in Chicago. Bradley, a veteran of the Civil War also called "Pa Bradley," had started his racing career at fairs around the state. He did well enough to buy Greenway Plantation, the birthplace of President John Tyler. In the 1890s, his well-known horses included Blitzen, Will Ellett, Clarus, Chucknut, and Sir John. In 1901, his horse's victory at the American Derby signaled his move onto the national scene.[10]

Around the same time, breeders of Thoroughbreds continued to ply their trade in the Old Dominion, such as the Garth, Pitts, and Dorrier families of Albemarle County.[11] Those who succeeded in the racing business did so by embracing Kentucky or by waiting until the 1920s and 1930s to make their move.

Albemarle County nurtured one lasting Thoroughbred dynasty during and after the Civil War. When a Confederate soldier from Alabama, Richard Johnson Hancock, recuperated from a wound in Charlottesville, he met a local woman, Thomasia Overton Harris. Her father, John, owned a large Albemarle County farm, Ellerslie. The young couple moved there after their marriage, and Hancock began raising Thoroughbreds. He formed an alliance with Thomas Doswell, of Hanover County's Bullfield Stud, the breeder of Planet. In 1895, the Hancocks' son Arthur struck up a partnership with his father, and in 1909 he took over the business. Arthur married Nancy Clay, of Paris, Kentucky, whose family owned the lush rolling pastures of a place there called Claiborne Farm. The younger Hancock ran the breeding operations in both states for many years, moving to Kentucky in 1912 but keeping Ellerslie going for three more decades.[12]

At the Virginia farm, the Hancocks used Doswell's outstanding stallion, Eolus, another descendant of Sir Archy, to produce winning horses, including Knight of Ellerslie, winner of the 1884 Preakness. With those two horses, plus a stakes horse of the 1890s named Morello, the Hancocks and Ellerslie restored some of Virginia's earlier reputation as a racehorse center.[13]

Ellerslie continued its achievements into the twentieth century, although Claiborne overtook it in importance and stature. In 1921, the leading Thoroughbred stallion in the United States was Ellerslie's Celt, and twenty years later the *Virginia Breeder* called Ellerslie the "oldest Thoroughbred nursery in the Old Dominion" and the "foundation of Claiborne, the greatest stud in the world." In the 1940s, the Hancocks stood at Ellerslie a horse they co-owned with Charles and Whitney Stone of nearby Morven Stud, Pompey, a son of the leading stallion Sun Briar; the English import and stakes winner Foray II; and Tintagel, owned by Marshall Field, the department store magnate (who lived in Orange County). A fine broodmare herd filled the Ellerslie pastures, and a family of expert horsemen named Gentry ran the place. In the late 1940s, the Hancocks sold Ellerslie and consolidated all operations at Claiborne Farm, thus ending one chapter of a legend in Virginia and continuing the next in Kentucky.[14]

This elite group of prominent Virginia breeders also included New Yorker Willis Sharpe Kilmer, owner of Sun Briar, a French-bred stallion. Kilmer had made his fortune with a potion called Swamp Root and spent the proceeds on racehorses. He owned another equine celebrity, the famous gelding Exterminator, the 1918 Kentucky Derby winner that Kilmer had bought to sharpen Sun Briar's competitive edge.

Thoroughbred stallion Pompey, a son of Sun Briar.

Instead, "Old Bones" had taken Sun Briar's place in the Derby, stunned the crowd with a decisive win, and raced successfully until he was nine. Kilmer imported European horses, bought American-breds, and raised his own. In the early 1920s, he bought a Shenandoah Valley farm, Court Manor, near New Market. In the winter, he also conducted operations at Remlik Hall in Middlesex County. Sun Briar's son Sun Beau, among other fine horses, was foaled there. In the 1930s, Kilmer moved Sun Briar, Exterminator, and Exterminator's sidekick, a pony named Peanuts, to Court Manor, where they enjoyed the Virginia grass until Kilmer's death in 1940. In October of that year, a dispersal sale brought in more than $200,000 for 101 horses, except for Sun Briar, Exterminator, and Peanuts, which lived out the rest of their days in New York, and Sun Beau, which was leased out to stud. Charles Howard, owner of the fabulous racehorse Seabiscuit (retired from the track that year), attended the sale, along with the Virginia horseman Christopher Chenery.[15]

Chenery, a Richmond native who grew up in Ashland, started The

Meadow Farm near the community of Doswell (named for the racing family) in the 1930s. He grew up without much money, worked hard to get an education, and became a wealthy utilities executive in New York. His love of Virginia and horses brought him back to his home state, where he invested wisely in broodmares and made good matches for them, accumulating fine breeding stock at home and numerous winners on the racetrack. Like Thomas Doswell, Chenery had a close relationship with the Hancocks. His tale is told at greater length in chapter 4, with a discussion of his most famous horse, Secretariat.[16]

In 1925, two-thirds of the best 155 Thoroughbred stallions in the United States lived in Kentucky. Nevertheless, of those top animals, thirty-six lived in Virginia, specifically in Albemarle, Clarke, Fauquier, Loudoun, Nelson, Orange, and Rockingham Counties. The owners of these animals were Valley breeders like Dr. Lewis M. Allen, who raised horses on Clifton, his nineteenth-century family farm near Berryville; William H. duPont, with Walnut Hall Stable in Clarke County (his sister, Marion duPont Scott, raised horses in Orange County at Montpelier); and Colonel Kenneth N. Gilpin, of Kentmere, also in Clarke County, a nucleus of Valley breeding. Most of these operations carried on into the 1940s, some even longer.[17]

The brothers Bernard and Montfort Jones stood Triple Crown winner Sir Barton at their Audley Farm, near Berryville. (Audley had been the final home of Eleanor Parke Custis Lewis, the granddaughter of Martha Washington and step-granddaughter of George Washington who had so enjoyed riding as a girl in the 1790s.) The Jones brothers hailed from Mississippi, although Montfort had been born in Virginia. They invested money made in the Oklahoma oil fields in the horseflesh and historical property of Virginia, raising racehorses, keeping broodmares like Princess Doreen, and standing an imported English stallion, Bright Knight, in addition to Sir Barton. A dispersal of the stock in 1939 brought more than $200,000.[18]

In northern Virginia, Dr. Cary T. Grayson, a Culpeper County native, bred racehorses on 1,500 acres at Blue Ridge Farm, in Upperville. He had been the presidential physician for Theodore Roosevelt, Woodrow Wilson, and William Howard Taft. Daniel Cox Sands, also a leading foxhunter, operated the Benton Stud in Middleburg, standing a horse named Prince of Wales. Joining Ellerslie in Albemarle County were the Nydrie Stud at Esmont, and Charles and Whitney Stone's Morven Stud. In addition to breeding racehorses, Whitney Stone led the National

Horse Show in many capacities from 1932 to 1979, held important offices with the United States Equestrian Team, and served in World War II. Over on the Northern Neck, scene of many a horse race in the eighteenth century, the Robert E. Lee Memorial Foundation bred horses for the track and the hunt field at Stratford Hall, the Lee ancestral home.[19]

By 1940, Clarke, Fauquier, Loudoun, and Warren Counties in northern Virginia formed the center of Thoroughbred breeding in the state. Several Kilmer horses raced and stood at stud. Westmoreland Davis, the Virginia governor from 1918 to 1922, raised horses at his Big Spring Farm in Leesburg, with a stallion named Teddy Beau that was related to Sun Beau. William F. Hitt stood Sun Meadow, a son of Sun Briar, at Homeland Farm in Middleburg, and rode hunters like Elf King in horse shows. William H. Lipscomb ran Raspberry Plains farm near Leesburg. Ernest Ashby's farm stood Dr. Freeland, a Preakness winner, for owner John E. Hughes of Chicago. Blue Ridge Farm was now owned by Mrs. George L. Harrison, widow of Cary Grayson, and stood the well-known stallion Happy Argo and the blind broodmare Modification. John S. Phipps owned Blenheim Farm near The Plains, and Mrs. David Buckley, at High Acres, stood Playfellow, a full brother to Man o' War owned by Daniel Cox Sands. Northern Virginia now held the same status that Southside Virginia had enjoyed more than a century before.[20]

Phipps's stallion, also named Blenheim, was American bred. He shared a name and an English sire (Blandford) with an English stallion, Blenheim II, who stood at the Hancocks' Claiborne Farm in Kentucky. Phipps bred him to mares of Sun Briar and Sun Beau lines and produced stakes winners. Although his Kentucky brother was a more productive sire, Virginia's Blenheim lived in "one of the most spacious abodes in Virginia," wrote Anne Hagner in the *Washington Post* in 1941. "His stall is so large, in fact, that he has plenty of room to exercise in it if he so desires."[21]

Blenheim (both horse and farm) had as a neighbor another good racing sire, Milkman, who stood at Rolling Plains Farm. In 1941, Mrs. W. Plunkett Stewart, who had owned the farm since the late 1920s, charged $650 for a mating to the stallion, who had broken two track records at Saratoga and won close to $100,000 during his racing days. Following the dairy theme, Milkman's get bore such names as Pasteurized, Buttermilk, Early Delivery, and Early Morn. At age fourteen, Milkman was a "beautifully built brown" horse "who looks more like a youngster than a middle-aged gentleman," found the *Washington Post*.[22]

Archie Randolph *(left)* and Sammy Knowles *(right),* MFH and whip, respectively, of the Piedmont Hunt.

During the 1930s, several wealthy women carved out a niche as breeders of racehorses. In addition to Mrs. Stewart and Mrs. Harrison, northern Virginia had Katherine Elkins Hitt, Leila Gaines Gwathmey, and Mary Elizabeth "Liz" Whitney (later Tippett).

Isabel Dodge Sloan kept them company. At Brookmeade Farm in Upperville, Sloan stood Psychic Bid, a grandson of the famed stallion Fair Play. During his racing days, Psychic Bid had won three stakes races and three handicaps and finished third in the Preakness. As of 1941, his foals were doing well in shows and races. The nine-year-old was "quiet as a pet hunter" except under saddle, when he demonstrated considerable "bucking prowess," wrote the *Washington Post.*[23]

David N. Rust started his Rockridge Farm in Loudoun County around 1911. At the Court Manor dispersal sale, he bought the stallion Gino for $19,500. In addition to the gray eleven-year-old, an import from England (his previous owner was the Aga Khan), Rust also stood Time Maker, age sixteen. He affectionately called the stallion, at a shade over 14.2 hands, "a little big horse." Time Maker had sired many stakes winners, including Time Supply. In 1941, having just added Gino to his string, Rust was eagerly awaiting his first crop of foals.[24]

The region had a living representative of the equine heritage of Virginia in the person of Archibald Cary Randolph, a descendant of the co-breeder and namesake of Sir Archy. (The modern-day Randolph called the famous horse "the Man 'o War of his day.") At Grafton Farm near Upperville, Randolph stood a former racehorse named Runantell in the 1930s and early 1940s, crossing him with Percheron, pony, and Thoroughbred mares. Randolph also owned a pony mare, Blue Wing, who had carried the Randolph children (once clearing a jump of 4' 6" at the Warrenton Horse Show) before retiring to a career as a broodmare.[25]

The horsemen of the area relished foxhunting and steeplechasing in addition to racing, and so they bred and rode horses that specialized in one or more of the disciplines. Many of them had a good eye for a draft horse as well.

## MARION DUPONT SCOTT

The twentieth century found in a woman its counterpart to the all-around, nineteenth-century racing man: Marion duPont Scott (1894–1983). She arrived in Virginia in 1902, when she was eight. The new home of the wealthy duPont family—Montpelier, a mansion in Orange County—dated from 1760 and had been the abode of James Madison, president of the United States from 1809 to 1817, and his wife, Dolley. The environment nurtured the young girl's interest in equines. "I guess it was a case of being brought up with horses," she said of her adult career, "more than anything else." Scott and her brother, William, who became a lifelong Virginia horseman as well, built a show ring they called Coney Island where she could put her ponies—Barbra, Bonnie Bell, Midget, and Grisette—through their paces. As she grew older, she preferred to ride sidesaddle, but at age twenty-one she was reportedly the first woman riding astride to win a blue ribbon at Madison Square Garden. Sidesaddle or astride, hunters or jumpers, Hackneys under harness or gaited saddle horses, she rode and drove them all, chasing the fox as well with the Montpelier Hounds.[26]

In 1928, after the deaths of her parents, Scott found herself the owner of Montpelier and heir to a considerable fortune. She invested in her increasing passion for steeplechasers and flat racers and even built courses for both sports at her home, which became the scene of the enduring Montpelier Hunt Races. She bought one of her best-known steeplechasers, Trouble Maker, in 1927. He raced unsuccessfully in England but did well in the United States, triumphing at the Maryland Hunt Cup in 1932. In 1935, the gallant horse died at the seventeenth jump of the Maryland course after suffering a heart attack. Even forty years later, the memory drew tears from Scott.[27]

In addition to Trouble Maker, Scott owned or bred famed racers over fences and on the flat. Battleship, a son of Man o' War, won the 1938 Grand National in England, the most famous steeplechase in the world. He was the first Grand National winner bred in the United States and owned by an American. The compact chestnut stallion—he was only 15.2—raced on the flat before trying his hand on the Virginia hunt field and then on the steeplechase course. Accra (a broodmare), Annapolis (also by Man o' War), Benguala, Mercator, Mongo, Neji, Proud Delta, Rouge Dragon, Shipboard, and Soothsayer brought in trophies and sent out winning offspring. She relied on the trainers Carroll Bassett, Frank A. (Downey) Bonsal, Peter Howe, Noel Laing (who rode Trouble Maker in his winning Maryland Hunt Cup), and Ray Woolfe Sr.[28]

Grand National winner Battleship and his owner, Marion duPont Scott.

"The land in Virginia is just as good as Kentucky for raising horses," stated Scott in 1976. She gave back to her home state by establishing the Marion duPont Scott Equine Medical Center, at Morven Park in Leesburg, with a gift of $4 million. The center, a referral hospital that opened in 1984, provides complete veterinary care as well as training of interns. It is one of three campuses of Virginia Tech's Virginia-Maryland Regional College of Veterinary Medicine. Scott also donated her extensive library on subjects equine and sporting to the University of Virginia.[29]

## ALEXANDER MACKAY-SMITH

In the Virginia horse world, Alexander Mackay-Smith (1903–1998) was "a man for all centuries, a renaissance individual."[30] During his long, rich, productive life, he wrote eleven books (six of them about foxhunting) and edited the *Chronicle of the Horse.* He founded, promoted, or served such important organizations as the U.S. Pony Club, the North American Riding for the Handicapped Association, the U.S. Combined Training Association (now the U.S. Eventing Association), the Museum of Foxhounds, the American Foxhound Club, the American Horse Show Association, the Virginia Thoroughbred Association, the National Sporting Library, the Cleveland Bay Society, the Morven Park International Equestrian Institute, the American Remount Association, the Clarke County Historical Association, the U.S. Dressage Foundation, and the American Academy of Equine Art. It was quite a résumé for a New Yorker and a Harvard man, a member of the Harvard Glee Club, a violinist, and a civil servant in the administration of Franklin Delano Roosevelt who didn't set foot in Virginia until 1932.

Once he arrived on Virginia soil, Mackay-Smith made up for lost time. He bought Farnley Farm in White Post, where he raised Cleveland Bays and his then-wife Joan (later Dunning) raised Welsh and Dartmoor ponies. He also began to pursue his love of foxhunting. "He believed that God had put him on earth to ride a horse behind hounds," said his son Matthew Mackay-Smith. In 1939, he served as Master of Foxhounds (MFH) of Raymond Guest's private Rockhill Hounds. When Rockhill joined the Blue Ridge Hunt, he became MFH for that group from 1942 to 1949 and from 1951 to 1960. Mackay-Smith hunted until he was seventy-seven. "He was nerveless on a horse," said his widow, Marilyn Mackay-Smith. "He would jump anything, and he would ride anything so he could go hunting."[31]

The renaissance horseman of Virginia, Alexander Mackay-Smith, in hunting attire, with an apt companion—a foxhound. Portrait by Jean Bowman, a well-known Virginia artist of equine and related subjects.

When he wasn't actually riding a horse, Mackay-Smith was organizing or writing or running something that had to do with horses. He even invented the competition known as a hunter pace. "He had a way of getting across to you that you had an obligation to the sport," said James C. Wofford, the eventing rider and trainer from Virginia.

"There is a tremendous amount of power in being the dean of American horse sports," said Charles L. Fletcher, a friend and fellow MFH. "And he handled it with grace and dignity and kindness."[32]

"He never did any of this for notoriety," said his widow. "His interests were genuine, and when he saw a need for something, he had . . . the ability to make it happen."[33]

Near the end of his life, Mackay-Smith declared, "I am just as fascinated with horses and hounds today at the age of 93 as when I moved from New York to Virginia at the age of 29." After his death, the Blue Ridge Hunt gave him a moving send-off. On December 22, 1998, the mourners sang a few foxhunting songs (another passion of Mackay-Smith's), and then his family rode into the Master's Spinney (a small grove of trees), which had been named for him, to scatter his ashes. Once the riders returned, the assemblage sang "Drink Puppy Drink" before the hunt plunged into the Master's Spinney, the huntsman's horn sounding through the winter air, riders, hounds, and horses headed for a day's sport. It's hard to imagine a more fitting tribute.[34]

## FOXHUNTING

After the Civil War, foxhunting regained its footing and grew in stature and popularity. Landowners continued to hunt their private packs, such as Richard Henry Dulany and his Piedmont Fox Hounds, but new takes on old traditions began to take hold. Virginians who had hunted in Britain and British newcomers to the state relished pursuing a fox over the Old Dominion's countryside. One such Englishman, Archibald Buchanan Bevan, came to Virginia in the late 1880s, serving as the first master and a huntsman of the Blue Ridge Hunt, established in 1888 in Clarke County on the lands that Lord Fairfax and George Washington had once enjoyed. Carter Hall, the magnificent old home of the Burwell family, became a landmark for the members. Englishmen also rode with the Warrenton Hunt, founded in 1887, which initiated a long tradition of steeplechasing and hunt races; its best-known huntsman was a member of an old local family, H. D. Bywaters.[35]

As with so many other aspects of Virginia culture over the centuries, the British imprimatur made hunting a desirable social pastime for the upper class. Once people had begun to recover economically from the war, they joined organizations like the Deep Run Hunt, founded in 1887 in Richmond. It first headquartered at a plantation called Chantilly outside of Richmond (near today's West Broad Street and Staples Mill Road). By 1896, Deep Run had moved to Ginter Park near the monument devoted to A. P. Hill, a Confederate officer, with stalls, a racetrack, and a golf course. Deep Run's members were a who's who of 1890s Richmond: Branch, Bryan, Carter, Langhorne, Scott. By 1900, it boasted 218 members and occasionally met at the new statue of Robert E. Lee on the western edge of the city (then open fields, now Monument Avenue).[36] Where horse racing had once filled a social function for respectable citizens of means who liked a good horse and a good party, foxhunting took its place.

Other hunts that sprang up before the turn of the century included the Loudoun Hunt (1892), which counted as members Governor Westmoreland Davis and E. B. McLean, publisher of the *Washington Post*, and the Keswick Hunt (1896) near Charlottesville. Gertrude Rives (Mrs. Allen) Potts was one of Keswick's top riders. During a 1903 hunt, in a snowstorm, she "ended the run in the lead and showed her usual exhibition of beautiful horsewomanship by putting Bachelor over a five-foot flank fence without a 'touch.'" A few years later, she headed her own Castle Hill Hunt and was putting Willow King through his paces in the Corinthian class at the Warrenton Show.[37]

Not every hunter of foxes rode a Thoroughbred and drank from a stirrup cup. Blanche Chenery Perrin wrote of the sport around 1900 around Ashland, where she grew up: "A fox hunter's pink coat with its attendant luxury and glamour, was in the past and in the future. The present contained the foxes—there were plenty in Hanover County and their raids on chicken houses much resented—the fox hounds, and the men eager to ride to the chase."[38]

Though the sport was truly on the upswing, it took the new century and another invasion from the North to solidify its importance once and for all in Virginia. It wasn't just Virginians and British who loved the sport; it seemed that more than a few Yankees hankered to spend a crisp fall morning on a fine Virginia-bred hunter, jumping fences, following the cries of the hounds in pursuit of a smart fox. They found land readily available as farms belonging to once-wealthy Virginians, still impoverished by the Civil War and its aftermath, went on the market. For example, in 1900 Edward H. Harriman, a railroad magnate from New York, founded the Orange County Hunt. He named it not for the Virginia county but for his home county in New York. Many a weekend Harriman would load up his railroad cars with New York friends for two days' hunting in Virginia. More than a century later, the organization remains just as exclusive and desirable.[39]

If Harriman retained an air of the outsider, another northerner, Harry Worcester Smith (1865–1945), made himself at home and won a place in the hearts of die-hard Virginia foxhunters. From 1905 to 1917, the Massachusetts man revived and redefined foxhunting in Virginia, putting the state once and for all on the map as a center of the sport. Smith first visited in 1898, befriended H. Rozier Dulany, of Upperville, a member of the Dulany family, and fell in love with northern Virginia. Before long he became a joint master of the Dulanys' Piedmont Fox Hounds. In 1905, he earned his reputation with the American Foxhound Match in northern Virginia. Convinced of the superiority of American-bred hounds over English hounds, he pitted C. C. Eastham's pack of American hounds from Flint Hill, in Rappahannock County, against A. Henry Higginson's English Middlesex pack, from Massachu-

Harry Frost and Daniel Cox Sands, well-known horseman of northern Virginia in the mid-twentieth century, out for a day's hunt.

setts. The match began at Welbourne, the Dulany home. It was a fox-hunter's dream: two November weeks of hunting every other day, with two fine packs of hounds to follow. The Virginians were eager to prevail, and they did—the American pack won the match and cemented northern Virginia's popularity as premier foxhunting territory. Smith was a memorable figure. He "rode hunched over a bit with his head tucked in," wrote Katherine "Kitty" Slater, a chronicler of the hunt, "and under his rather frazzled velvet hunting cap was a thick suit of curly grey hair and a deeply furrowed brow."[40]

Another transplanted northerner, Daniel Cox Sands, also settled right in, serving as the master of foxhounds of the Middleburg Hunt (established 1906) from 1915 to 1953. The Casanova Hunt came along in 1909, with territory near Warrenton in Fauquier and Culpeper Counties.

A prominent Virginian of the time, Charlotte Noland, was an avid rider who hunted sidesaddle and partnered with Sands as joint master of the Middleburg Hunt in the 1930s and 1940s. One of her best horses, Rokeby, was a homebred from Cary Grayson's Blue Ridge Farm. In 1914, she combined education with foxhunting by founding the Foxcroft School for girls on family land in northern Virginia. Noland called the

Charlotte Noland, ca. 1938, about to go hunting on a handsome gray. She is riding sidesaddle, not astride as most women did by the mid-twentieth century.

school teams "Foxes" and "Hounds" and named her home The Covert, after the fox's hiding place. She lived by one maxim and expected her pupils to do the same: "Take your jumps clean and straight; talk clean and straight; live clean and straight." Further, opined Noland, "Fox-hunting calls forth quick and fateful judgement . . . and is, therefore, the ideal corrective for the one thing most lacking in women—decision." The firm-minded equestrian headed her school until her retirement in 1961.[41]

The 1920s gave rise to the Old Dominion Hounds (1924), with the first joint masters Joe Thomas and Major Louis E. Beard of the U.S. Army's Remount Depot in Front Royal, and then MFH Sterling Larrabee, and local huntsmen from the Poe and Chadwell families; the Rappahannock Hunt (1926); and the Fairfax Hunt (1927), founded by A. Smith Bowman. (The original Fairfax territory is now covered by the town of Reston, Dulles International Airport, and Wolf Trap, so it hunts in Loudoun County, north of Middleburg.) The Williamsburg area had the Princess Anne Hunt (1927). Charlottesville-area hunters rode with the Albemarle Hunt Club until it ended with World War I, then with its successor, the Farmington Hunt Club (1929), when Randolph Ortman, of Blue Ridge Farm, in Greenwood, got it up and running. Farmington became known for its horse show held from 1934 to 1944. The Glenmore Hunt Club (1930) covered the Shenandoah Valley between Staunton and Stuarts Draft, and the Middlebrook Hounds (1930) emerged from Glenmore. Bull Run Hunt came along in 1937, enjoying a few years of sport before World War II placed foxhunting, along with so many other recreational pursuits, on hold.[42]

Before he became one of that war's signal figures, George S. Patton Jr. (1885–1945) rode many a day with the Cobbler, Middleburg, Piedmont, and Warrenton Hunts. The son and grandson of Virginians and VMI graduates, Patton attended VMI for one year (1903–4) before graduating from West Point. He studied at the French Cavalry School and at the cavalry courses at Fort Riley, Kansas. In 1912, he placed fifth in the Olympics' modern pentathlon, which required prowess at shooting, fencing, swimming, running—and riding. He took up polo in 1920. During the 1920s and 1930s, stationed three times with the Third Cavalry at Fort Myer, Virginia, Patton and his family rode to the hounds three horses they had brought from a posting in Hawaii: Hukupu, Khonakki, and Heonakula (no doubt the only horses with such names in Virginia at the time). They also owned a show hunter named Silver King. Patton and his wife, Beatrice, were joint MFHs of the Cobbler Hunt. He bought his breeches from the Upperville tailor Shirley Kines and even wore them with his uniform during World War II. In 1944, at the peak of his controversial fame, the *Washington Post* called him "the ridin'est man who ever donned expensive hunting boots and dashed across Cobbler's beautiful rolling territory around Del[a]plane."[43]

In the relatively brief interval between the arrival of Harry Worcester Smith and the start of World War II, Virginia foxhunting carved out a king-sized niche in the equestrian and sporting worlds. "Virginia is now all agog over the fox-hunt," wrote the *Washington Post* in 1933, also pointing out the sport's financial benefits to the state—increasing land values and employment for locals. The newspaper called the foxhunters themselves, "the folk who have made northern Virginia the mecca of the old sportsmanship," adding, "they were riding to hounds, suh, in Virginia when the 13 original colonies were just about getting on their feet."

One of foxhunting's devotees, Alexander Mackay-Smith, described the sport with an experienced eye:

> Foxhunting means a great many different things to different people. There are the cut-me-downs who measure hunting in terms of how fast they can gallop and how big the fences are. There are the dyed-in-the-wool hound men, many of them indifferent riders, who get just as much pleasure in seeing a pack work up the cold line as they

The traditional hunting whip this rider carries is used to communicate with the hounds by making a popping sound with the lash. It can also be used to open gates from horseback by hooking them with the handle.

do in the run that follows after the fox has been burst out of his kennel. There are those who come to see their friends, those who like to show off their horses, those who have hunter prospects to school and those who simply love cross-country riding. There are good riders and bad, children, and long standing members who can no longer go the pace, but deserve special consideration.[44]

Joseph B. Thomas, MFH of the Piedmont Fox Hounds, thought that all a good season of foxhunting needed was the cooperation of the landowners, fences in good repair, plenty of foxes, and well-conditioned horses and hounds. He had an ideal day on December 13 of the season of 1916–17: "Four foxes viewed away, four foxes run to earth—about twenty five miles of galloping behind the pack—the shortest run no less than three to four miles, the longest twelve to fourteen. A bit of snow on the ground, the most marvelous sky effects and views of the Blue Ridge Mountains in distant sunshine occasionally cut off by snow squalls."[45]

## STEEPLECHASING

Steeplechasing provided even more sport for daredevil riders and mettlesome horses. Although virtually suspended in Virginia during the Civil War, along with most horse sports, at least one steeplechase did occur then, at Falmouth on St. Patrick's Day, 1863. The competitors were the Irish Brigade of the Army of the Potomac—Union troops.

Steeplechases and other races sprang up under the aegis of the mushrooming hunt clubs. As foxhunting grew, so did the steeplechases. Where Virginians had once imported English Thoroughbreds for flat racing, now a few brought foreign horses for steeplechasing, such as Robert Neville, of Loudoun County, who imported a French Thoroughbred named Rigoletto in 1893. The sport drew enthusiastic audiences, such as the crowd at the 1902 Spring Race Meet of the Deep Run Hunt Club. Smiling and chatting with friends while they watched the races, Governor and Mrs. Andrew Montague worked the crowd, along with two of the famous Langhorne sisters, Nancy Langhorne Shaw (later Lady Astor and the first woman in the British Parliament) and Irene Langhorne Gibson (wife of the illustrator Charles Dana Gibson and a model for his famous Gibson Girl). The Deep Run races shuttled around and about Richmond, starting in Ginter Park, then moving to what is now the Country Club of Virginia, then Curles Neck Farm, and then to the state fair when it was on Strawberry Hill on Laburnum Avenue, before shuttling to Colonial Downs. Along the way, the meet became known as the Strawberry Hill Races.[46]

In 1906, the Warrenton area had enough men interested in the sport to float a proposal for a country club featuring a steeplechase course. The interested parties included northerners who had recently moved to Virginia, such as H. C. Groome, of Philadelphia, and Temple Gwathmey, of New York. They wanted "to revive racing in Virginia as it existed many years ago," said the *Washington Post.* Top riders in Warrenton stayed busy on the circuit, riding mostly at county fairs: Lee Evans, Dion Kerr, James K. Maddux, Charles Daniels, Percy Evans, Charles Harris, and F. A. B. Portman.[47]

From 1926 to 1944, one of the best-known jockeys on Virginia courses was Colonel "Not" Brooks (1911–1993), an African American from Upperville. His father had trained horses for the Dulany family. Brooks won more than one hundred steeplechases with his old-fashioned, English-

Steeplechase images helped sell Virginia tobacco, illustrating the popularity of the sport in the Old Dominion.

hunting-print style of riding—leaning back over the horse's rump, arms and legs thrust straight out in front. Everyone had ridden that way once, but the forward-seat method of the Italian cavalryman Federico Caprilli, which he'd devised around 1900, was gaining currency everywhere people rode hunters and jumpers.[48]

In addition to fine riders for the steeplechase, Virginia produced quality horses, such as Sandy Creeker from Aftongreen Stud in Culpeper, owned by William T. Townes. In 1909, in the middle of an exciting career, the horse broke a leg during a race and had to be shot on the spot. Another fine horse, Oracle II, hunted and raced in the 1920s. In the late 1930s and early 1940s, Blockade, a horse bred in Upperville, dominated the field by winning the prestigious Maryland Hunt Cup three times in a row. The champion's career ended when he broke his neck in a fall at the Virginia Gold Cup. The Gold Cup, second only to the Maryland Hunt Cup as the top timber race in the United States, began in 1922 as the Virginia Hunt Cup at the Oakwood estate near Warrenton. It changed locations a few times until finding a home at Great Meadow in 1984. (The steeplechasing fan Arthur W. Arundel bought and donated the property.) The oldest race in Virginia, born in 1921, occurs in Middleburg at Glenwood Park.[49]

## POLO

Toward the end of the nineteenth century, polo swung into Virginia. The thrilling, centuries-old sport came not from Britain but from China, India, Japan, and Persia. Two teams of riders pursue a ball while wielding mallets and attempting to score goals at either end of a large field, as long as three football fields and as wide as one and a half. Each team has four players, and the match occupies six, seven-minute chukkers, thus requiring several horses per player. The galloping, stopping, sliding, bumping, and turning require a speedy, agile, responsive horse, called a polo pony. The British and other Europeans in India latched onto the game in 1863, and in 1876 polo came to the United States via James Gordon Bennett, a New Yorker. After he introduced it to his area, players were soon buying Texas horses for ten dollars apiece and competing at a riding academy. The sport caught on right away with such horsemen as future president Theodore Roosevelt, who played in the 1880s and 1890s, and with members of the U.S. Cavalry, who fielded teams at Fort Monroe, Virginia, among other posts. By the 1890s, a handful

Virginia Military Institute cadets *(left to right)* Girard, Penniman, Daube, and Barrow composed the VMI Polo Team.

of teams competed at Keswick, near Charlottesville. Over the next few years, boosted especially by its popularity with army players (including George S. Patton Jr.), polo took its place in the history of American and Virginian equestrian sport.[50]

In 1906, in the same social trend that was giving new vitality to fox-hunting, wealthy newcomers from the North planned a polo field near Warrenton. Horsemen in Norfolk and Richmond watched the developments from afar. "While polo has never flourished in this section of the country," reported the *Washington Post* about the Warrenton area, "it is thought that if once a start was given polo would be a success here." From 1908 to 1910, Fauquier County players did their best to fulfill that prophecy. They competed at Airlie, at Glenara, and at Sinclair's Field. In 1910, a Fauquier team traveled to a tournament in Rhode Island, where its rider John Butler Swan died in an accident on the playing field. With the sobering reminder of the sport's risk in mind, county players went on hiatus for a few years.[51]

During the 1920s and 1930s, however, polo shone its brightest. By 1920, the Fauquier County Country Club (with Fairfax Harrison, president, and Archibald Cary Randolph, member) had turned thirty-one acres near Marshall into a playing field. The Fauquier/Loudoun Polo Club (later called Middleburg Polo) formed in 1921, and other players and clubs followed. Competitions took place on Phipps Field (later Kent Field) along Goose Creek, in Upperville, built by the polo-loving Phipps family, who also played the sport and bred mounts. In 1922, the Virginia

Military Institute formed a team, and in 1925 gave it the nod as an official school sport.[52]

In the 1930s, the Fauquier/Loudoun team, among others, continued to play, and newcomers like William Ziegler Jr., of New York, kept a string of ponies in northern Virginia. Matches entertained guests at posh resorts in Virginia and neighboring states. In 1935, the War Department Invitation tournament in Washington, D.C., drew the Fort Myer and Fauquier/Loudoun teams. A few years later, Fauquier/Loudoun lost its player Johnny Walker due to a bad fall during a game. The next month, the team regrouped with Captain Richard Kirkpatrick, Robert V. Clark, Hubert Phipps, and Henry Skinker playing at Phipps Field. The sport took a charitable turn in 1940, when Charlotte Noland, head of the Foxcroft School, held a match as a benefit for the relief of wartime Britain. After the United States joined Britain in the fight against Germany, polo players joined the armed forces, and polo fields became wheat fields. The sport went on hiatus for the duration of World War II.[53]

## TROT ON

Galloping and jumping weren't the only things Virginians liked to see their horses do. Although fast trotters had been around a good long while, they came into their own as a separate breed, the Standardbred, in the late nineteenth century.

During the eighteenth century, a few Narragansett Pacers, colonial-era riding horses that flourished in Rhode Island, had paced and ambled their way into Virginia. When someone hitched up a Virginia horse—be it an imported Thoroughbred, a Hobby, or a visiting Narragansett Pacer—they discovered how fast the animals could move at the trot or the pace. Trotting races came about in a casual way, like the early quarter races, with a couple of owners matching their animals. George Washington competed one of his pacers in 1768, Virginia pacers and Narragansett Pacers faced each other down in both states, and some Narragansetts stayed behind in Virginia. In 1799, Thomas Mann Randolph Jr., a son-in-law of Thomas Jefferson, stood a Chickasaw pacer named Hiatoga at his Edge Hill, in Albemarle County. After a move to Kentucky, Hiatoga became an original foundation sire of the American Saddlebred. Canadian horses of French breeding had also been contributing their trotting and pacing genes since the seventeenth century, influencing Morgans, Saddlebreds, and Standardbreds.[54]

In 1849, a horse named Rysdyk's Hambletonian was born in New York. Though a descendant of many good imported Thoroughbreds, he produced trotters, not runners. English Thoroughbreds and their descendants, such as Boston and Planet, contributed their speedy genes to the pool of existing trotters and pacers, and breeders refined the type into a breed, with Rysdyk's Hambletonian a founding sire. The Standardbred was born, and Virginians extended their love of racing to the new horse. Its popularity really took off in the late nineteenth century, after a modicum of normality had been established after the Civil War and Reconstruction and a new racing business could emerge.[55]

Quite different from flat racing, where the big-time owners left the training and riding to professionals, harness racing attracted many middle-class do-it-yourselfers and fewer elites. In 1882, Captain Foxhall A. Daingerfield, of Rockingham County, stood a trotting stallion named Sam Purdy along with a flat racer named Dan Sparling. William J. Carter, a Richmond reporter who covered the equestrian scene for the *Richmond Times,* called Daingerfield "one of the best posted men on pedigree and blood lines in the county" when it came to trotters. In the early 1890s, the Richmonder W. S. Forbes, who owned many good trotters, drove a fine team, both by a stallion named Roanoke, and took

Judging Albemarle County harness horses, 1916.

The standardbred mare Lou Dillon and her foal belonged to C. K. G. Billings, who raised trotters on his Curles Neck estate on the James River.

"pleasure in handling the ribbons over a good roadster at any time." Other Richmonders of those years found wintertime pleasure by hitching their harness horses to sleighs and racing them down Franklin and Grace streets. A horse by the name of Toodles Jr. often took the prize.[56]

In 1892, a group of Richmonders discussed development of the Broad Rock Driving Park Association on or near the site of the old Broad Rock racetrack. H. C. Chamblin, of Whitby Stock Farm, in Chesterfield County, one of the leading Standardbred breeders in Virginia—the Floyd brothers were the other—was involved, along with officials of the Virginia Trotting Horse Breeders Association. Carter called Whitby, formerly a Goode family property, "the home of the high bred horse for over a century." Preston Belvin's Acca Stock Farm also raised good trotters, as did Dr. D. D. Carter, of Woodstock, with his well-bred stallion Supremacy. E. T. Cox and Brother of Hundred Stock Farm, Bermuda Hundred, in Chesterfield County, stood Phalanx. Up in Fredericksburg, M. B. Rowe & Co. bred Standardbreds, as did Albemarle County's William J. Ficklin, who had once imported Percherons to the Belmont Stock Farm, and A. A. Payne at the Annita Stud Farm.[57]

By 1893, trotting was "the fascinating pursuit, which, with measured strides, is steadily forcing its way to the front in all sections of the Old Dominion," wrote Carter. Even down in Tazewell County, in southwest Virginia, a good broodmare, Lutie Dawson, turned out foals for her owner, Major Samuel Walton. Up in Loudoun County, T. J. Ross raised trotters. And at Westover, former headquarters of the colonial Byrd family and Thoroughbreds, the current owner, Major A. H. Drewry, had a few good harness horses. In 1913, Drewry gained a neighbor who also enjoyed a good trotter, C. K. G. Billings. From New York and Chicago, he bought the Curles Neck estate on the James River (once home to various Randolphs) and for three years bred fine trotters such as The Harvester, Lou Dillon, Baroness Virginia, and William.[58]

After 1900, the Northern Neck claimed a good many trotting horses and enthusiasts. Tappahannock, once teeming with Thoroughbreds and flat racing, became a center of harness racing, with tracks at Brockenbrough's Track, Jack's Fork, the Essex County fairgrounds, Booth Eubank's farm at Dunnsville, Mannfield Farm at Millers Tavern, and even the Tayloes' Mount Airy, like Westover once the home of blue-blooded, galloping Thoroughbreds. Eubank, a prominent horseman, owned and raced a successful pacer named S. K. Bedworth. In the 1920s and 1930s, W. Henley Broache built two trotting tracks. Other prominent harness

The well-known trotter The Harvester was another occupant of Billings's Curles Neck.

The horse Dick Watts, of Tazewell County, was a champion trotter.

enthusiasts of the region were Melvin Blake, the Kilmarnock postmaster, and Lewis Latane Trice.[59]

County fairs usually featured harness races, like the July 4, 1893, meet of the Rockingham County Agricultural Society. Matches might occur at as grand a facility as the Broad Rock track, or they might speed down the main street of tiny Buena Vista, in Rockbridge County. Owners called their trotter a Standardbred if they knew its ancestors, a non-Standardbred if not.[60]

In those days of legal segregation, African Americans had their own fairs with their own trotting races. In the 1890s, John Scott, of Hobson & Scott, African American barbers in Richmond, owned both flat racers and trotters, including Lucy, a Thoroughbred granddaughter of Planet.[61]

Residents of the Eastern Shore liked to race their trotters and drive them just for fun. In the 1890s, followers of the pastime knew such horses as Stephen A. Maxwell, Modoc, Maggie Morrill, Black Magnolia, and Highlight. In the 1930s, in Accomac and Northampton Counties, William L. Bull dominated the scene, along with the Turlington family, John S. Turner, M. J. Duer, Walter Daugherty, John R. James, and H. P. James.

Elsewhere, W. A. Horner raised horses in Chesterfield County, as did Walter Roach, of King William County; J. J. McIntyre, of Hobby Horse Farm at Hollins, who raced a horse in the Hambletonian (trotting's version of the Kentucky Derby); and Daniel L. Porter, of Orange. In 1939, the *Virginia Breeder* summed up the current scene: Following a dismal period after World War I of "cheap and tawdry midway offerings" at county fairs, "the light harness horse is rapidly trotting and pacing his way back to the high place he once held in the estimation and affection of Virginians who turn to horses for their sport." Harness racing was more prevalent on the Northern Neck and the Eastern Shore than in other regions. In the 1920s, however, the advent of automobiles contributed to its decline.[62]

Another kind of trotter, the Hackney, made its mark not on the racetrack but in the show ring. The compact English horses, which arrived in the United States in the early nineteenth century, had pulled vehicles until railroads took over transportation routes. With its high-stepping, proud carriage, the Hackney was a natural for the show ring in harness competitions. Virginians of the early 1890s, such as Elijah B. White, of Leesburg's Selma Farm, and Senator Henry Fairfax, of Oak Hill Stud in Loudoun County, with his half-bred Lord Loudoun, showed their Hackneys around the state and at the National Horse Show at New York's Madison Square Garden. Fairfax imported the animals from England and bred his own, such as Danesfort, Matchless, and Northern Light. Hackney ponies, bred since the 1870s, provided an equally pleasing pic-

C. W. Watson had a fancy pair of ponies: Ruffles and Chiffon.

Hackney pony in the show ring, 2004.

ture. Fairfax called the breed "the best type of the all-around general-purpose horse. . . . He is active, hardy, and cheerful in disposition." Though on the small side, "still he is powerfully built, and can draw weight at a brisk clip and keep it up hour after hour, and will finish a drive dapper and be as lively as you please."[63]

## HOMEGROWN HUNTERS

With the early twentieth century's growing interest in foxhunting, Virginians needed more horses. They usually turned to half-breds, meaning horses that were part (though not necessarily half) Thoroughbred. The *Half-Bred Stud Book* was first published in 1918, with the Virginia Half-Bred Association coming along more than forty years later. When riders in other areas of the United States wanted a hunter, they specified a Virginia horse. Some experts even recommended copyrighting the name "Virginia Hunter." "The project of breeding hunters is no job for the inexperienced," read a 1944 editorial in the *Eastern Breeder*. "In its way it is as intricate as breeding race horses, but with the goal of weight carrying ability, a smooth way of going, an even disposition, and above all, a real hunter must have sense and the quickness to get out of a bad place." The magazine thought neither weedy Thoroughbreds nor "clumsy and stupid cold-blooded [draft] mares" would do the job.[64]

Breeders echoed the practices of Hoomes, Tayloe, Jefferson, and other horsemen of the late eighteenth and early nineteenth centuries who had used their Thoroughbreds under harness and saddle, not just on the racetrack. Ideally, half-bred mares performed under saddle in the Virginia hunt field one day, under harness in the wheat field the next, and produced foals by Thoroughbred sires once a year. (Horses have a gestation period of eleven months.) For a reliable cash crop, farmers sold the young horses to be trained as hunters.

By the 1920s, a handful of prominent hunter breeders were doing business in the Shenandoah Valley. George H. Burwell, John Towns, and B. F. Garber lived in Rockingham County. William B. Watkins, of Philadelphia, resided in Clarke County. In the 1940s, Ernest L. Redmon, of Middleburg, owned a fine show mare named Lucille II, a standout at the National Capital Horse Show and other events. As a broodmare, she turned out colts and fillies like St. Mary, Our Time, Out of the Way, and Royalty II, who went on to success at the Upperville show as well as Madison Square Garden. As of 1941, James P. McCormick and his ancestors had been breeding horses at Dover Farm between Middleburg and Aldie for 125 years. One gray homebred hunter, by David Rust's Time Maker, was showing at Upperville. Farmers of lesser means also supplied plenty of good mounts, even if their names didn't make it into the livestock press.[65]

Breeders of racehorses also turned out hunters, as did Llangollen Farm, in Upperville, which stood the jumper stallion Bonne Nuit. Llan-

Bonne Nuit and his owner, Liz Whitney, in 1940, taking a large coop with style and grace. The gray stallion is remembered today as a leading sire of jumpers.

Ellie Wood Page and her young cousin, May Speed, in 1913, near the University of Virginia. Page's daughter, Ellie Wood Keith Baxter, would become a well-known Virginia equestrian.

gollen's original owner, the wealthy John Hay Whitney, had given the estate to his former wife, Liz Whitney, one of the area's leading hostesses and horsewomen. By 1938, Harry Worcester Smith could observe that in northern Virginia, "there are more well-mannered, perfectly-schooled Thoroughbred hunters than can be found anywhere else in the world." Virginia hunters and jumpers proved his point in 1940, bringing home many ribbons and trophies from the National Horse Show, at Madison Square Garden in New York.[66]

Ponies also had their place on the hunt field and in the show ring. Ellie Wood Keith Baxter, a well-known Charlottesville rider of hunters, imported and bred Welsh ponies. In the 1930s, a Colonel Elliott raised Shetland ponies at his Belle Meade Farm, near Front Royal. The animals grew tough and hardy from life in the pastures and received thorough training when they were young. After they had learned the basics, Elliott farmed out the ponies to local youths who were good riders and seasoned the animals on the hunt field. Elliott then sold the ponies through a catalog that might list as many as

Ponies and riders, Albemarle County, ca. 1920.

three hundred animals. One of his young riders was a boy named Melvin Poe, who became a well-known huntsman for the Orange County Hunt and others. One of Elliott's customers was Margaret Cabell Self, a member of the distinguished Cabell family of Virginia, who grew up in Nelson County and went on to a career as a riding teacher and an author of many well-regarded books about horses.[67]

Alexander Mackay-Smith had a plan to keep the state well supplied with good hunters and a good reputation. "Northern Virginia was at one time a hunter breeding center," he wrote. "We might just as well face the facts and admit that at the present time it is nothing of the kind." Since cars had taken over the roads, he thought, the offspring of harness mares and draft stallions were too heavy for riding; if the sires were Thoroughbred stallions, too often the foals turned out "weedy and small." Mackay-Smith was doing his part to solve the problem by crossing his Cleveland Bay stallion with Percheron and Thoroughbred mares, and he thought farmers should try breeding their work mares with Morgan stallions belonging to the U.S. Army.[68]

The army's Remount Service constituted the military's contribution to Virginia horseflesh. Its purpose was to ensure a sufficient supply of well-bred horses for use as cavalry horses in war or peace. The army preferred mixes of Thoroughbreds and other breeds, 15.2 to 16 hands, weighing between 775 and 1,300 pounds. To that end, the army stationed its own stallions (a few Arabians, Morgans, and Saddlebreds, but mostly Thoroughbreds) with individuals and with Remount Depots around the country. Locals with good mares could breed them to the stallions for a modest stud fee and keep the fillies and colts, thereby improving the horse population in general. (The plan echoed Dulany's introduction of out-of-state stallions to northern Virginia before the Civil War). In 1912, the army established a depot on five thousand acres in Front Royal, in the Shenandoah Valley, drawn by the lush grass, the freshwater, and the area's long and welcoming history of horses. There it stood stallions, kept a herd of broodmares, and trained the foals for the army. In 1940, the service placed twenty-three stallions, mostly Thoroughbreds, throughout Virginia.[69]

The depot supplied many of the horses at Fort Myer, Virginia, which boasted Battery C, Sixteenth Field Artillery, also called the Grey-Horse Battery. The unit had seen service in World War I, and it honed its edge by performing at horse shows in Virginia, at Fort Myer, and even at the 1939 National Horse Show in New York City. "Each appearance of the sleek, well-groomed horses, spotless equipment, accurate driving, and general all-around snappy appearance of the battery," wrote the *Virginia Breeder*, "brought forth thunderous applause from the appreciative and responsive audiences."[70]

A talented cavalry horse shows off at Fort Myer, ca. 1915.

Persimmon's Pride, a Remount stallion from Britain, stood at Sterling Larrabee's Oakwood Farm in the 1920s.

## FAVORING HORSE POWER

Most of the state's draft horses had disappeared into the maw of the Civil War, so Virginians started breeding and importing replacements. Percherons, an ancient breed from the Normandy region of France, led the way. They are dapple gray or black, exhibit elegant gaits, and have a refined head thanks to Arabian blood. In 1866, Slaughter W. Ficklin and his son, William, brought six of the animals from France to their Belmont Farm in Albemarle County. The newcomers soon repopulated farms all over the state, with O. E. Jordan of southwest Virginia breeding them in the 1880s, and John F. Lewis, a breeder of both saddle and draft horses in Rockingham County, buying a four-year-old stallion named King Victor from Slaughter Ficklin's estate in 1890. The son of an imported stallion, King Victor was "a beautiful dapple gray . . . with a smooth, shapely body; flat, cordy legs, luxuriant mane and tail and an extra fine head and neck," said the *Rockingham Register*. "In fact, he is an all around good one." By the 1920s, Percherons also graced the pastures of Loudoun and Fauquier Counties, and in 1940, Labes, one of the top ten Percherons in the United States, stood in Winchester for J. H. Funkhouser.[71]

In the 1930s, Virginia added the name of a Percheron stallion, Laet, to its long list of illustrious horses. Elijah B. White (1864–1926), of Selma Farm, in Leesburg, had been breeding Percherons since 1903, importing French mares and buying American show mares to improve his stock. (He also had Hackneys.) Laet was born at Selma Farm in 1916. "His bold, masculine appearance, his smart little ear flicking this way and that, his high crest, his beautiful top and spring of rib, his great size" added up to a champion in the show ring and a potent sire that produced many top horses. In 1919, White sold Laet, his dam Couceorous, and some mares to W. H. Butler, of Ohio, who said of White that "no one man in America has done more for the Percheron horse." The same could be said of Laet, one of the breed's greatest sires.[72]

Other European draft breeds soon lumbered across the state—English Shires and Suffolk Punches, Scottish Clydesdales, and Belgians. Shires are the biggest of the big, with distinctive feathered legs. Suffolks boast chestnut coats and flaxen manes and tails. Clydesdales are usually bay with white stockings, white feathers, and snappy gaits. (In the late twentieth century, they gained fame as the stars of television commercials for Budweiser beer.) Clydesdale owners in northern Virginia and

# MULES

As much as he loved horses and horse sports, George Washington really loved mules. Intrigued with the hardy beasts, the sterile offspring of a male donkey and a female horse, he asked King Charles II of Spain for Spanish donkeys to breed with Virginia horses. Such an import was illegal, but the two leaders found a way around the laws in the interest of diplomacy and husbandry. In 1785, the king dispatched two jacks (male donkeys) and two jennies (females) from Andalusia. One of the jacks died at sea, but the other three donkeys arrived at Mount Vernon. Washington named the jack Royal Gift and put him to stud with his broodmares. He obtained other animals from South America by trading twenty-five barrels of flour for molasses, coffee, and a jenny, and from his friend the Marquis de Lafayette, who sent three Maltese donkeys, including a jack named Knight of Malta. Washington advertised the stud services of Royal Gift and Knight of Malta in newspapers and even displayed the pair at an election of the Maryland General Assembly in 1788 to drum up business. He came to prefer the animals for certain work; after fourteen years, most of his draft stock comprised mules and donkeys, not horses.

Washington's mules eventually won over many other Virginians. They served as draft and pack animals in the Civil War and pulled plows and wagons for farmers. Throughout the last part of the nineteenth and into the mid-twentieth century, the animals worked on sugar, rice, and cotton plantations; on levees, in mines, for railroads, and as pack animals. In the mid-twentieth century, mules experienced a decline across the South, even though the animals were strong, hardy, and easy to keep. Black farmers used them more than anyone. Into the early 1940s,

*(Opposite page)* Mule teams bringing in the hay.

A peddler named Moses and his mule, Spider, were well-known figures on the streets of Richmond around 1900.

Richmond-area breeders raised mules for markets in southeastern Virginia and the Carolinas. In the Tidewater of the 1930s, people used horses (Thoroughbreds, Saddlebreds, and Standardbreds) only for pleasure and sport, not work, as most draft animals there were mules. (Mule breeders of the 1930s and 1940s included Curles Neck Farm, L. M. Walker Jr., A. W. Broaddus, G. O. Townsend, Maude Low, Jim and T. V. Luck of Ashland, H. D. and A. C. Dabney of Rockville, and R. G. Todds of King and Queen County.)

George Washington would be happy to know that mules still had plenty of aficionados in the early twenty-first century, like Steve Foster of Front Royal, who owned champion jumping mules such as Prissy Missy. The Virginia Horse Center hosted an annual show called Cheers for Ears, with classes in halter, English, and western subjects, costume, trail, and driving.

*Sources:* Travis, *The Mule,* 17–18; Twohig, *George Washington's Diaries,* 328; Flexner, *Indispensable Man,* 191–92; *Encyclopedia of Southern Culture,* 511–12; *EB,* January 1942, 26; *VB,* December 1939, 58; *Roanoke Times,* April 21, 2004; conversation with Steve Foster, October 2002; program, 2004 Cheers for Ears; *Richmond Times-Dispatch,* March 15, 2004.

Mules in western tack at a Cheers for Ears show, 2004.

A powerful lineup of draft horses at the Virginia State Fair drew an appreciative audience.

Charlottesville of the late 1930s believed that "a free-moving, acting type of draft horse is best designed to fit the picture of modern-day farming and its future developments," according to John C. Butler, of Kelvedore Farm in Fauquier County. The country of Belgium actively exported Belgians, with their reddish coats, after Americans caught on to them in 1903 at the St. Louis World's Fair and the International Livestock Exposition in Chicago. In 1930s Virginia, they were bred in Clarke, Loudoun, Fauquier, Culpeper, and Campbell Counties.[73]

By the early 1940s, however, American farmers had added 218,000 tractors to their fields and subtracted approximately thirty thousand draft animals. Virginia farmers followed suit. "The days of the big, four-horse teams on the road and the heavy drays in the city are over," wrote the *Virginia Breeder.* Nonetheless, plenty of Virginians still preferred draft horses. Enthusiasts thought the state's "smaller farms and hilly terrain will always favor horse power over tractor power."[74] The large horses that weighed 1,800 pounds, such as Shires, were falling out of favor; a horse of 1,500 or 1,600 pounds could "walk faster, stand the heat better and eat less feed than the Belgians and Percherons," wrote Alexander Mackay-Smith.

"The way to compete with tractors is not merely to point out to small farmers that they are uneconomical, but to offer them a source of power they like better."[75]

## STYLISH SADDLE HORSES

In the late nineteenth century, Virginia once again helped to develop a new breed. This time, however, most of the credit had to go to Kentucky. The Saddlebred emerged to fill a new niche as well-to-do Americans rode purely for pleasure. In addition, plantation owners wanted a flashy saddle horse with smooth gaits that could also pull a carriage with style.

To obtain this new type of horse, initially called the Kentucky Saddler, breeders combined Thoroughbreds, Arabians, and Morgans. Thoroughbreds contributed their refined looks and speed, with a stallion named Denmark becoming a Saddlebred foundation sire. Morgans, especially the Black Hawk line, donated their strength. Arabians, such as a stallion named Zilcaldi, imparted their reliable and uncanny ability to improve any breed. In 1891, the American Saddle Horse Breeders Association formed and named fourteen foundation sires, including Copperbottom (a son of Sir Archy and also an important ancestor of Quarter Horses). In 1908, the association pared down the list, leaving Denmark as the sole foundation sire. Other breeds contributed some of their qualities to the Saddlebred: Narragansett Pacers, Canadian Pacers, and various trotting horses.[76]

As descendants of those beloved amblers, Saddlebreds fit the bill for a comfortable riding horse. Riders used wider, flatter saddles and developed a new style of equitation, behind rather than over the horse's center and therefore encouraging high action of the animal's front legs. Riders learned to rise out of the saddle at the diagonal trot, a move called "posting," rather than sitting. Three-gaited Saddlebreds exhibit a flat-footed walk and a high-stepping trot and canter. Five-gaited horses do those three gaits plus a slow-gait or single-foot—a kind of slow amble—and the fast, high-stepping, four-beat rack. When people used horses and buggies to get around, they set their Saddlebreds to work in harness; today they ride and drive them at horse shows. Some owners and trainers of Saddlebreds, striving for a show-stopping appearance, have traditionally broken the horses' tails and set them up high, grown their hooves extra-long, affixed weights to their feet, and placed ginger under their tails to make them look bold and fiery—a practice not without controversy.[77]

Saddlebred stallion King Cole.

The popularity of the breed flowed back into Virginia from Kentucky, with the crest of the wave in the 1930s and 1940s. In 1939, for example, Laurence E. Tierney Jr. and Lewis Clark Tierney established Leatherwood Farms. Although their mail arrived in Bluefield, West Virginia, the brothers' farm straddled the border with Virginia. The lavish spread boasted a barn, box stalls, a trophy room, a lounge, a show ring, a training stable, an indoor ring, and housing for manager John A. Lucas (imported from Kentucky) and a groom. Leatherwood horses such as the well-known, well-bred animals Dixiana Helen, Sugar Foot, Ebony April, Cream de la Cream, and Golden Sensation showed successfully in the heart of Saddlebred country at the Kentucky State Fair and in Virginia.[78]

"Followers of the sport are coming from all over the country to get the Virginia-breds," boasted the *Virginia Breeder.* Shows of the 1930s in northern Virginia, a bastion of hunters and jumpers, sometimes had classes for Saddlebreds, such as the Bassett show organized by J. E. Bassett, F. A. Stanley, and C. V. Stanley. It even had a Tennessee judge and classes for Virginia-bred horses. Southwest Virginia, however, was Saddlebred country, with breeders and owners like Mr. and Mrs. G. D. Cassell and Mountain Brook Farm, R. J. Kinsley and Gordon Felts in Galax, and S. T. Crockett in Wytheville. In 1941 at least twenty-five Saddlebred stallions lived in Virginia. "There is a definite boom in the Saddle Horse industry in this state," wrote the *Virginia Breeder* that year. "More people are entering it, bringing top stock to the state. Bigger and better shows were held. Many fair grounds were dusted off for the first time in many years and became scenes of rare racking exhibitions."[79]

The versatile horses could flash around the show ring and also provide a pleasant ride over the farm. Addie Muncy, a southwestern Virginia writer for the *Virginia Breeder*, was an unabashed fan. She thought the Virginia saddle horse was "more 'breedy'" than the Tennessee Walking Horse, an even newer breed, with a "finer head on an impressively poised back, the symmetry complemented by a natural highly arched tail," along with "the head well up." (That tail may have been set or broken to achieve the desired effect.) Further, "these well grounded, easily gaited premiers of Virginia's grass land," she wrote, "are a poet's fulfillment of both an eye (symmetry) and an ear (rhythm)," with "almost unbelievable loyalty and devotion to their masters."[80]

The Tennessee Walking Horse did not measure up, at least in the eyes of Saddlebred owners. Of the same back-

A paint Tennessee Walking Horse, named Pocahontas for her unusual marking, lived in Craigsville.

A flat-shod Tennessee Walking Horse of the early twenty-first century.

ground stock as Saddlebreds, they were slower and less animated. They move in three gaits: a flat-footed walk; a running walk (a four-beat gait in which the hind feet overstep the forefeet and the head bobs up and down in rhythm); and the canter, which is often described as resembling a rocking chair. One can imagine that the running walk is pretty close to what a seventeenth-century lady experienced on her palfrey, for the rider's head stays absolutely level as the horse goes its way. As with the Saddlebred, humans sometimes use gadgets to exaggerate and animate the horse's natural gaits for the show ring. The breed association formed in 1935, and Tennessee and North Carolina claimed the largest populations. A few made their comfortable way into Virginia. H. B. Johnson, of Haymarket, owned Big Knight; J. P. Sapp, of Martinsville, showed Mary Souvenir; and C. C. Turner, of Broadway, had Go Boy's Prince Rockingham, and a champion, Merry Go Boy. Nonetheless, the Saddlebred reigned supreme in the state for those who preferred their horses stylish and high-stepping. Muncy, for one, thought Saddlebreds and Tennessee Walkers were just as good as saddle horses from the West.[81]

## OTHER BREEDS

Despite the emphasis on Thoroughbreds, draft horses, Standardbreds, and Saddlebreds, other breeds made their way to the Old Dominion.

Arabians, once so prominent in the form of the earliest imported Thoroughbreds, arrived in opposite ends of the state. In the 1920s and 1930s, Arabians of the rare Al Khamsa strain, which belonged to the Bedouins of Saudi Arabia, ended up in the Tidewater at Westover, once the home of the colonial Byrd family. The oilman Charles Crane, who lived in New York and Massachusetts, had imported the horses, even managing to obtain a few desert-bred mares, which the Arabian breeders valued above all else and rarely allowed to leave the country. His son and daughter-in-law, Richard and Ellen Bruce Crane, now occupied Westover, as did a gray Arabian stallion with the exotic name of Mulhalhil and three mares called Saoudia, LaTisa, and Masudha. Ellen Crane bred the horses and passed them on to her grandchildren, including Frederick Fisher. For many years, the Cranes and Fishers crossed the animals with Arabians belonging to other Virginia breeders and even with a Chincoteague pony. Around the same time in the other end of the state, the Abingdon farm of G. Y. Booker boarded Arabians in the summertime for a South Carolinian named John Hutton, who had imported them from England along with Fell ponies. Hutton rode the animals when he hunted waterfowl in South Carolina.[82]

In 1940, the Stones' Morven Stud, near Charlottesville, bred Morgans and used a four-horse team of the Vermont breed. A few years later,

The Crane family raised Arabians at Westover Plantation. This 1930s photo is probably the stallion Mulhalhil and his groom, Jack Porter.

Nelson Moyer's Cleethrow Stock Farm, in Orange, imported twenty-five Palomino mares and foals and one stallion from Pennsylvania. The animals with the golden coats and white manes and tails may have been Quarter Horses or Saddlebreds, but not Thoroughbreds, which never exhibit that coloration. Moyer planned to breed hunters and jumpers, no doubt hoping that riders wanted horses with the Palomino's eye-catching appearance.[83]

## SCHOOLS

Virginia Military Institute, in Lexington, had used horses as work animals since its founding in 1839. Stonewall Jackson had appropriated them to pull the cannons when he taught artillery to cadets. The school also borrowed and rented horses on occasion to serve as artillery and cavalry horses. The cadets took their primary training in artillery and infantry, however, not in cavalry. Toward the end of the Civil War, nevertheless, Governor William Smith approached VMI with a plan: Desperate Richmonders would furnish one hundred cadets with horses if they would come to the defense of the city. Lacking cavalry training, the boys reported for duty, but on foot.[84]

In 1916, with World War I just around the corner, cavalry finally came to VMI under the auspices of the new Reserve Officers' Training Corps (ROTC). Alumni donated funds to build the stables, and in 1919 the army sent one hundred horses, forty for artillery and sixty for cavalry, plus forty enlisted men to serve as blacksmiths, grooms, and stablehands. By 1930, more than 130 horses lived at VMI. Regardless of their equine background, the cadets learned horsemanship, equitation, and cavalry drills. When student Harry W. Easterly Jr. arrived in the early 1940s, the novice horseman found himself not only on a horse but also jumping a fence without a saddle. In 1925, Captain Kent Craig Lambert of the U.S. Cavalry assembled the school's first mounted unit, which displayed its expertise at reviews and parades. From 1920 to 1947, First Sergeant Edward L. Henson, a Rockbridge County native, taught riding and horsemanship and rewarded deserving pupils with Sunday passes to ride off campus. In addition to guiding young men, he oversaw the rehabilitation of a wild, unmanageable young horse, Jack Knife, into a winning jumper.[85]

In the 1920s, VMI added a troop of cavalry to its infantry battalion and artillery battery. During the weekly garrison reviews, the cav-

Horses once enjoyed a prominent place at the Virginia Military Institute. *Left,* a jumping demonstration on the parade ground, ca. 1930; *bottom,* one of the last cavalry displays at VMI, 1946.

alry demonstrated at a walk, a trot, and then a gallop. Between 1933 and 1938, the cavalry shone throughout Virginia at horse shows, polo matches, and on the interscholastic team circuit, with favorite mounts including Dark Cloud, Midnight, and Silver Bell. The school also kept a pack of hounds, and cadets sometimes rode with the Deep Run Hunt, in Richmond. By 1941, cadets and their horses practiced in an indoor riding hall.[86]

World War II brought an end to the riding program at VMI, transforming that part of the school's equestrian culture just as it did other areas of the horse business in Virginia and elsewhere. Its equine population peaked in 1945 with 180 animals, but during the war, the school dismantled its horse artillery and ROTC temporarily disappeared. The last

Horse husbandry at Hampton Normal and Agricultural Institute (now Hampton University), ca. 1900.

The first-ever horse show at Hollins College, 1931.

The Arlington Hall Mounted Lancers Troop. *Left to right:* Carol Norton, Virginia Smith, Sally Seward, and Eleanor Leh.

parade of horses came at the end of the school year in 1948. VMI transferred some horses to the Remount Depot in Front Royal and the Marines at Quantico, and sold others. Sgt. Henson, following military tradition but no doubt with a heavy heart, shot those animals deemed old and unsound. The indoor riding hall became the athletic facility known as the Pit, and the remodeled stables housed the reinstated ROTC program.[87] The cadets put away their boots and saddles, and a stirring part of the history of both VMI and the army vanished.

In the 1940s, other Virginia schools had plenty of students for their own riding programs. Hollins College, near Roanoke, taught a rigorous course for women riders of hunters and jumpers; Virginia Tech (then called Virginia Polytechnic Institute) offered classes in riding and breeding; Virginia Intermont College, in Bristol, had seventy-five female riders. Sullins College, also in Bristol, advertised an extensive program for its female pupils. The junior college owned forty-five Saddlebreds, "carefully selected for their aristocracy and show ways," which the women could ride on a Sullins bridle path or in the Sullins show ring. The school even stood a Tennessee Walking Horse stallion.[88]

## HORSE SHOWS: NONE BUT CLASSY STEEDS

Horse shows became more than just an occasion to enjoy competition and admire good horseflesh. The National Capital Show in Washington,

The appeal of jousting tournaments carried over from antebellum times. *Top,* participants at an 1890s tournament; *right,* a tournament contestant attempting to catch the ring with her spear—while at a gallop.

D.C., for example, was a highlight of the year for skilled Virginia horsemen as well as for debutantes and politicians eager to experience the social whirl. On opening day in 1914, the seats overflowed with "members of the diplomatic corps, officers from Fort Myer, and leaders of the smart sets of this and other cities of the East and the South," reported the *Washington Post.* Margaret Wilson, daughter of President Woodrow Wilson, and the others wore "gay raiment and high spirits." In the ring, "crack horse show animals" provided the raison d'être for the event.[89]

Tournaments, with their antebellum southern trappings of romance and chivalry, continued even after the Civil War and into the twentieth century. In the immediate postwar years, they took on a Confederate cast, with knights in Confederate uniforms calling themselves things like "Knight of Liberty Lost" and "Knight of the Fallen Banner," and with a tournament at the 1868 Augusta County Fair in honor of Robert E. Lee's visit. An 1870 competition at Amelia Springs reached back to colonial days by featuring an old-fashioned gander-pull (G. A. Miller, calling himself the "Knight of Dry So," won), as did a 1931 event where the knights wore powdered wigs and brocade coats to mark the 150th anniversary of the British surrender at Yorktown. County and state fairs, horse shows, and horse races often included a tournament. The holdover from a previous century was a fun and popular way for the community to socialize and for riders, like future huntsman Melvin Poe, to show off their horsemanship.[90]

The association that had established the Upperville Union Club Colt Show in 1853 lost little time in resuming operations. In 1869, it dropped "Union" from its name (which reminded listeners of the late war) and changed it to the Upperville Colt Show, then added the word "horse" in 1902. The Dulany family continued its involvement, with Richard Henry Dulany (now called "Colonel" due to his wartime service) acting as president until he died in 1906. They hosted the show on their property, originally called Number Six, later called Grafton. In 1902, Upperville became a two-day show, with classes for harness, park, and gaited horses as well as for hunters, along with Thoroughbred breeding classes and the popular and thrilling high jump. In the 1920s, the Dulanys showed a fine hunter mare, Silver Crest, a winner of many national championships. When she died, she was buried at her birthplace—the Upperville show grounds.[91]

Another tradition began in 1899 with the Warrenton Horse Show, in Fauquier County. The area horsemen Julian Keith and Charlie W. Smith led the way. The association bought the show grounds in 1900, with one ring only. It has never added another. By 1910, two thousand spectators a day cheered on draft horses, Thoroughbreds, hunters, polo ponies, and entries in a combination saddle and harness class. "None but classy steeds ever are shown," opined the *Washington Post*. The crowd was "the annual gathering of Virginia's aristocracy, with all of the old families well represented." In 1920, local children started and ran the Warrenton Pony Show, another event still going strong with plenty of classy steeds.[92]

A saddle horse competition in Albemarle County, 1916.

Mattie Williams shows off her prize horse in Tazewell County, ca. 1909.

Other shows proved ephemeral. In 1900, horsemen formed the Albemarle Horse Show Association and held an annual show at Fry's Spring, with dances and music adding to the festivities. In 1905, they claimed that twelve thousand spectators showed up. "We have the very best blooded horses, horses with pedigrees that go far back beyond any of our lives," boasted the show's association, "[so] that the exhibition is one of the greatest sights of the United States." The exhibition, nonetheless, was gone by 1920.[93]

Communities all over the Commonwealth sponsored horse shows. The Deep Run Hunt Club built on the tradition of the Richmond Horse Show, initially allowing only members to compete but then soliciting entries from all over the state. In 1898, a horse named Waterford won the Deep Run's high-jump contest, clearing five feet and earning thirty-five dollars. Second place and fifteen dollars went to Folic, a grandson of the Doswell and Hancock stallion Eolus, and third prize, a bridle, to Buck. The 1904 Fredericksburg Horse Show displayed roadsters, hacks, park horses, and hunters, with classes for women and men. Harrisonburg had its Rockingham Horse and Colt Show and classes for gaited saddle horses, Hackneys, trotters, draft horses, and Thoroughbreds. Perhaps unsurprisingly, given the number of foxhunters in Albemarle County, hunters dominated the Keswick show. The Homestead resort in Bath County sponsored a horse show and a point-to-point for Virginia horsemen as well as guests at the hotel. From 1928 to 1966, the Bath County National Horse Show at the Homestead was an A-rated production. Competitors had their pick of classes for hunters, gaited horses, and draft horses.[94]

In the late 1930s, horse shows took place at county fairs from Fincastle and Abingdon to Luray and Lynchburg, from Manassas and Roanoke to Staunton and Norfolk, from Covington and Rocky Mount to Blackstone, Lexington, Farmville, and Warsaw. The Front Royal Remount Horse Show encouraged "the breeding of hunters by bonafide farmer breeders." The Galax Fair and Show had plantation horses, five-gaited animals, jumpers, roadsters, and ponies.

The Radford Fair and Horse Show advertised Virginia-bred five-gaited horses, hunters, jumpers, and ponies. Tazewell's premium list contained the usual classes plus "Open Plantation or Walking" horses, and the Bland Fair and Horse Show had a class just for local saddle horses. The mix of classes reflected Virginians' varied interests.[95]

Professionals could make a career in the show ring. The 1930s, for instance, saw the rise of Morton W. "Cappy" Smith. A rider and trainer

Women and their horses. *Top,* on the McConnell Farm, Halifax County, ca. 1940; *right,* near Virginia Beach, 1939.

of hunters and jumpers, a successful competitor at the National Horse Show, and the master of the Orange County Hunt, he had the three-year-old hunter champion of Virginia for five years in a row. A member of several halls of fame (for show jumping, hunters, and Virginia horse shows), Smith epitomized the professional show rider. George Morris, a leading trainer of hunter and jumper riders in the late twentieth century, called Smith a "giant in his field, bigger than life," with "movie-star looks and a personality to go with it . . . a great, great horseman."[96]

At many shows of the late 1920s, however, local farmers and their children dominated the ring. They showed their homebreds and often wore blue jeans instead of breeches. This practice dovetailed with an increasing trend toward participation by ordinary horse owners, not just the pros or the wealthy. "It is possible to place horses in professional training at a very reasonable price for a few months," wrote the *Virginia Breeder* in 1939 in a discussion focusing on Saddlebreds, "and have the satisfaction of either seeing them exhibited by the stables or the pleasure of being in the merry-go-round yourself on a horse you would not have had the time to prepare."[97]

The magazine's words underline a significant shift in the horse world of Virginia. Horses were gradually becoming less necessary as work animals, and they no longer belonged only to rich owners of purebred racehorses. Someone with a little extra money could buy a Saddlebred and pay to have it trained, then exhibit it themselves. Children of farmers could raise their own horses and show them alongside those of their wealthy neighbors. A horse could be a pet or a form of recreation. "The socially smart thing is to own a good horse," wrote Addie Muncy of the *Virginia Breeder* in 1941. "A healthful thing to do is to ride him." Even during World War II, the market for riding horses increased because more and more people were riding for pleasure.[98]

## CHANGING HORSES IN MIDSTREAM

It would have taken a clairvoyant to foresee the earth-shattering cultural changes that World War II was about to bring to the United States and the Commonwealth. Virginia horsemen, however, had always been an irrepressible, optimistic lot. The *Virginia Breeder* magazine, published by Hubert Phipps, of Rockburn Farm in northern Virginia, had begun publishing from Warrenton in the 1930s and changed its focus along with its name (to *Eastern Breeder*) in 1941. It led the cheering section.

"This is the big moment for Virginia to grab a hunk of deserved publicity," the *Breeder* trumpeted in 1941. "In the state are representatives of numerous ranking horse families; let the breeding world know what line your stallion represents so he can decide what crosses or line breeding will best serve his interest." Virginia raised such wonderful horses because it was "blessed with a soil and climate ideally suited to the raising of pure-bred animals[,] and with the natural inheritance of the people for the art of raising the best, Virginia need never fear fair competition." Addie Muncy averred that "aside from the Sport of Kings, the horse is a necessity to the topography and agronomy of the state." Further, farmers still used horses because "they can't breed tractors or raise gas."[99]

In the spring of 1941, horsemen from all over the state met at the Red Fox Tavern in Middleburg to form the Virginia Horsemen's Association. Their plan was to promote the state's draft horses, ponies, hunters, and Thoroughbreds. The guiding lights of the gathering were Kenneth Gilpin, the Boyce Thoroughbred breeder; David Rust Jr., Leesburg; Henry Frost Jr., a steeplechase rider and trainer, Middleburg; Colin MacLeod, a Middleburg breeder of Thoroughbreds and Clydesdales; Colonel Pleas

A versatile group of Virginia horses.

B. Rogers, the commander of the army's remount depot; A. Alexander Baldwin, another Thoroughbred breeder, from White Post; Alexander Mackay-Smith; Heyward Thompson, a Percheron breeder from Round Hill; and William Worth and Hubert Phipps, the managing editor and publisher, respectively, of the *Eastern Breeder.* Former Governor Westmoreland Davis, H. Rozier Dulany Jr., and Walter Craigie, a writer for the *Richmond Times-Dispatch,* joined in. The association received a small appropriation from the state. By December of that year, the association's field secretary, Nick Saegmuller, was visiting stables, inspecting herds of broodmares and foals, attending horse shows and hunt races, corresponding with horsemen, and compiling racing and show records of horses by Virginia stallions.[100]

Not to be outdone, the Southwestern Virginia Horse Breeders' Association got under way around the same time. Whereas its northern counterpart was top heavy with owners and breeders of Thoroughbreds, most of the SVHBA members owned Saddlebreds. Its organizers included Dr. Huston St. Clair, of Chilliridge Farm, Tazewell; Lewis Tierney, from Leatherwood Stable; and James L. Wiley, Dixie Stable. "Southwest Virginia is a stock raising section of large farms or estates with many lovely old colonial homes, and all modern conveniences are available for even the humblest living," said the *Eastern Breeder.*"[101]

During World War I, from 1917 to 1918, the United States had exported to Europe thousands of horses and mules (probably some from Virginia) for use in military operations. Although they pulled artillery and carried cavalrymen, the animals labored in the shadows of tractors and trucks. Their wartime utility was nearing an end. Nevertheless, in the late 1930s, some Virginia horsemen and army officers at Front Royal thought the cavalry could still serve in the raging European war. Accordingly, in preparation for possible U.S. involvement in what would become World War II, the army transferred horses from army posts in Virginia and elsewhere to central locations. (The action depleted the supply of riding horses at Fort Monroe in the Hampton Roads area, sending officers and their families to ride at local stables, hardly a wartime hardship.) After December 7, 1941, when American involvement in the global conflict became a reality, the cavalry advocates in the U.S. Army had to admit their error in the face of the annihilation of European cavalry by modern armaments such as tanks and machine guns.

If European horses faced death and privation on the battle front, American horses on the home front found a reprieve. "The importance of the horse in the national crisis is driven home by day by day events," wrote Addie Muncy in the *Eastern Breeder*. "Many, many errands of normal duty and grave necessity can be safely and economically accomplished via 'dobbin,' . . . a short sprint to town can be a real pleasure . . . every trip can mean a defense stamp and a saving of essential materials for fighting armaments." She had a point. Plantation supervisors, busy growing food for citizens and soldiers, swapped their gas-guzzling cars for gaited horses to inspect the fields. R. E. Hunt, the head of the animal husbandry department at Virginia Polytechnic Institute, recommended that farmers use large hitches of horses—three, four, even six or eight—to help with their extra duties growing crops for soldiers and civilians, and VPI offered free teamster training.[102]

One of the ritziest of all horse operations in northern Virginia, Llangollen Farm, surrendered its prewar identity as the home of pampered Thoroughbreds. Llangollen's owner, the socialite and horsewoman Liz Whitney, oversaw the farm's transformation after undergoing one of her own. Withdrawing from her usual social whirl of horse races and Hollywood, she sold most of her show horses and donated some of her canines to Dogs for Defense. Llangollen's cattle and chickens produced meat, milk, and eggs, and its fields yielded enough crops to feed its own inhabitants. Draft horses pulled the plows, and Bonne Nuit, the famed Thoroughbred show hunter, now earned his oats as a cow pony. Whitney herded her cattle from a Western saddle aboard either the stallion or a pinto named Chief.[103]

Much too far from Virginia and all too close to the fighting, a Virginia soldier, Charles Hancock Reed, helped save a European breed, the Lipizzan, from near-certain obliteration. The highly schooled Austrian horses, of Spanish descent and known for their white coats and elegant gaits, had performed at the Spanish Riding School in Vienna for hundreds of years. Threatened with destruction by the Germans, the animals and their caretakers had retreated to Czechoslovakia. There the armored cavalry division under General George Patton took the horses under its protection and escorted the Lipizzans back to Austria. Reed, a member of the Deep Run Hunt, was one of the division's officers.[104] A horseman was a horseman, after all, whether in peacetime Virginia or wartime Europe.

A light schedule of horse racing continued in Virginia, with some people justifying it as much-needed recreation and as a way to contribute to the economy and raise money for the war effort. "Every true horseman, whether at home or in the service," opined the *Eastern Breeder*, was happy that racing was alive and that breeding, while lessened, had kept going. Prices for hunters (and presumably all types of horses) declined. For example, a gelding offered for $10,000 in 1940 sold for $2,700 in 1942. In January 1944, however, the Remount Depot auctioned off 1,512 horses and mules in front of a mostly Pennsylvania crowd of three thousand. A good pair of mules brought $520. Polo fields sprouted crops, and most of that sport's players served in the military, such as A. Alexander Baldwin of Millwood, a trainer; George H. Bostwick, a New Yorker who also lived and rode in Middleburg; Louis E. Stoddard Jr., of Middleburg, a steeplechase rider and polo player; and Charles von Stade, a New York polo player with a place in Middleburg. Like the rest of the United States during World War II, the Virginia horse world cut back and changed gears.[105]

## ONE ERA ENDS, ANOTHER BEGINS

The end of World War II in 1945 was wonderful news for Americans—but not for their horses. The country's horse population dropped by more than half between the 1920s and the 1950s; by 1959, the country had just a sliver, about a seventh, of the farm horses it had counted in 1918. During the 1950s alone, American farmers sold off more than 357,000 horses and mules, half of them for pet food. At the Front Royal Live Stock Market, farmers sold draft horses that they'd replaced with tractors. Two-thirds of the animals were slaughtered, bringing five cents per pound if they were intended for human consumption, only three cents if they ended up in a can of dog food. Virginia grocery stores of the time even sold frozen horsemeat.[106]

Some Virginia horses ended up not on the American dinner table but behind European plows. The United Nations Relief and Rehabilitation Administration and Heifer Project shipped cattle and horses from all over the United States to Europe, where they restocked farms and helped put in new crops. In a mirror image of their ancestors' ocean voyages from Europe to Virginia, the animals sailed across the Atlantic on ships that embarked from Newport News. Caretakers called "sea cowboys" accompanied the animals, including Maynard Garber, of Staunton, who traveled with 750 horses to Greece.[107]

In 1948, the same year VMI gave up its horses, the federal government transferred the Remount Depot at Front Royal from the aegis of the army to the Department of Agriculture. Its new purpose: to breed horses for farm and ranch work—not for show, racing, or polo—and to breed cattle. Eventually it became a research center for the Smithsonian Institution. The U.S. Cavalry in its prewar form ceased to exist.[108]

With the cavalry gone, tractors taking over farms, and workhorses disappearing into slaughterhouses, life for Virginia equines looked bleak.

The old world gives way to the new.

# 1946–2009 AND BEYOND

## THE ROMANCE OF THE HORSE

*The Virginians have a large number of fine horses, and are accused of devoting too much attention to that beautiful animal.*—Richard Mason, *The Gentleman's New Pocket Farrier,* 1820

In the late twentieth century, velvet hunt caps came to coexist alongside cowboy hats in the Commonwealth. Virginians no longer used horses only for work, war, or wealth, but also for pleasure. And a lot of those horsemen fell in the junior category. "Almost simultaneously and practically throughout the country, children of all ages suddenly discovered the romance and fascination of the horse," wrote Margaret Cabell Self, the Virginia-born riding teacher and writer. A child who grew up listening to Westerns on the radio, watching them at the movies, and following them on television yearned to be a cowpoke. A horse, whether a backyard pet or a well-bred show animal, completed the picture.[1]

A change in the composition of the Olympic riding teams further enhanced the picture for devotees of English-style sports. The squad had heretofore drawn its members from the army. With the end of the cavalry, civilians could compete at the highest levels of equestrian sport. Before long, a good many of those skilled civilians were women, with show jumping, dressage, and eventing among the few sports where men

By 1984, the sight of horses in downtown Richmond was so rare that passersby stopped to gawk at Prissy and Buck, who'd been ridden down from Ashland.

and women compete on equal footing. In an astonishingly few decades, sports with their origins in the hunt field, such as three-day eventing and show jumping, took off, with many of their best practitioners from Virginia. The Quarter Horse even returned from the West to its birthplace, and with it riders toting western saddles and cowboy boots.

## THOROUGHBRED RACING

In the immediate postwar years, Thoroughbreds composed the biggest breed in Virginia, followed by Tennessee Walkers. The Virginia Horsemen's Association (VHA), suspended during wartime, resumed operations in 1946 and became the Virginia Thoroughbred Association (VTA) in 1957. The organization had its work cut out for it in the 1940s. Help came in the form of the VHA official Kenneth Gilpin, who bought the Fasig-Tipton Company, which conducted sales of Thoroughbreds. After the war, Kentucky breeders kept their sales in Kentucky, thus allowing Virginia breeders to dominate the Fasig-Tipton sales at Saratoga, New York. The organization sponsored a tour of breeding farms in connection with the sale, with visitors seeing Nydrie, Morven, the Augustuses' Old Keswick, the O'Keefes' Pine Brook, Gilpin's Kentmere, Taylor Hardin's Newstead, the Churches' North Cliff Farm, and the Phippses' Rockburn Farm.[2]

Melvin "Judge" Church II and Gordon Grayson headed the VHA after Gilpin's death in 1947. A parallel organization, Virginians for Horse Racing, joined the VHA/VTA in its effort to resume pari-mutuel betting in Virginia, which would give breeding and racing a boost. In pari-mutuel betting, the track operator pools the total money wagered and then divides it proportionally among the winning bettors based on how much money each one put down. The operator keeps a cut. During his term in the House of Delegates in the 1970s, Daniel Van Clief worked for the legislation.[3]

While the state waited to see about pari-mutuel betting, Never Say Die, a Kentucky-bred horse owned by Robert Sterling Clark, of Upperville, won the 1954 Epsom Derby, in England. In the 1960s, horse racing was still important to places like Albemarle County, but Virginia was losing ground as a Thoroughbred center to beef cattle, the number-one livestock crop. Nearly 115,000 horses and ponies of all breeds lived on more than five thousand breeding farms, owned by sixty thousand people and worth $95 million to the state. The VTA was concerned that people didn't realize the importance and worth of the horse industry, mentioning its perceived "improper image." The organization thought that people outside the horse world needed to learn about the business; that Virginia Tech and other educational institutions should have classes and courses; that taxes should encourage the industry; that the state needed pari-mutuel racing; and that the industry needed better marketing.[4]

Marion duPont Scott thought a solution lay in another direction. Comparing Virginia breeders to Kentuckians, she said: "The trouble is, the breeders in Virginia think they know so much, you can't tell them anything. If one of the top people would stand a good horse in Virginia, and not worry about the number of mares, it would make other people want to do it, too." By the early 1970s, Virginia had 7,500 breeding farms and 125,000 horses and ponies, a healthy measure, and it was the number-four breeding state after Kentucky, Florida, and California. The Morven Stud, near Charlottesville, had produced a top filly, Shuvee. By 1981, however, Virginia, despite its reputation as the home of the 1973 Triple Crown winner, Secretariat, had dropped from its spot as the number-three producer of Thoroughbreds in 1978 to number eleven.[5]

Virginia horsemen had a reason to cheer in 1988, when the General Assembly finally approved pari-mutuel racing. In 1997, an elaborate new racetrack, Colonial Downs, opened in New Kent County and sponsored Virginia-bred and Virginia-sired stakes races. The 2001 meet was its most successful since the opening, with an average take of $1 million a day. In 2004, the top turf horse in the United States, Kitten's Joy, won the $500,000 Virginia Derby. Colonial Downs also conducted races on the Secretariat Turf Course.[6]

Virginia breeders of the late twentieth and early twenty-first centuries included Diana and Bertram Firestone, who bred Paradise Creek, a million-dollar-winning racehorse, and owned Genuine Risk, the 1980 Kentucky Derby winner. Keswick Stables bred winners like Simply Majestic and owned prize broodmares, such as the dam of Northern Dancer. Daniel G. Van Clief Sr. still ran the Nydrie Stud in Albemarle County. Alice duPont Mills, of Hickory Tree Farm in Middleburg, received the Thoroughbred Owners and Breeders Association Award in 1991 for her contributions, including a founding membership of the Marion duPont Scott Equine Medical Center. In 2003, Blue Ridge Farm in Upperville turned one hundred, making it one of Virginia's oldest racing establishments. And in 2005, Nellie Mae Cox, of Rose Retreat Farm, sold her Virginia mare Be Gentle, a stakes winner and 2003 Virginia-Bred Horse of the Year, for the staggering sum of $2.1 million at the Keeneland (Kentucky) November Sale.[7] Virginia still had what it took to produce great Thoroughbreds.

As of 2002, one thousand Thoroughbred breeders lived in the state, mostly in Fauquier and Loudoun Counties. Those areas had 29,500 horses worth more than a half billion dollars. From 2001 to 2003, Virginia breeders won approximately $5 million on the track, including Warrenton's Edward P. Evans, a publishing executive. His horses earned $2.3 million in 2003, making him seventeenth in the nation in earnings.[8]

The Virginia Thoroughbred Association, continuing its promotion of the industry, conducted a yearly auction of stud services from Kentucky stallions. The fee ran about half the usual stud fee and was a great chance for small breeders to match their mares with a top or promising stallion. The proceeds supported VTA, which also administered a Virginia Breeders Fund, funded by a percentage of live and simulcast gambling, to give incentive awards to Virginia breeders, owners, and stallions. It also offered instruction, a library, pedigree research, annual meetings and awards, directories, bulletins, and live racing on TV at its Warrenton headquarters.[9]

Marion duPont Scott's Montpelier found a way to help Thoroughbreds in 2003. The facility welcomed retired racehorses from all over the country to two hundred acres of green pastures and renovated barns. The Thoroughbred Retirement Foundation took the animals off racetracks and away from slaughterhouses and retrained them for a variety of uses.[10]

Trainer A. Ferris Allen III, from Varina, represented another side of Virginia horseracing. He lived in Maryland and trained forty-five to fifty racehorses for tracks in West Virginia, Maryland, Virginia, and Delaware. In 1985, Miracle Wood, a horse he and his father trained, finished fifth in the Preakness, one of racing's Triple Crown. "You have to make some balance between being a human being and being a top athlete. With me, it was not aspiring to go to Southern California or New York," he told the *Richmond Times-Dispatch* in 2002. "I wanted the best year-round circuit I could find, where I could make a good living and a name for myself and, if a good horse came along, I could keep it." Content with his position, Allen said he didn't want to attend the Kentucky Derby until he ran a horse in it.[11] A good living, a good name, and a good horse—many a Virginian before and after Allen would be pleased with those three possessions.

## SECRETARIAT

In 1969, breeding, serendipity, and the flip of a coin produced one of the greatest horses in the history of Thoroughbred racing, let alone in the history of Virginia: Secretariat.

We can thank a Virginian named Christopher Chenery. Born in Richmond in 1886, he grew up poor in Ashland, working odd jobs to help the family finances and enjoying the outdoors. He especially liked riding horses that belonged to a relative on a farm in nearby Caroline County. He scraped and saved his way to college, first at Randolph-Macon in Ashland, then to Washington and Lee University, where he earned a degree in engineering in 1909. He worked as a surveyor and engineer in Virginia and the Pacific Northwest before marrying and starting a family. By the 1930s, he had become a well-to-do utilities executive.[12]

Chenery held onto his love for horses and for his home state, and in 1936 he bought the Caroline County farm, near Doswell, that had belonged to his kin. "He was determined to breed horses in Virginia," said his daughter, Penny Chenery. He told the New York–born girl, thirteen

Secretariat exhibits his awe-inspiring stride during a workout.

at the time, "Don't answer when people ask where you're from." When she asked why, he replied, "Because you'll have to say you're *not* from Virginia." Proud to say he hailed from the Old Dominion, he lavished attention on the flooded lowlands and depleted soil, built proper facilities, restored the house, and started buying Thoroughbreds for the farm he called The Meadow. It was an auspicious location due to its heritage, for Thomas Doswell's Bullfield Stud, breeder of the star 1850s racehorse Planet, had operated right across the North Anna River. Chenery chose blue and white racing silks to honor his alma mater, Washington and Lee.[13]

Chenery bought and raised many fine horses. Hildene, a mare he purchased for less than $1,000, produced the colt Hill Prince, sired by Princequillo. (Princequillo stood at the Ellerslie Farm in Albemarle County of Arthur "Bull" Hancock Jr., son of the nineteenth-century Virginia breeder Arthur Hancock Sr.) Hill Prince grew up to be the 1950 Horse of the Year and win the Preakness. First Landing, another colt of Hildene, was named for the 350th anniversary of Jamestown and sired another Chenery horse, Riva Ridge, winner of the 1972 Kentucky Derby and Belmont Stakes. Chenery's broodmare Imperatrice gave birth to Somethingroyal, a daughter of Princequillo and later the dam of Sir Gaylord, a leading stud. With the success of Chenery and others, Virginia enjoyed a renaissance of its early-nineteenth-century status as a center of Thoroughbred breeding.[14]

In 1965, Chenery decided on an unusual business deal. Joining him were Bull Hancock, proprietor of the Claiborne Farm, in Paris, Kentucky, and Gladys (Mrs. Henry) Phipps, owner of the famed racehorse and sire Bold Ruler, which stood at the Hancock farm. Each year Chenery sent two of his broodmares to Claiborne for breeding with Bold Ruler. The first mating would usually produce two foals, and the second mating soon after their births would result in two more foals within a year. After the birth of the first pair and before the second arrived, Phipps and Chenery or their proxies would flip a coin. The winner received first choice of the first pair of foals, while the loser had first choice of the second.

In 1968, with Chenery elderly and failing, his daughter, Penny Chenery (then Tweedy), stepped into the family horse business. Following the arrangement, she sent two mares, Somethingroyal and Hasty Matelda, from Virginia to Kentucky. They each mated with Bold Ruler and gave birth to a foal in the spring of 1969. Soon after, Somethingroyal was again bred to Bold Ruler and conceived. A horse named Cicada, a champion filly during her racing days, served as the second broodmare for The Meadow in 1969, but her rendezvous with Bold Ruler did not take, leaving only three foals up for grabs (two from Somethingroyal, one from Hasty Matelda). That year the Phippses won the toss and therefore had first choice of the first pair. Penny Chenery lost and so possessed Somethingroyal's yet-to-be-born second baby. The Meadow may have lost the coin toss, but it had won something beyond the Chenerys' wildest dreams.[15]

Back home in Virginia on March 30, 1970, shortly after midnight, Somethingroyal gave birth to a big chestnut colt with three white feet and a white star on his face. He grew up romping in the rich pastures. At four months of age, he made his first impression in print when Christopher Chenery's secretary, Elizabeth Ham, jotted in her notes: "You would have to like him." After his weaning in October, it was time for a name. Following official procedures, Ham and Penny Chenery submitted six names to the Jockey Club: Deo Volente, Games of Chance, Royal

Line, Secretariat, Scepter, and Something Special. The organization accepted one of Ham's candidates: Secretariat.[16]

In the late summer of 1971, the yearling began his training as a racehorse. He learned about saddles, bridles, horseshoes, riders, and racetracks. On September 20, 1971, he met his trainer, sixty-year-old Lucien Laurin. The French Canadian veteran had been working a short time for The Meadow, guiding Riva Ridge to a stellar year on the track. Now he had another candidate.[17]

A few months later, on January 20, 1972, Secretariat, now considered two years old by Thoroughbred rules, and other colts and fillies boarded a van headed for Hialeah Park, Florida. The chestnut colt left Virginia for the first and last time.[18]

In Florida, Secretariat met another important person: jockey Ron Turcotte. A French Canadian like his boss, Laurin, he also rode Riva Ridge. Other members of the team included Eddie Sweatt, his groom, who provided expert care and plenty

Secretariat at the Preakness, with Ron Turcotte on board and Eddie Sweatt leading him.

of stability, and Billy Silver, a plain old horse who kept the blue-blooded Thoroughbred company.[19]

Turcotte and the exercise riders liked the young horse's kind, easy-going personality. They taught him new lessons about running and strength and holding his own on the track with a crowd of galloping horses. In the spring, he was sent to Belmont Park, in New York, to continue his schooling. On July 4, 1972, the red colt ran his first race, at Aqueduct Racetrack, New York, with jockey Paul Feliciano up.[20]

Secretariat got off to an inauspicious start when another horse ran into him right out of the gate. He nearly fell but regained his equilibrium and managed to fight his way from eleventh place to fourth. On July 15, he ran his second race, again piloted by Feliciano, and won by six lengths. For his third race, Ron Turcotte took the reins. Another victory forged a winning partnership that would last for all but one race of the rest of Secretariat's career.[21]

When Secretariat ran, he scrambled around at the start before he figured out what he was going to do. Before his style became apparent, the colt's hesitation could etch worry lines on the foreheads of owner and trainer. Once Secretariat got the picture, though, he engaged his perfect body into flawless running form and moved smoothly to the front, picking off the other horses like a champion skeet shooter picking off clay pigeons. Effortlessly, swiftly, neatly, the chestnut colt would run around the pack or thread his way through. One competitor after another felt the whoosh and saw a reddish blur as he passed them with his long strides, breath chuffing, running faster and faster, winning.[22]

The sportswriter Charles Hatton, with fifty years of watching racehorses under his belt, got his first look at the Virginia horse that summer of 1972. Stunned, he compared the animal to the perfection of the Kohinoor diamond. The experts—members of the Thoroughbred Racing Associations, the National Turfwriters Association, and the Daily Racing Form—agreed and named him the 1972 Horse of the Year. Older horses usually received the award, but this time it belonged to the two-year-old. As a three-year-old, he would tackle the Triple Crown.[23]

Secretariat's outstanding performance in 1972 created a bittersweet dilemma for The Meadow. Christopher Chenery, too ill to relish his superstar, died on January 3, 1973. The inheritance taxes on his estate were staggering. In order to keep The Meadow alive, the Chenerys would have to sell some of their eighty horses. Riva Ridge would bring at least $2 million. Secretariat's price tag ran from $5 million to $7 million.

Secretariat winning the Preakness on May 19, 1973, the second leg of the Triple Crown.

However, if he failed to take the Triple Crown—which was a possibility, as Bold Ruler's offspring often peaked as two-year-olds—he might sell for $3 million.[24]

The alternative to selling any horses at all was to syndicate Secretariat—to sell shares in his future as a breeding stallion. Even though he had not yet seen the steeples of Churchill Downs, home of the Kentucky Derby, the Chenerys set a record price of $190,000 a share and put twenty-eight of thirty-two shares up for sale, keeping four for themselves. Seth Hancock, son of Bull Hancock and president of Claiborne Farm, handled the deal over four nail-biting days, selling the twenty-eight shares for a total of $5.32 million to Ogden Phipps (son of Gladys and Henry Phipps), the Virginia breeders Paul Mellon (Rokeby Farm) and Richard Stokes (Shenstone Farm), and others.[25]

In the spring of 1973, with a stupendous sum and sky-high expectations riding on his broad back, Secretariat began his three-year-old racing career. Between Turcotte's arrival in July 1972 and the Kentucky Derby on May 5, 1973, Secretariat ran ten races, three of them in 1973. He won eight of the ten. In October 1972, he crossed the finish line first, but was disqualified for bumping another horse and officially placed second. He tied the track record at the Gotham Stakes on April 7. But in the Wood Memorial two weeks later, he ran a lackluster third due to an undetected abscess in his mouth. Was he going to take the Triple Crown, or was he going to disappoint his thousands of admirers, not to mention the syndicate's members?[26]

The Triple Crown it was. On May 5, Secretariat won the Derby by two and a half lengths in a new track record, running every quarter mile of the mile-and-a-quarter race faster than the one before. On May 19, he took the Preakness by the same margin in what many expert observers thought was another track record. (The official record, which relied on an electric timer, called it more than a second slower.) On June 9 at the Belmont, he confirmed his place in history with an astounding victory—thirty-one lengths ahead of the second-place horse and a new *world* record.[27]

Secretariat was a phenomenon. He appeared on the covers of three national magazines: *Time, Newsweek,* and *Sports Illustrated.* Newspapers and television featured story after story about the Virginia horse. He even had a talent agency, William Morris, to deal with requests for his name and image. Once again, he was Horse of the Year.[28]

In the remaining six races of his career, Secretariat won four, setting

When Secretariat crossed the Belmont finish line on June 9, 1973—thirty-one lengths ahead of the second-place horse—he won the Triple Crown.

another course record and a world record, and placed second in two. He rang up total winnings of $1,316,808. On November 6, 1973, at Aqueduct, Turcotte rode him for the last time at a public farewell ceremony. Six days later, Secretariat arrived in Kentucky at his new home, Claiborne Farm, and took up residence in the stall that had belonged to his sire, Bold Ruler. One can only imagine what new heights he might have reached on the track as a more mature four-year-old, but his syndication called for his retirement at age three. Although he never produced a carbon copy of himself—none of his offspring came anywhere near his record-breaking speed—in sixteen years he sired plenty of fine racehorses and, especially, excellent broodmares. One of his fillies, Terlingua, raced well and then produced Storm Cat, *the* Thoroughbred stallion of the early twenty-first century.[29]

In his new life, Secretariat galloped and grazed on Kentucky bluegrass. The powerful stallion mellowed enough to let small children sit on his back while their parents snapped a photo. "He loved to hear the cameras click," said Penny Chenery. "His head would come up, ears pricked, as he gazed regally into the distance."[30]

The great horse died on October 4, 1989. Suffering from severe laminitis, a debilitating and painful hoof disease, Secretariat was euthanized to prevent further suffering. He was only nineteen. On every subsequent October 4, visitors line up outside the gate to Claiborne, eager to place red roses on his grave.[31]

Virginians remembered the big red horse. "Secretariat was born in a shed right outside my window," said the then-owner of The Meadow, Ross Sternheimer, in 1988. "From the horse-racing standpoint, that's a very significant event in Virginia." In June 1990, fifty people gathered on the side of the road that runs through the farm to unveil a state historical marker dedicated to Secretariat. The Clay Spring Garden Club, of Hanover, had gathered donations for the marker. Postage stamps, statues, even license plates honored him. In 2003, the State Fair of Virginia bought the property to house the fair and other events, with plans to preserve its heritage. "If Virginia ever had a piece of horse history that put it on the map, it is The Meadow," said Sue Mullins, a fair official.[32]

Those who knew Secretariat best remembered him too. "I miss the atmosphere of perfection around Secretariat and want to be touched by something like that again," said the sportswriter William Nack, who accompanied the horse and his entourage during his racing career and wrote the definitive book *Secretariat: The Making of a Champion.*[33]

"Having a horse like Secretariat," Penny Chenery told the crowd at his retirement ceremony, "is something that you pray might happen to you once in a lifetime."

"He was the greatest racehorse who ever lived," said Ron Turcotte.[34]

It all began with a poor boy who dreamed of raising horses in Virginia—and the toss of a coin.

## PAUL MELLON: THE LOVE OF A HORSE

Paul Mellon (1907–1999), heir to an immense fortune, used his wealth to enjoy art, literature, philanthropy—and horses. From Rokeby, his home in Upperville, he viewed the animals with an educated and appreciative eye. Born in Pittsburgh to an English mother who rode to the hounds, he learned how to groom his ponies, Topaz and Hotspur, at a young age. As a youth, he competed in horse shows and rode the trails of Bath County when the family vacationed at Hot Springs, Virginia. The college-aged Mellon studied his books and his horses in Europe, hunting with the Cottesmore and Pytchley Hunts in England and riding at the Saumur Cavalry School in France.[35]

His mother, Nora McMullen Mellon, owned a farm in Upperville. From there, mother and son rode with the Piedmont, Middleburg, and

Warrenton Hunts. Membership in the Orange County Hunt required residency in the county, so Mellon bought a farm there too. (It would become the site of the Virginia Tech Experimental Farm.) His mother gave him his favorite hunter, Dublin, who "could have jumped the Eiffel Tower," he wrote. When he wanted to hunt in Ireland, he took Dublin with him and had their portrait made. He loved foxhunting because of its "physical skill, good judgment, quick thinking, and the age-old thrill of the chase and the kill." During World War II, Mellon, then thirty-four, ended up at the Cavalry Replacement Training Center at Fort Riley, Kansas, thanks to his foxhunting friend General George S. Patton. He learned how to pack a mule and shoot a Colt .45 from a galloping horse, and taught horsemanship. He loved riding on the open prairie, hunting coyotes instead of foxes.[36]

Mellon raced in point-to-points and hunted in the United States and Britain, shipping and flying his horses to and fro. A season of hunting on English terrain reduced his horses to "just skin and bones," he wrote. "They were all Thoroughbreds, not used to slogging in the mud." In Virginia, he served as joint master of the Piedmont Fox Hounds in the 1950s, a time when he found a new equestrian pursuit: endurance riding. From 1959 to 1979, Mellon competed seventeen times in the Vir-

Paul Mellon *(right)* at a sporting event. The Upperville resident and famed philanthropist enjoyed horses during the entirety of his long life.

ginia 100-Mile Trail Ride in Hot Springs, a three-day event that covered forty miles on the first two days, twenty on the last. He won five times, three times in a row on the same horse, Christmas Goose. In his later years, he rode in the fifty-mile version of the ride. His human partner in these Virginia adventures was his head groom, the Reverend William Parker. The former pastor of a Baptist church in McGaheysville, Virginia, Parker would follow Mellon and his friends in a car that held water for the horses, martinis for the riders.[37]

Mellon admired racehorses as well. He started with steeplechasers, buying his first racehorse, an Irish Thoroughbred steeplechaser named Drinmore Lad, in 1933. He also owned an English mare, Makista, which he rode in point-to-points, and his Welbourne Jake won the Maryland Hunt Cup in 1937. He dedicated himself to breeding flat racehorses after World War II, feeling he could make more of a profit than with steeplechasers. His trainers included Elliott Burch, Peter Hastings-Bass, Mackenzie Miller, Jim Ryan, and Jack Skinner. Casting himself as Rokeby's chairman of the board, and his trainer as chief executive officer, Mellon set to work buying fillies, breeding horses, and holding biannual meetings with an agronomist, a veterinarian, a nutritionist, the trainer, and the managers of the stallions and farm.

His horse Quadrangle won the Belmont, as did Arts and Letters, who placed second in the Kentucky Derby and the Preakness. Sea Hero won the Kentucky Derby in 1993. Fort Marcy was Horse of the Year in 1970, and the famous Mill Reef triumphed abroad, winning the Coronation Cup, Epsom Derby, Eclipse Stakes, King George VI, Queen Elizabeth Stakes, and Prix de l'Arc de Triomphe. A statue of Mill Reef is exhibited at the Virginia Museum of Fine Arts, the home of many artistic donations from Mellon, who thought "the enjoyment of British sporting art and literature has always been inseparable from the enjoyment of racing, 'chasing, and hunting."[38]

The horse world honored and respected Mellon for his interest and contributions. In 1975, he received an award for distinguished service to racing from the Thoroughbred Club of America. He served as a trustee of the National Museum of Racing, in Saratoga, New York, helped with the Sport and the Horse exhibition at the Virginia Museum in 1960, and provided seed money for the Middleburg Training Center for Thoroughbreds. Further, Mellon paid special attention to the National Sporting Library, in Middleburg, just down the road from Rokeby, and to the Virginia Historical Society, donating to both institutions a bronze statue honoring the horses and mules of the Civil War. He also set up a timber-racing course at Rokeby and hosted the Piedmont Point-to-Point for nearly twenty years, with its coveted prize, the Rokeby Bowl. The man who knew and loved art found in racing an "aesthetic quality. . . . It is the colour, the movement, the speed, the excitement, the competition, the skill of riding, the cleverness of the horses, and the primitive element of luck. . . . But it is mostly the love of the horse, the well-kept, well-trained, beautifully moving horse, the horse as an object of art."[39]

The Middleburg Steeplechase, 1962. Virginia has had many steeplechase enthusiasts, including the well-known horsemen Marion duPont Scott, Peter Winants, and Paul Mellon.

## STEEPLECHASING

In the early 1970s, the introduction of off-track betting led to the elimination of races over fences at some flat racetracks. The racing public was reluctant to bet on the jumpers. Further, it was expensive to build steeplechase courses with fences of cedar and brush, so the portable National fence, made of synthetic material, came along. Some American steeple-

The Piedmont Hunt Point-to-Point, 1972.

Jay Trump winning the Grand National in 1965, with jockey Tommy Smith Jr., of Middleburg, grandson of Harry Worcester Smith.

chases used timber fences, big and solid, but others had high and formidable brush fences, similar to those used in Britain. Many followers of the sport preferred timber and brush. "Steeplechasing needs to have elements that truly set it apart from its flat racing cousin," wrote John Strassburger, editor of the *Chronicle of the Horse*. "It's a great test of riders, because it's far harder to negotiate a big hedge while making a winning move than it is to skim over a plastic rolltop [i.e., a National fence]." Marion duPont Scott and Arthur W. Arundel, among others, encouraged a revival of the sport. A circuit emerged in the early 1970s, and meets eventually occurred across the state in the guise of point-to-points, hunt races, and official steeplechases. In 1999, Colonial Downs, the new racetrack in New Kent County, began offering races over fences.[40]

In the early years of the twenty-first century, Kinross Farm was one of Virginia's leading steeplechase institutions. Lisa and Zohar Ben-Dov (an avid foxhunter) owned the spread, and Neil Morris (a former eventer) trained the horses. Matt McCarron, one of the sport's leading jockeys, rode regularly for Kinross, and horses like Chinese Whisper and Sur La Tete led to the farm's reputation as a "juggernaut."[41]

Great steeplechase horses came out of Virginia. In 1975, L'Escargot won the English Grand National. Raymond Guest, of Powhatan Stable in King George, owned the horse. Saluter, bred by Rose M. Estes, born in Hillsboro, owned by Ann Stern of Richmond, won six Virginia Gold Cups in a row from 1994 to 1999. He also competed in England and earned more than $400,000. In 1965, Crompton "Tommy" Smith Jr., of Middleburg, grandson of Harry Worcester Smith, rode a horse named Jay Trump to victory in the Grand National. An unprepossessing dam with good breeding and a sire related to Native Dancer produced the horse in 1957. He raced unsuccessfully at Charles Town, West Virginia, until Smith got a look at him and bought him for $1,250. He carried foxhunters, competed in point-to-points, and just got better and better, winning the Maryland Hunt Cup in 1963 and 1964. He crossed the Atlantic to take the Grand National and retired after a third win at the Maryland Hunt Cup in 1966.[42]

Another American winner of the Grand National, Bon Nouvel, was born in 1960 at Theodora Randolph's Oakley Farm in Upperville. After a racing career, Bon Nouvel took to the hunt field. Peter Winants, the editor of the *Chronicle of the Horse* and author of a book about steeplechasing, once watched Bon Nouvel, with Erskine Bedford, MFH of the Piedmont Fox Hounds, on his back, as they galloped across Paul Mellon's Rokeby Farm: "We had a long, fast run . . . riding hard to keep up with a marvelous pack of hounds and one of the best steeplechase horses in history. It doesn't get any better."[43]

## HARNESS RACING

The Northern Neck and Eastern Shore continued as centers of the sport. Seabrook Smith, from Mathews, was a nationally recognized starter of trotting races. He worked in the field for fifty years, breeding, training, racing, and working at races.[44]

Horses such as Quick Trick, Nansemond, Pecatone, and Orange Blossom kept up Virginia's trotting reputation. Bache Gill, who built a track near Kilmarnock around 1945, raced Quick Trick, a Pennsylvania pacer. In 1972, Nansemond, another pacer, sold for $1.2 million, the highest price to date for a Virginia harness horse. Pecatone made money for Howard Scott and his sons through the 1980s, as did Orange Blossom for Bob Crowther, of Kilmarnock.[45]

The Eastern Shore produced the Standardbred driver and expert Howard Camden. A native of Machipongo, born in 1930, he grew up around harness horses and had a job grooming horses after he graduated from high school. John S. Turner, a farmer on the Eastern Shore, had bred two trotting mares, Cindy M. Jr. and Carrie Castle, to a Pennsylvania stallion named Adios. Carrie Castle produced a pacing colt named Adios Boy. Camden went to work for Turner, breaking Adios Boy at the Keller fairgrounds. In the early 1950s, he drove Adios Boy in many races, breaking the world record for the pacing mile and helping the colt become the champion three-year-old pacer. The partnership lasted until Adios Boy retired at age five.[46]

In 1998, Colonial Downs added fall harness racing to its schedule of flat races and steeplechases. Ron McLenaghan, a Canadian building contractor and part-time Standardbred breeder who helped build the facility, moved his family, horses, and livelihood to the racetrack's home, New Kent County, in 1997. He and his son, Ryan, trained and drove their six horses themselves while holding down other jobs as well. "I was raised in it, but I love the horses," said Ryan. "I love racing." Like many a Virginia owner of trotting horses before him, Ron found that "the joy of harness racing is anyone can do it."[47]

## FOXHUNTING

In the late twentieth century, foxhunters all over the world knew Virginia as a place "where the ladies and gentlemen take their preeminence in American hunting for granted and very seriously," according to R. W. F. Poole, a British MFH. Virginians illustrated his point by establishing at least nine new hunts after World War II: the Rockbridge Hunt, the Southampton Foxhounds, the Commonwealth Fox Hounds, the Smith Mountain Hounds, the Fort Valley Hunt, the Oak Ridge Fox Hunt (originally an 1887 club, revived in the 1990s by the novelist Rita Mae Brown), the Colonial Fox Hounds, the Caroline Hunt, the Reedy Creek Hounds, and the Stonewall Hounds.[48]

Virginians provided plenty of other examples to back up Poole's assertion. In the early 1950s, rabies killed many foxes, so huntsmen like Melvin Poe captured the animals, inoculated them, and freed them for another day's hunting. Poe also imported foxes from Iowa to supplement the Virginia stock. A 1960s documentary, *Thoughts on Foxhunting*, featured Poe, Alexander Mackay-Smith, and other well-known members of the hunting community. In 1970, Nancy Johnson, of Roanoke, represented the significant numbers of foxhunters who didn't necessarily have a lot of money to back up their love of the sport. When she and

Jacqueline Kennedy Onassis giving daughter Caroline a ride in 1962. Onassis, a skilled equestrian, often hunted and showed in Virginia, beginning during the presidency of her husband John F. Kennedy. Her friends Eve and Paul Fout bred this horse, Rufus. Caroline's famous pony Macaroni, who commuted between the White House and Middleburg, came from the Virginia breeder Barney Brittle.

## COLORS

*Top:* A judge rides an Appaloosa to monitor a Warrenton race, 1941. *Bottom:* A buckskin and a paint race around their paddock.

APPALOOSA—A breed, not a color, but known for its spots. An Appaloosa can be one main color (bay, brown, black) with small white spots; white with black or brown spots; a dark main color with a white blanket over the hindquarters; a dark main color with a white blanket dotted with black or brown spots; and other variations.

BAY—Reddish brown, with black mane, tail, and legs.

BLACK—A true black horse has not one hair of another color, such as brown.

BROWN—May appear black but actually has brown hairs when viewed up close.

CHESTNUT OR SORREL—Reddish, with mane and tail of the same color. Sometimes the mane and tail are blond, called "flaxen."

DUN—Tan, with a stripe down the back and, often, a black mane, tail, and legs. Called "buckskin" when the horse is a light shade.

GRAY—A mix of black and white hairs. A gray horse is born almost black and lightens to white in old age. Dapple grays appear to have a coat of subtle oval gray spots. Flea-bitten grays are white with speckles of gray.

PAINT OR PINTO—Large splotches of white and either brown or black.

*Clockwise from top left:* Chestnut, gray (note the darker patches on muzzle and ears), Palomino, and a Paint Tennessee Walking Horse.

PALOMINO—Gold with a light mane and tail.

ROAN—Mix of white and other colors to make strawberry (chestnut), blue (black), or red (chestnut) roans.

WHITE—A true white horse is born that way and has no other hair color. Albinos are white because they lack pigmentation.

Horses may be further marked by white socks and stockings on their legs, and white stars, snips, and blazes on their faces.

Source: Ensminger, *Horses and Horsemanship,* 39–40.

Melvin Poe *(front, center)* and the Orange County Hunt.

her horse Sassy weren't on the field with the Bedford County Hunt, they could be found combing the countryside as census workers. Many foxhunters like Johnson worked extra jobs to pay for feed and board, drove long distances, and trained their own horses. In 2001, a shining example of preeminence, the Virginia-bred Dr. No was voted grand champion foxhunter of the United States.[49]

"To a scholar fox hunting is pageantry, history and tradition; to a poet it is the rising mist of an early, frosty dawn; to the uninitiated it is a group of men huddled around a fire and a moonshine keg on a high hill in the night," wrote Oliver Jackson Sands of the Deep Run Hunt. "But to all who love to hunt, fox hunting is a way of life."[50]

That beloved way of life faced a number of obstacles toward the end of the twentieth century and into the twenty-first. Suburban sprawl pushed pastures and horses out of the way, forcing hunts to seek new territory. As early as 1948, in fact, the Deep Run Hunt Club had to move all the way to Goochland County to escape the growth of Richmond. Veterans puzzled over newcomers who wanted to participate but didn't know how to ride, let alone know anything about horses. Finally, some people concerned with animal welfare raised their flag and declared their opposition to the sport.[51]

"Just because it's a tradition doesn't mean it is right," an official with the Fund for Animals told the *Richmond Times-Dispatch* in 2001.

"This is not just some benign social activity. Animals are being killed." Virginia hunters pointed out that while English foxhunters kill the fox, Americans rarely do, preferring the thrill of the chase to the death of the prey. "In one season, we may kill one fox max," said the joint master of the Deep Run Hunt. "And it is always a sickly fox." Balancing tradition with the present challenged everyone involved. With the outlawing of the sport in Britain in 2004, American foxhunters wondered if it was "time for civil disobedience," as an editorial in the *Chronicle of the Horse* proclaimed.[52]

Perhaps Alexander Mackay-Smith best described foxhunting as Virginian devotees relish and understand it. After a January 1949 day with the Blue Ridge Hunt, a bad day weatherwise when only twelve "die-hards" made it, he remembered: "We looked at each other and grinned with that smugness which can only be found in the inveterate foxhunter who has achieved Nirvana—the first flight of a classic run and the prospect of telling practically everyone else . . . exactly what they missed."[53]

A quintessential Virginia scene: The Blue Ridge Hunt at Carter Hall, Millwood, in 1968. The house dates to the 1790s; Stonewall Jackson headquartered there in 1862.

Field hunters earned their keep with a reliable performance while foxhunting; looks and form mattered less than reliability and heart. Their talents lay either in galloping over flat, open country or over "trappy"—hilly, wooded—terrain. Show hunters, however, needed a sleek appearance and stylish form over fences. Jumpers in the show ring must jump high, avoid knocking down the fences, and compete against the clock. These women and men of the late twentieth century excelled at horse shows as riders and trainers of hunters and jumpers, and their accomplishments added luster to Virginia's reputation, both at home and around the world.

Jane Marshall Dillon (1915–2000), born in Fauquier County, first climbed on a horse when she was three. She foxhunted and bred horses, including April Dawn, a champion hunter of the 1950s, but she made her greatest contribution through her tutelage of children and teenagers. Dillon opened her Junior Equitation School in Hayfield in 1950. Urban sprawl pushed it to Full Cry Farm in Vienna in 1955 and then to Clifton in 1989. Wherever she taught, she imparted a strong foundation in the basics as well as a sense of fun. "It was the perfect start for a young child," said Joe Fargis, one of her most famous and successful pupils. "Mrs. Dillon ran a happy camp in terms of both ambiance and environment." Her books, *Form over Fences: A Pictorial Critique of Jumping for the Junior Rider* (1961) and *School for Young Riders* (1958), instructed riders with a pleasant mixture of fun and responsibility.[54]

Joe Fargis grew serious about horses as a Virginia second-grader in the 1950s, when he met a classmate's mother, Jane Marshall Dillon. Fargis found a home at her Full Cry Farm for the next eleven years. A star pupil, he shone on the cover photograph of her 1961 book, *Form over Fences.* "By the time he was ten or so, his exceptional talent was obvious," remembered Dillon in 1985. Headed for a career at the pinnacle of show jumping, from 1966 to 1978 he worked with another legendary Virginia horsewoman, Frances Rowe, who taught him, he said, that "the horse is a living, breathing creature, not a machine or vehicle for the achievement of success." Worldwide recognition came in 1984, when Fargis and a former racehorse mare named Touch of Class won two Olympic gold medals, one as a member of the show-jumping team, the other as an individual pair. In 1988, he rode on the U.S. team that captured a silver Olympic medal. Long after the Olympics, he trained and continued to show at the top level of the sport, averring that his favorite win was always his last one.[55]

Rodney Jenkins gave jumper riders everywhere a run for their money from the 1960s through the 1980s, becoming what the Show Jumping Hall of Fame called "the winningest rider in the history of U.S. show jumping." A native Virginian, with a father who was a well-known huntsman, the man easily recognized by his red hair racked up win after win in the show ring, especially with grands prix, and with a spot on the United States Equestrian Team (USET) in the Pan American Games. "The horse makes the rider," he said. "I don't care how good you are." Jenkins also showed hunters, raced horses on the flat and in steeplechases, and judged hunter classes. Later in his career, he trained racehorses at major racetracks.[56]

Kathy Kusner, born in Arlington in 1940, was a poster girl for the explosion in women's riding after World War II. She taught herself to ride on a pony—bareback. She upgraded to instruction at Dillon's Full

The leading show jumper Kathy Kusner on Unusual, 1962. Kusner doubled for an actor in the riding scenes of the 1968 Disney movie *The Horse in the Gray Flannel Suit.*

Cry Farm, became a leading show jumper, and by the age of twenty-one competed on the USET. In 1958, she set a U.S. record for the high jump at the Upperville show, clearing 7'3" on a horse named Freckles. Kusner found her most famous mount, Untouchable, through Ben O'Meara, a Brooklyn-born show jumper and supporter of the USET who had a sharp eye for a good horse. Kusner rode Untouchable to many open jumper championships and wins in the early 1960s, with a sixth team finish and thirteenth individual at the 1964 Olympics and a slot on the 1968 team. On another horse, she competed at the 1972 Olympics on the silver-winning team. Her skills took her to the steeplechase course, when she became one of the first licensed female jockeys in the United States in 1968, going on to compete as the first woman in the Maryland Hunt Cup. She moved to California and worked with Horses in the Hood, a nonprofit group that introduced inner-city children to horses, while also doing course design, conducting clinics, and serving as an expert witness and appraiser in equine legal cases. "She broke into a man's sport in the '50s and shattered the idea that men were the only ones who could show-jump," said Karen Lende O'Connor, an eventer who debuted at the Olympics in 1996. "As a child, I was excited to see that happen. It gave me hope."[57]

A spectacularly successful show jumper, Katie Monahan Prudent was "the greatest all-round woman rider I've ever seen," said George Morris, a leading teacher of equitation. She dominated the field in the 1970s and 1980s. Growing up in the Midwest, she rode a Quarter Horse that had been a barrel racer, and then graduated to foxhunting. As a teenager, she worked with Virginians Bill Queen and Sallie Sexton, and ended up with New Jersey–based Morris, winning the American Horse Show Association (AHSA) Medal Finals and ASPCA Maclay Finals, the major classes for young equestrians. In 1981, she opened her own operation, Plain Bay Farm, in Middleburg. She partnered with Bert and Diana Firestone. Monahan Prudent led a bicontinental existence after her 1986 marriage to Henri Prudent, a French horseman she met at the Virginia State Horse Show. Their son, Adam, showed jumpers in Virginia, and Monahan Prudent continued training and competing.[58]

Frances Newbill Rowe (ca. 1926–1985), born in Essex County, graduated from Mary Washington College, in Fredericksburg, which had a riding program. In the 1950s, she showed professionally, and in the 1960s, she trained jumpers and hunters and their riders, including Joe Fargis, Conrad Homfeld, and Kathy Kusner, Olympic competitors all.

From her Goochland County home, Foxwood Farm, she also worked with race horses, designed courses, and judged. She developed jumpers and owned a piece of Touch of Class, Fargis's Olympic mount. Rowe also promoted the Virginia State Horse Show, hoping to make it more attractive to the general public.[59]

A queen of the hunter show ring, Sallie Sexton (1912–1998) rode Welsh ponies as a child, showed in the Midwest as a young woman, and foxhunted. In 1941, she showed with great success a hunter named Runancarry, a son of Archibald Cary Randolph's stallion Runantell. She came to Middleburg in 1976, raising horses (as well as rabbits and chickens) and dominating the ring with her homebreds. Sexton trained hunters and sidesaddle riders and held strong opinions and high standards.[60]

Sallie Busch Wheeler (1931–2001), a member of the horse-loving Busch family, was eulogized as "the grande dame of horse shows" by the *Chronicle of the Horse* when she died in 2001. She spent her life with Hackney ponies, Saddlebreds, and hunters in partnership with her husband, Kenneth Wheeler, on their Cismont Manor Farm in Keswick. Not only did she own, train, judge, and show the animals with incredible success—the couple averaged two hundred or three hundred first-place showings every year—but she also led the way in the horse-show world in the state and the nation. She was identified particularly with the National Horse Show, traditionally held at Madison Square Garden in New York City, serving as its president and chairman of the board. After the show moved to New Jersey, she brought it back to New York in 1996, even adding bull riding to the schedule to attract bigger crowds. "She came from that tradition of giving and giving to the sport," Alan Balch of the AHSA told the *Chronicle*. "And in so many ways, her contributions . . . were infinite."[61]

## EVENTING

Virginia was made for the demanding sport of three-day eventing. "We have the ideal climate, turf, footing, and scenic courses with trees and rolling hills," observed Major General Jonathan R. Burton of Fort Belvoir, an army post near Mount Vernon. He should know—he rode on the army's team in the 1940s and in the Olympics in 1956. "We have the perfect terrain for these 3-day events." Another sport with military origins, eventing—also known as combined training—made its first Olympic appearance in 1912. In a competition that originally challenged a cavalry horse and rider under simulated combat conditions, participants perform a dressage test, and then gallop and leap over a long outdoor course studded with obstacles, and finally jump a series of fences in an arena. At the top level, additional phases called roads and tracks (miles of walking and trotting) and steeplechase (two-plus miles at a gallop over fences) provide an even more thorough test.[62]

As a British expert wrote, "success demands the complete horse, sufficiently supple and obedient to complete the dressage test, bold and courageous across a range of solid and demanding cross country fences, and then after these exertions still able to complete a small but twisty show jumping course with control and accuracy." The first American Olympians to compete in the discipline were army men from the Cavalry School at Fort Riley, Kansas. Their last appearance in the Olympics came in 1948.[63]

During the infancy of the sport, the state produced Jenny Camp, one of the discipline's most famous horses. Foaled in 1926 at the Remount Depot in Front Royal, by the Thoroughbred sire Gordon Russell and out of a Thoroughbred/Standardbred dam, the athletic mare won individual silvers at the 1932 and 1936 Olympics and the team gold in 1932. During the adolescence of U.S. eventing, the 1950s and 1960s, introductory levels were called Jenny Camp Divisions in her honor.[64]

Interested riders of the 1950s had to train and compete in Europe, since the United States lacked any kind of organization in the sport. Horsemen of all ages in the United States and Virginia had plenty of interest. The U.S. Pony Club, organized in 1954 with Alexander Mackay-Smith at the helm, teemed with eager young riders looking for new ways to compete with horses. Adult steeplechasers and foxhunters also sought new challenges. In 1959, the growing interest coalesced into the United States Combined Training Association (USCTA; later called the United States Eventing Association, USEA). Mackay-Smith was one of the founders, along with the Virginians Jonathan Burton; H. Steward Treviranus, a neighbor of Mackay-Smith's who had ridden for Canada at the 1952 Olympics; and Whitney Stone, president of the United States Equestrian Team. In Virginia and in Maryland, a rudimentary circuit operated in the spring and fall. At the 1964 Olympics, eventing took a giant step when women competed for the first time. Starting in the 1970s, the sport matured and welcomed many Virginians to its ranks.[65]

Stephen Bradley, of Leesburg, began his international career in 1989. He rode Sassy Reason on the 1992 Olympic team and became the second

American ever to win at Burghley (the four-star event in England) in 1993, when the Olympic committee named him Equestrian Athlete of the Year. He won Rolex Kentucky in 1996 and took the top spot at the Checkmate International for three years in the early 1990s. In the early years of the twenty-first century, he and a Russian Thoroughbred gelding named Fröm competed at Rolex Kentucky and Burghley.[66]

Tad Coffin, a team and individual gold medallist in the 1976 Olympics on Bally Cor, moved to Charlottesville from Vermont. Retired from eventing, he ran a saddle-making business there.[67]

Phyllis Dawson began competing in the 1970s. Riding Albany II, she served on the Olympic team in 1988. On Snowy River, as a member of the USET, Dawson competed in the Open European Championships at Burghley. She moved on to training and selling event horses at Windchase, a farm in Loudoun County.[68]

Becky Douglas came to Virginia from Kansas after foxhunting and earning a B level from the Pony Club. Training with Karen and David O'Connor, she rode a bay Thoroughbred named Highland Hogan to high placings at the 2000 Rolex Kentucky and other competitions. In 2000, they made the pool comprising the Olympic short list, from which the bronze-medal team of four Virginians emerged.[69]

Nina Fout, of Middleburg, came from a horse-loving family. Her father, Paul Fout, rode hunters and jumpers and trained flat racers and steeplechasers; brother Douglas was a steeplechaser rider and trainer; her sister, Virginia, rode show hunters; and her mother, Eve, was a foxhunter and well-known artist. "The bulk of my childhood," said Fout, "was spent running and jumping up and down the hills here in the heart of Virginia hunt country where I'm lucky enough to live—foxhunting, going to Pony Club, playing cowboys and Indians with my friends." All that running and jumping led to a career as an international eventer, beginning in 1972. In 1979, riding Rimrock, she earned the title of National Junior Champion. In the early 1990s, Fout, who trained with Jim Wofford, found a superb horse through her brother. Doug was considering a 17.1-hand Thoroughbred gelding, 3 Magic Beans, as a steeplechaser, but Nina decided he'd make a better eventer. The pair made good showings in Maryland, Ireland, and England, including at Blenheim in 1997, where Beans won the Ryan's Cross Award as best young horse. A career high point came in 2000, when Fout rode 3 Magic Beans on the bronze-medal Olympic team—Fout, David O'Connor, Karen Lende O'Connor, and Linden Weisman, Virginians all. Fout was amazed and grateful:

"What were the odds that the final team would be composed of four riders not only from the same state, but the same town? For me, being able to take a family steeplechaser down a path that would take us to . . . the Olympics . . . was more than I could ever dream would happen."[70]

A leading rider of the late 1990s and early years of the twenty-first century, Karen Lende O'Connor grew up in Massachusetts, where membership in the Pony Club piqued her passion for eventing. In the mid-1970s, she worked for Tad Coffin (before he retired to Virginia to build saddles). "He has a tremendous work ethic," she said of the Olympian. "He taught that if you're going to be at the top of this sport, you really have to work very hard." Putting that advice into action, in 1977 she moved to Virginia and began training with the top rider and trainer Jim Wofford. Two years later, she entered international competition and began accumulating a string of victories. Her career included a stint as the USEA's Female Equestrian Athlete of the Year.[71]

One of her best-known horses was Biko, her 1996 Olympic mount and the 2000 USCTA Horse of the Year. Belonging to Richard and Vita Thompson, of Pennsylvania, the tall Irish Thoroughbred with the

Karen O'Connor and her pony, Teddy O'Connor, on the cross-country course of the 2008 Rolex Kentucky, where they placed sixth.

David O'Connor in the show-jumping phase of a cross-country event.

blaze face "had the grace of a ballerina and the strength of a giant," said his rider, "along with the eye of an eagle, the greatest heart, and elegance. There wasn't anything he couldn't do; he was a hero, and everything I always dreamed of in a horse." On another outstanding mount, Prince Panache (called Nash), she helped win the team bronze at the 2000 Olympics. "Nash has always been loving and sensitive," she said. "A lovely horse to be around, who would try his heart out for you." Perhaps her most popular equine partner, however, was a pony named Theodore O'Connor. At only 14.1 hands, Teddy, a mix of Arabian, Thoroughbred, and Shetland, carried her to team and individual gold medals at the 2007 Pan American Games and finishes in the top six at Rolex Kentucky in 2007 and 2008. The unpredictability of sport showed its hand in 2008, after the pair had made the short list for the Olympics. The pony was so severely injured in a freak accident at home that O'Connor had to euthanize him. "His trust for me went beyond what I thought was possible," she told the *Chronicle of the Horse*.[72]

At not one but two Olympics—1996 and 2000—one of her teammates on the winner's stand was her husband, David O'Connor. They were the first married couple ever to achieve such a feat. "Being married to your teammate intensifies the glory," said David O'Connor, "making the most of an already incredibly special experience." They wed in 1993. "It's great to have two eventers in the family because we enjoy so much in common," the O'Connors stated in their 2004 autobiography. "But we don't coach each other unless the other person asks." After a stint in England, the pair returned to Virginia in 1994 to run an eventing operation for Jacqueline Mars, of Stonehall Farm, in Middleburg. Like most eventers at the higher levels, they trained and rode horses owned by others. The couple created an entity they called Team O'Connor because, they reasoned, "Why should we split our effort into separate camps when we actually could double our effort?" They further wanted to make sure they had plenty of good horses on hand and to establish a recognizable brand. "We also knew we had to become more accessible to the public," they wrote. "We made a conscious decision to become public personalities."[73]

The male half of the O'Connors grew up in Maryland, the son of a British horse-loving mother and an American father. He belonged to the Pony Club and played other sports. At age eleven, he, his mother, Sally, and his brother, Brian, undertook a three-month trail ride from Maryland to Oregon. His mother's and brother's interests in eventing ensured his youthful introduction to Jim Wofford. After he became an eventer himself, O'Connor moved to Virginia in 1986 to work for Wofford. Starting that year, he was winning international and national competitions on well-known mounts like Custom Made, Giltedge, and Rattle 'N' Hum.[74]

"It's one thing to have one good horse," O'Connor wrote of Giltedge (owned by Jacqueline Mars) and Custom Made (owned by Joseph Zada). "But to have two with careers like theirs, and to have them play the game the way they did—I was just incredibly lucky." Giltedge, a tall Irish Thoroughbred, took his time to reach his full potential. "It was just a question of getting his body to catch up to his mind," wrote O'Connor, "and to have him understand what I wanted." Giltedge joined his stablemate Custom Made at the 2000 Olympics, when O'Connor rode Giltedge for the team bronze and Custom Made for the individual gold. In 2002, Giltedge and O'Connor rode on the gold-medal team at the World Equestrian Games.[75]

Custom Made, a dark bay, seven-eighths Thoroughbred, first captured O'Connor's attention by running away with a rider. Nonetheless, "when I first looked into the horse's eyes," he remembered, "we had a connection right there." The bond paid off. At the 1996 Olympics,

O'Connor and "Tailor" earned an individual fifth place. In 1997, they won at Badminton, in England, which many experts call the toughest event in the world. Three years later, man and horse nearly lost the 2000 Olympic gold during the final, show-jumping phase, when O'Connor momentarily forgot the course. "I turned my head, swiveling to find the right fence," he remembered. "That got everyone in the stands gasping." He recovered, jumped the correct fence, and sped up Custom Made through the rest of the round for the individual gold medal, the first one for the United States in eventing in twenty-four years since Tad Coffin won at Montreal in 1976. Such accomplishments earned Custom Made the title of 2000 USCTA Horse of the Year and a well-deserved retirement in 2004.[76]

The O'Connors expressed their appreciation for the sport by giving clinics, training other riders and horses, and, in David's case, by serving as president of the United States Equestrian Federation, the national governing body of horse sports. The couple called themselves "fortunate as riders from Virginia to have at our fingertips three of the premier equestrian facilities in the United States": the Virginia Horse Center at

Kim Severson and Tsunami tackle the cross-country course at the Virginia Horse Center.

Lexington, Great Meadow at the Plains, and Morven Park at Leesburg. The state was equally fortunate to have athletes like the O'Connors and their peers making Virginia the home of the very best in the sport.[77]

Kim Vinoski Severson, of Scottsville, proved another top competitor of the early years of the twenty-first century. Riding Linda E. A. Wachtmeister's Winsome Adante, she received such accolades as USCTA Lady Rider, while "Dan" won his own acclaim as the *Chronicle of the Horse*'s Eventing Horse of the Year in 2001 and 2004 and the USCTA's 2001 Horse of the Year. In 2004 she won the Rolex Kentucky CCI**** plus a team bronze and the individual silver at the Olympics. Winsome Adante, an English Thoroughbred, 16.1 hands tall, arrived at Wachtmeister's Plain Dealing Farm in 1999. "You're rubbing your hands together when he and Kim are on a team together beside you," David O'Connor told the *Chronicle*. "You know he'll have a good dressage, one of the fastest cross-country rounds, and his show jumping keeps getting better and better." His status as a celebrity only increased after the 2004 Olympics. "I was at a horse trial after the Olympics," said Wachtmeister. "And some kids . . . realized I was Dan's owner and started squealing like I was a rock star."[78]

Virginia-born Torrance Watkins starred in the 1970s and early 1980s. Her compact (15.1 hands) Paint mare, Poltroon, matched a flashy appearance with winning performances. Watkins began riding at age four. She became the first woman to win an Olympic medal in eventing, the team gold in 1984, on Fin Varra, a former racehorse. After moving to Massachusetts, she participated in the sport by designing courses.[79]

Linden Weisman, of Bluemont, and her horse Anderoo competed at the Sydney Olympics in 2000. A relative novice at that level, Weisman did well at dressage but suffered two falls in the cross-country phase, thus dropping them out of the running. She credited her trainers, Karen and David O'Connor, with helping her see the larger picture and work even harder at her sport.[80]

Jim Wofford, of Upperville, capped an illustrious career in the 1960s and 1970s with the individual and team silver medals in the 1980 Olympics. He added the disks to a collection of two other team silvers, earned while riding Kilkenny at the 1968 and 1972 games, along with five national championships, a 1970 World Championship bronze, and a team gold from the 1967 Pan Am Games. A love and aptitude for the sport flowed through his veins: his father, John W. Wofford, competed at the 1932 Olympics; his brother J. E. D. followed at the 1952 games; his brother Warren carried the family flag at the 1956 Olympics. "It wasn't a question of if I wanted to ride in the Olympics," Jim Wofford said. "It was a question of when I was going to ride." After his retirement in 1986, he became a full-time and highly successful coach. Since 1978, in fact, each Olympic, Pan American, and World Championship team contained at least one Wofford student, and the 2000 Olympic team comprised all current and former pupils. A foxhunter, horse-show competitor, and steeplechaser, Wofford also wrote two educational books and a memoir. "Teaching makes me a better teacher," said Wofford in 1995. His teaching certainly made better riders out of many Virginians.[81]

If anyone doubted Virginia's preeminent place in the world of eventing, a look at the short list for the 2004 Olympic team would erase any questions. Stephen Bradley, Holly Hepp, Abigail Lufkin, David O'Connor, Kim Severson, Jan Thompson, and John Williams—seven of the thirteen on the list—all lived, trained, and competed in Virginia. The alternate list was equally stellar, including Karen O'Connor as well as Lufkin, Severson, Thompson, and Williams on different mounts. Severson on Winsome Adante and Williams on Carrick made the five-member team, which won the team bronze medal. Severson took the individual silver.[82]

By 2001, an official of the United States Equestrian Team could say, "Virginia has a lot to offer the event world. Some of the best riders, coaches, farriers, and veterinarians call Virginia home. Where else can a person run into Karen O'Connor at the grocery store, Linden Weisman on the track, Becky Douglas trotting beside the road, Nina Fout at the tack shop, and Jimmy Wofford at the gas station—all in the same day?" Virginia kept offering the sport talented eventers in the twenty-first century. "We are proud to see some of our young riders go on to compete at upper levels during recognized horse trials and three-day events, and to see their brothers and sisters at our schooling shows," said Penny Ross in 2003. She and her husband, Brian, of Rockbridge County, ran events and related competitions in the 1990s and early twenty-first century, often at the Virginia Horse Center, which hosted the Virginia Horse Trials, the Virginia International Three Day Event CCC*, and lower-level events for novice riders. "That is what it is all about," she said.[83]

## DRESSAGE

In the 1970s, the discipline called dressage made its stately way into the United States and Virginia. The ancient and classical form of riding,

Horse and rider commune at a high level in dressage.

born in Europe, calls for superb and subtle communication between horse and rider. While following a pattern in a large arena marked off by letters of the alphabet, the horse performs moves that can be the most basic—a four-beat walk, a brisk trot, a canter on the correct lead. At the highest levels, the moves are complicated, elegant, and sometimes spectacular. In the pirouette, for example, the horse spins in a circle around a hind leg. Trotting in place, moving neither forward nor backward, produces the piaffe. The famous white Lipizzans leap into the air from a standstill and kick out their hind feet, the capriole. Dressage, as much an art as a sport, demonstrates the utmost obedience and suppleness on the part of the horse. As with three-day eventing, Europeans and military riders dominated the field, which joined the Olympics in 1912. European warm-blooded horses such as Westphalians, Hanoverians, and Trakheners filled arenas with their elegance and versatility.[84]

A few practitioners of dressage lived in Virginia before the 1970s, including television personality Arthur Godfrey, who owned Beacon Hill Farm near Leesburg. He gave exhibitions at the major shows in the 1950s. The sport gradually expanded its territory and popularity, especially with riders' introduction to it through Pony Club. Competitors in three-day eventing developed their skills, with dressage the first part of the tests they performed. Dressage specialists emerged within the borders of the state, such as Lendon Gray, a well-known trainer on the national scene, who attended Sweet Briar College and rode under Paul Cronin before returning to teach there.[85]

The Virginia Dressage Association sponsored, among other activities, the popular Christopher Reeve Celebrity Freestyle in Keswick. The fund-raising event, named for the late actor who became paralyzed in an eventing accident, drew celebrity judges and an enthusiastic crowd to watch riders and horses perform dressage to music. The association also conducted a large dressage show at the Virginia Horse Center, in Lexington, called the Colonel Bengt Ljunquist Memorial Championships. Of the dressage scene in 2001, "Virginia is a horse-loving state with lots of talent and potential," said Sarah Reuter, a proprietor of European Performance Horses in Barboursville. "And we need to pull closer together." Although far more Virginians participated in hunting, jumping, and eventing, in 2004 more than twenty riders from the state won awards from the United States Dressage Association. They seem to have heeded Reuter's advice as they wrote a new chapter in Virginia's equine history.[86]

## POLO

A period of dormancy for polo in the early 1950s turned into one of vitality by the 1960s. The Virginia Polo Association was formed in 1952, and the next year, the University of Virginia's alumni-supported Virginia Polo Club came along at the instigation of three students. They played on a former corn field called Brook Hill Polo Field. By 1963, it was one of the best college teams in the United States. Over the years the students won national intercollegiate championships with members who had played in high school and students who had learned while on the team.[87]

By the early 1960s, Virginia teams competed in tournaments in and out of the state. In 1963, for example, the Goose Creek Polo Club played

Virginians such as General George Patton, novelist Rita Mae Brown, and illustrator Wesley Dennis have played polo.

at Phipps Field and at the Izaak Walton League grounds near Leesburg. Top players of the time included Texan Will Farish (a veteran of the University of Virginia team), Juan Rodriguez of Argentina, Vinnie Rizzo, Hap Puelicher, George Oliver (nationally ranked), Cunny Cunningham (a native of the state), Wayne Brown (coach of Goose Creek), and Colonel Jim Spurrier, from Fort Belvoir. In 1967, Thomas N. Lavery added a new venue, Black Cat Field, in Keswick. It featured parking on two levels for optimum viewing. Spectators and riders liked Phipps Field (later Kent Field) for its idyllic setting and gorgeous turf.[88]

In the 1990s, the Northern Virginia Polo League comprised clubs from Great Meadow, Rappahannock, Charlottesville, Middleburg, and Potomac. Vineyards and luxury car dealerships often sponsored the teams. "We want . . . to make the game available to everyone who wants to play," said a spokesperson for the Great Meadow Polo Club, which was started by Peter Arundel, publisher of the *Fauquier Times-Democrat,* in 1993. Many spectators received their first introduction to polo at charity matches, and schools—in The Plains and the town of Washington, to name two—offered lessons for aspiring players. Players came from the United States Polo Association clubs of Bleu Rock, in the town of Washington; Bull Run, Clifton; Charlottesville; Goose Creek, Middleburg; Great Meadow, The Plains; Old Dominion, Great Falls; Piedmont

Polo at Phipps Field.

Women's, Charlottesville; Powhatan Plantation, King George; Rappahannock, Alexandria; Shirley Plantation, Charles City; the University of Virginia; and Virginia Beach.[89]

Many of the players of the 1990s were foreign professionals, mostly from Argentina, who traveled to practice their trade, subsidized by enthusiastic amateur patrons who owned the ponies and took lessons. Both professionals and amateurs played a new variation, arena polo, in an enclosed arena about one-third the size of a traditional field, with three players per side (instead of four) and four chukkers (instead of six) of seven and a half minutes. In 1997, one of the Argentine players, Roberto Villegas, made headlines on the front page, not the sports page, when he was shot and killed by Fauquier County's Susan Cummings, his girlfriend as well as his employer.[90]

The sport gained audiences and adherents through the rest of the twentieth century. The Virginia author and horsewoman Rita Mae Brown took it up in 1988. "Most polo people are fabulous," she said. "I wouldn't give two cents for a lot of the people on the sidelines down at Palm Beach [a popular Florida venue for polo]. . . . But the folks out there on the pitch, they are the best people in the world."[91]

## ENDURANCE AND TRAIL RIDING

Endurance riding, like three-day eventing, sprang from a military background. The discipline pits horses and riders against distances of twenty-five, fifty, even one hundred miles, with trails winding through all sorts of terrain. The winner may be the horse that comes in first, or it may be the best-conditioned animal, depending on the type of contest. Competitors ride all breeds of horses, but Arabians excel because of their desert backgrounds and a build particularly suited to long distances.

As early as 1939 and 1940, Virginia-bred horses did well in the sport, including King George VI, a Saddlebred-Standardbred cross who took second place in the 100-Mile Trail Ride in Woodstock, Vermont, and Bo Peep, a half-bred mare by a government stallion who won it in 1940. The horseman Paul Mellon was an enthusiastic and successful competitor at all distances well into his golden years, at The Homestead's ride and other events. In the 1970s, the Old Dominion 100-Mile Ride in Front Royal started up, with Matthew Mackay-Smith (son of Andrew Mackay-Smith) among the organizers. Mackay-Smith, a veterinarian, and his wife, Winkie, competed all over the country, with Matthew winning

Valerie Kanavy, a leading endurance rider, competes all over the world. Here she rides Saagre Gold.

both the Tevis Cup in California (100 miles) and the Old Dominion in Virginia (100 miles) in the same year. A founder and the medical editor of *Equus* magazine, and a foxhunter, Mackay-Smith said that "in distance riding, you discover how much deeper your resources are than you believed."[92]

The star endurance rider from Virginia was Valerie Kanavy, of Fort Valley. On Arabian horses, Kanavy won world and national prizes and, as of 2003, had ridden more than 15,000 miles in competition. Born in California, she rode in Kansas and in Pennsylvania, trying western pleasure, barrel racing, and foxhunting. Conditioning her horse for the hunt field led her to try competitive trail riding. She won her first event in 1972. She and her family—daughter Danielle was a successful competitor as well—came to love Virginia when they attended events here, so when their territory in Pennsylvania grew overcrowded with suburbs, they moved to Fort Valley. She competed as far away as Abu Dhabi and as close as Virginia.[93]

The state produced other leading competitors. Brenda Baird, a psychology professor at Hollins University in Roanoke, took up the sport after forays into other equine events. "No other professional, academic, athletic, or personal endeavor in my life satisfied me mentally, emotionally, and physically like endurance riding," she said in 2001. Lexington's Sally Mann, a photographer of international repute, won a fifty-mile race in North Carolina in 2006. Lynn Gilbert of Glasgow competed in national events like the Pan American Endurance Championship, in Washington state, and in Abu Dhabi, as well as the Old Dominion. To help such riders and their mounts, the Virginia Tech Middleburg Agriculture Research and Extension Center gave trail rides and conducted research with Arabians and part-Arabians.[94]

Thousands of Virginians enjoyed the trails of the state on their own, with trail-riding organizations, and in competitions that test a horse's common sense. Trails wind through state, private, and federal land. Clubs have included at one time or another the Patrick Henry Saddle Club, the Nokesville Horse Society, the Jack Jouett Bridle Trails Club, the Battlefield Equestrian Society, the Clifton Horse Society, and the Buffalo Riders of Hampton Roads. Inns, farms, and stables rented horses and facilities for the pastime.

As Virginia's population grew, trail riders and other horsemen concentrated on preserving open space for trail riding and other horse activities. National organizations like the Equestrian Land Conservation Resource and Back Country Horsemen of America, and state groups like the Land Trust of Virginia and Northern Virginia Coalition of Equestrian Organizations, promoted the cause, as did the Virginia Horse Council. "We need to educate spectators, get them out to enjoy the sport and protect our open spaces," said Margaret Good of Morven Park, speaking of eventing. "Where we have land, we need to protect it." John Strassburger, editor at the time of the *Chronicle of the Horse,* headed up the Land Trust of Virginia in 2002. A foxhunter, eventer, and endurance rider, he and the other members worked "to ensure that Virginia's most scenic and historic lands are not lost forever."[95]

## DRIVING

Until the advent of the internal combustion engine, Virginians always used four-wheeled vehicles powered by horses. Many Amish and Mennonite residents of Virginia still do, with Standardbreds between the shafts of their buggies. When automobiles took over, however, some people

Viola Winmill takes Howard Linn for a spin in Warrenton, 1941. Winmill, an avid collector and passionate driver of horse-drawn vehicles, made a museum out of her possessions, the Winmill Carriage Collection at Morven Park.

turned driving a team of horses from a necessary skill into a sport. Viola Townsend Winmill, of Warrenton, transformed her love of carriages and driving into a historical collection that benefited Virginia long after her passing. As MFH of the Warrenton Hunt from 1925 to 1931, Winmill rode sidesaddle. She found another way to enjoy horses by assembling all manner of four- and two-wheeled horse-drawn vehicles into a private museum at her home, Clovelly Farm. (She dubbed her house Whiffle Tree Manor.) Her husband, Robert, gave her the first coach as a birthday present. She was entranced. After learning how to drive, Winmill began buying vehicles from Europe (Austria, England, France, Italy, Spain) and the United States (New York and Texas) and receiving them as gifts. A familiar sight to residents of the Warrenton area, she led parades at race meets or trotted smartly along the road.

At first Winmill drove a full-size coach pulled by four horses (called four-in-hand), but after two accidents—one that broke her husband's hip and shattered the coach, another that broke her father's collarbone—she switched to smaller and ostensibly safer vehicles. (Combining practicality with her hobby, she incorporated into her home décor fragments of the first ruined coach, along with bits and pieces from carriages, horse blankets, and wagon wheels.) Her new prizes included a coach called a Tom Thumb after its previous owner, the famous midget Tom Thumb, who entertained as a member of the Barnum and Bailey circus. Four or six

Welsh ponies (Happy Boy, Happy Girl, Dimples, Dapples, Peanuts, and Snapper) pulled them. Winmill competed successfully at horse shows, including Warrenton and Pennsylvania's famous Devon, and drove a small Wells Fargo stagecoach in the 1953 inaugural parade of President Dwight D. Eisenhower. In 1960, she helped found the Carriage Association of Virginia, and in 1970, she gave her prizes, 130 by now, to a facility at Morven Park called the Winmill Carriage Collection. She celebrated by taking her six-in-hand for a spin around the park. When she died in 1974, a horse-drawn hearse carried her to her final resting place.[96]

Winmill set the pace for a sport that increased in popularity after World War II. The historical aspect was one attraction, and its viability as an alternative to riding was another. "Driving is a way of keeping horses in our lives if riding is no longer possible or practical," as Darlene Jacobson, editor of the *Virginia Horse Journal,* pointed out in 2001. For example, Flora Hillman, of northern Virginia, drove two Welsh ponies after years of endurance riding, foxhunting, and eventing. When her hunter developed navicular, a hoof disease, she switched both herself and the horse to driving. She also liked it because a nonriding family member could accompany her.[97]

As of 2000, Virginia had four driving clubs: the Piedmont Driving Club, formed around 1980, the James River Driving Club, the Shenandoah Valley Driving Society, and the Potomac River Driving Association. They promoted safety, shared techniques, and offered friendship and competition. Enthusiasts drove carriages, coaches, and all manner of vehicles.

Steeplechase meets often featured a carriage parade before the races, and the Maymont Floral Carriage Festival in Richmond and the semiannual Coaching Day event at Stratford Hall offered many handsome carriages and teams. The Upperville show and others had driving classes, and the Virginia Horse Center added a course to its property. The Carriage Association of America, recognizing a welcoming state, has met at Colonial Williamsburg and The Homestead.[98]

Anyone who thought that driving competition meant a quiet trot down a shady lane changed their mind when they attended a combined driving event. Like its saddled counterpart, the three-day event, it tests drivers and horses with dressage in a ring; a marathon that plunges through streams, trees, and hills; and an obstacle course around cones. Competitors must have a spanking and appropriate turnout, from the grooming of the horse to the attire of the driver and the cleanliness of

Combined driving competition at the Virginia Horse Center.

the vehicle. Drivers, whether in shows or at leisure, handle one horse; two, either side by side or one in front of the other; three, side by side or two together and one in front, called unicorn; or four horses.[99]

Some of the discipline's top competitors lived in Virginia. Kate Shields, of Middleburg, bred Welsh Cobs and competed internationally, serving as team alternate in 2004 for the World Single Driving Championship. Muffy Seaton, an international competitor from Bluemont, was well known for her team of Dartmoor ponies, Farnley Brent and Farnley Maurice, affectionately known to their many devoted fans as "The Fleas." They capped a career of wins with a third place overall in combined driving at the 1997 Royal Windsor Horse Show, in England. What Seaton valued most about driving was "the gameness of my ponies, their sheer determination." Further, she said, "you don't have to be as physically fit, or as brave, as for foxhunting, so it appeals to older people." Seaton also judged shows and taught driving clinics.[100]

Other driving enthusiasts in the Old Dominion included Frank Calhoun, who drove Morgans from his Rockbridge Baths farm, Battersea Morgans, and Clay Camp, formerly of Keswick. Camp grew up with Saddlebreds, rode hunters as an adult, was heavily involved with Thoroughbreds, and drove draft horses for fun. He ended up with Dutch Warmbloods and became the first Virginia competitor at the World Four-in-Hand Driving Championships.[101]

Horse-drawn vehicles served tourists as well. Colonial Williamsburg had a fine collection of historic vehicles. And the Lexington Carriage Company began horse-drawn tours of the community in 1985. The clip-clop of the horses' hooves, the creak of the wagon, and the jingling of the harnesses fit right into the historic downtown.[102]

## WESTERN RIDING AND THE RETURN OF THE QUARTER HORSE

Quarter Horses began their comeback in Virginia in the early 1960s. With westerners enjoying their versatility, it was only a matter of time before horsemen on the East Coast wanted to see for themselves. Breeders of the time included the North Wales Stud, owned by Dr. Don Wade and Victor Orsinger, near Warrenton, which crossed them with Thoroughbreds; Cloverdale Farms, near Danville, owned by Fred Leggett Jr. and Larry Miller; and Max Tappero, of Forest. Owners and breeders

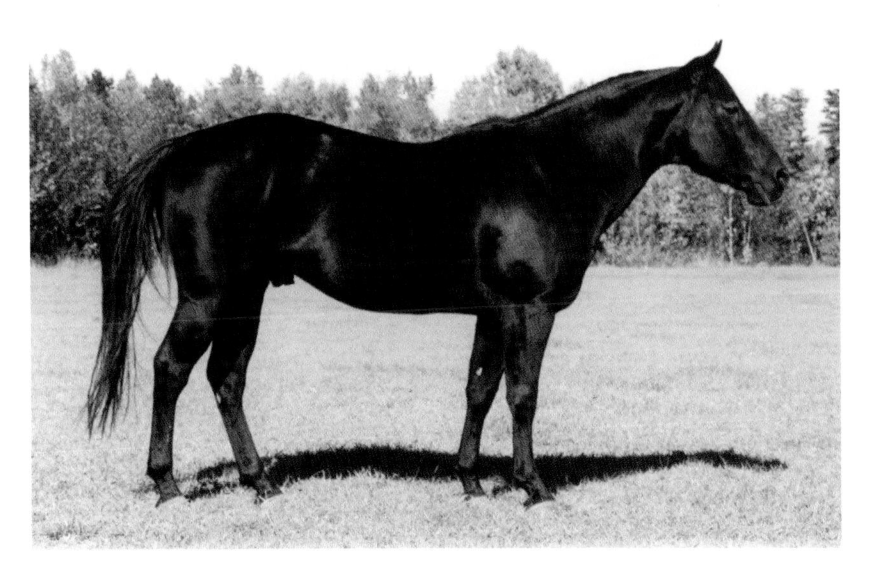

Jack, a black Quarter Horse stallion, exhibited the traditional so-called bulldog appearance of the breed.

of the more than four hundred registered animals formed the Virginia Quarter Horse Association in 1962 and entered their horses in point-to-points, foxhunts, trail riding, and even quarter races at Camptown, West Virginia. "If the real people are suddenly getting high on the quarter horse," said *Commonwealth* magazine in 1963, "the plain people have been leading the way."[103]

The ranks of Quarter Horses and their enthusiasts grew so much that by the early years of the twenty-first century, the breed came second only to Thoroughbreds in the state. Some English riders used them for dressage or sidesaddle. Plenty of Quarter Horses cantered around the hunter show ring, and eventers Phyllis Dawson and Stephen Bradley took appendix Quarter Horses (meaning part Thoroughbred) to high levels in the sport. Foxhunter Joan Batterton, of Berryville, said her Quarter Horse "was just about the best foxhunter I ever had. The only thing he didn't like was cattle."[104]

Shows just for Quarter Horses took place at the Virginia Horse Cen-

A ringful of Paints warming up for a western class at a Lexington horse show.

The sport of pole bending requires horse and rider to zig-zag through a line of uprights at a fast speed.

ter and other locales. In 2001, more than 3,500 competitors attended the East Coast Championship for Quarter Horses at the horse center, with classes for hunters, trail horses, and jumpers as well as at halter, with both western and English styles of riding on display. Competitors in western events favored Quarter Horses for their natural abilities in cutting, team roping, team penning, trail riding, and barrel racing. Team roper Fareed Miran, of northern Virginia, rode them "because Thoroughbreds can't take too much of the stopping and spinning that team roping requires." Trainer Connie Christopher, of Criswood Farm, Manassas, agreed. "I focus on Quarter Horses because to me they are the all-around horse," she said in 2003. She worked with many different breeds but had come to favor Quarter Horses because "they can do everything."[105]

Western horse sports made strong inroads into a state long in love with English pursuits like foxhunting and show jumping. In the late 1980s, some Virginia cowboys used horses to herd sheep and cattle in Tazewell County (although some of them switched to all-terrain vehicles). Western riding hooked some Virginians with its romantic images of cowboys, cattle, and riding the range. Ronald V. Marshall, a black barber from Stafford, began fantasizing as a child about life in the western saddle when his grandmother gave him a toy horse. He bought a real

In barrel racing, the contestants gallop around a clover-leaf pattern of barrels.

live horse when he was a teenager and competed in team penning and calf roping, owned Quarter Horses and Appaloosas, and served on the Virginia Equine Center Foundation board. In 2004, officials at the Virginia Horse Center named the gatehouse for him.[106]

The influx of Quarter Horses and Appaloosas, another western breed, came mostly in western pursuits like team roping. As of 2004, northern Virginia, traditionally a stronghold of English horse sports, also housed team ropers like Mark Price, who hoped to buy a horse in Virginia instead of going all the way to Texas. One of its most avid practitioners was Fareed Miran, born in Afghanistan, who came to Virginia in 1977. Why western riding instead of English? "I guess every little boy wants to be a cowboy," he said. Team penning, where three riders drive three calves (cutting them out of a herd of thirty) into a pen in ninety seconds or less, was popular at the state fair with competitors and spectators alike. Most of the riders used Quarter Horses.[107]

The Virginia High School Rodeo Association began in 1995 to accommodate the interests of younger cowhands, with an offshoot called the Virginia Junior Rodeo Association. In 2002, high school students Kurt Kight and Russ Hutchison, of the Richmond area, competed in the National High School Rodeo Finals at calf roping and team roping.[108]

Barrel racing, where horse and rider speed around a course of three barrels, drew competitors like Warren Morgan, of Madison County. He often rode his championship horse Mr. Frosty Smith, a Quarter Horse, and in 2003 won a world championship. Jessica Green belonged to the younger generation of barrel racers. In 2002, the sixteen-year-old from Powhatan competed nationally and around the state, winning five thousand dollars. "I don't compete for money," she said, "I do this for fun." In 2002, barrel racers in Fauquier County formed a club so they'd have some competition.[109]

A number of Virginians competed in cutting, where the horse maneuvers a cow or steer away from the herd. Tracy Barton, of Union Hall, one of the leading trainers on the East Coast, found Quarter Horses made the best cutting horses, along with Paints and Appaloosas. He thought Virginia was ideal for his pursuits. "The climate here is great, I like the four seasons," he said. "In addition, there's enough land, plenty of cattle, and a variety of competitions all within a four-hour drive." The National Cutting Horse Association had two chapters in Virginia, based in Abingdon and in Herndon, and Frying Pan Park in Herndon and the Virginia Horse Center hosted cutting competitions.[110]

One other sure sign that western horse sports had caught on in Virginia: the 2004 debut of a store at the Virginia Horse Center featuring products from Wrangler, a leading retailer of western-style clothing.[111]

Cutting competition at the State Fair of Virginia.

## HORSES AND HISTORY

Colonial Williamsburg, dedicated to re-creating an eighteenth-century town, reenacted horse races and even an auction of coach horses as part of its exploration and presentation of history. The organization used Percherons, Tennessee Walkers, Polish warmbloods, draft crosses, Hackneys, Standardbreds, and Gelderlands (Dutch Warmbloods) to pull coaches and plows and carry riders dressed in their colonial best. When the organization was pondering what other horses could portray eighteenth-century breeds, it found little information about ordinary workhorses of the era. So it decided to add rare existing breeds: the American Cream horse, which dates from the early twentieth century, and the Canadian horse, a breed the colonists did know. (It rejected Thoroughbreds, figuring that only a few colonists owned them and that they were temperamentally unsuited to working with crowds.) The amber-eyed American Cream hails from Iowa, standing 15 to 16.3 hands and weighing at least 1,500 pounds. By the 1970s, fewer than four hundred Canadian horses existed, so Colonial Williamsburg chose them in order to preserve them as much as for their historical accuracy and good temperaments. Of medium size, they are usually black, dark brown, bay, and chestnut. Richard Nicoll, director of the organization's coach and live-

A Colonial Williamsburg street scene, 1948.

Horses on and off the job at Colonial Williamsburg. *Left,* an American Cream horse; *bottom,* Canadian horses. Both are historic breeds and somewhat rare, so Colonial Williamsburg is helping to preserve them.

stock program, received the American Livestock Breeds Conservancy's award for his work with the rare animals.[112]

Other institutions around the state used horses and promoted their history as well. Mount Vernon, the home of George Washington, used different breeds of horses to demonstrate wheat threshing in Washington's self-designed treading barn, as well as mules, reflecting Washington's preference for them as draft animals. Busch Gardens, in Williamsburg, showed off the Budweiser Clydesdales, and the Frontier Culture Museum in Staunton had Percherons plowing its fields.

The National Sporting Library, in Middleburg, began in 1954. It contained a treasury of books on all kinds of sports, such as shooting and falconry, but was best known for its extensive collection of books related to horses—breeds, disciplines, people, fiction—just about any aspect of the subject. It also housed rare books dating from the sixteenth century. Horsemen like George Ohrstrom Sr. and George Ohrstrom Jr., Paul Mellon, Alexander Mackay-Smith, and Peter Winants promoted and strengthened it over the years. The library's first home was the basement of a handsome brick house, built in 1804, with the *Chronicle of the Horse* occupying the upper floor. In the late 1990s, both library and magazine received modern, spacious new homes next door.[113]

The Museum of Hounds and Hunting in Morven Park was a storehouse of information on two subjects dear to the hearts of many Virginians. Housed on the former estate of Governor Westmoreland Davis, a horseman who lived there from 1903 to 1942, the museum displayed hunting artwork and paraphernalia from around the world and had a library of videos, music, and books.[114]

## MILITARY

After World War II, the army no longer used horses to fight battles and carry soldiers. One special unit, however, continued to perform a solemn ceremonial function. The Caisson Platoon of the Third U.S. Infantry Regiment at Fort Myer, Arlington, carried members of the military to their final resting places at Arlington National Cemetery. The Old Guard, as it was called, supplied one caisson pulled by six black horses, another pulled by a white team; a rider accompanied them on a seventh horse.

The caissons date from World War I. The soldiers and horses worked eighty or one hundred hours a week, depending on the funeral schedule. The regiment preferred black and gray horses weighing 1,200 to 1,500 pounds, draft (especially Percheron) crosses with Morgans, Thoroughbreds, or Quarter Horses, which it bought from private parties. In 1995, it received a transfer of Lipizzan mares from the U.S. Marines. Like police horses, the caisson horses had to be calm, well-mannered, and broken to saddle as well as to harness. They underwent training at Fort Belvoir, near Mount Vernon. The caparison horse—the riderless animal that follows the casket—was used only for commissioned officers, colonel

Black Jack, famed caparison horse of the Caisson Platoon of the Third U.S. Infantry Regiment, stationed at Fort Myer, Virginia. He did his duty at Arlington National Cemetery and at the funeral of President John F. Kennedy.

or above, of the army or the marines. The caparison horse named Black Jack, a Morgan–Quarter Horse cross, gained fame from his appearance in President John F. Kennedy's funeral procession in 1963. In 2006, the caisson horses added a new duty to their job description: therapist. Soldiers who lost legs in Iraq worked on balance, mobility, and physical confidence while riding these horses.[115]

## MOUNTED LAW ENFORCEMENT

One police officer on a horse is ten feet tall, said police departments all over Virginia. The corollary to that statement is that one officer on a horse equals ten officers on foot. No matter how it's measured, the existence of mounted officers added a commanding element to police work as well as an appealing public-relations side.

The Richmond Mounted Squad was a good microcosm of squads across the state. In the 1860s, the city had mounted protection called outriders. Around 1896 a squad officially formed, providing a useful service until cars overtook horses in that area of life as in many others. It re-formed during World War II, when gas rationing took cars

Police horses in Richmond have worked with two- and four-legged partners. *Right:* Prince the police horse seems a little dubious about his canine counterpart, Fritz. The pair appeared at the Richmond Policeman Fireman Show in 1969. *Bottom:* Richmond's finest at the Lee Monument, 2005.

Civil War reenactors depict the cavalrymen of North and South at events across Virginia.

off the street. The squad has gone on and off active duty over the years, sometimes chasing criminals and making arrests, sometimes only writing parking tickets, as in the 1970s and 1980s. In the 1990s and on into the next century, however, the squad showed its effectiveness at crowd control, and both the police department and the community realized its value.

The officers, many of whom had no prior experience with horses before joining the squad, worked hard on their equitation and on their relationship with their mounts. Several of the animals were retired Standardbreds; eventually all of the horses underwent round-pen work and desensitization to such city features as loud cars, sewer grates, white lines on pavement, trashcans, buses, and recalcitrant wrongdoers. The officers, with the help of a volunteer group called Friends of the Richmond Mounted Squad, trained and competed at national events. They still wrote speeding tickets—drivers just didn't expect to see a mounted officer at the roadside—but they also could break up an unruly crowd at the state fair without injury to anyone and surround a stolen car in a flash. Perhaps most satisfying were their partnerships with their horses, which can be a bond "as strong as I've ever had with a human," said Sergeant Eric Bardon, leader of the Richmond squad.[116]

Cities like Charlottesville, Roanoke, Virginia Beach, Portsmouth, and Fredericksburg also knew the worth of mounted police, as did Henrico County. In 2002, the Fredericksburg Police Department sponsored the national Police Equestrian Competition. The Roanoke officers testified to an additional benefit. People like horses, so "droves of people come out of the house and just talk to us," said Officer Jason Holt, who rode a Friesian named Robbie. "Next thing you know, they're telling us about a problem house or something going on in the neighborhood." Most mounted units, like Richmond's and Virginia Beach's, relied heavily on volunteers and donations to maintain their missions. The National Park Service also used mounted rangers to patrol their properties, such as Manassas National Battlefield Park. The Cedar Creek Mounted Guard, an all-volunteer group, performed security and crowd control at Civil War reenactments (populated by people and horses portraying cavalry and artillery) and other events.[117]

## YOUTH ORGANIZATIONS

The Pony Club arrived in the United States in 1954 from Britain. Alexander Mackay-Smith, with his usual perspicacity, served as one of the founders. Horsemen in England had formed it after World War I. Virginians signed up right away, with the Deep Run, Blue Ridge, and Rappahannock Hunts starting clubs in 1954. Eve Prime Fout organized

Pony Club events bring kids and grown-ups together.

4-H competitors, both human and horse, at the Virginia Horse Center.

the Middleburg–Orange County Pony Club a few years later. The organization promotes all branches of English riding for children and teenagers, emphasizing knowledge, safety, handling, first aid, and all-around horsemanship. Members progress through various levels and tests until they reach age twenty-one. The organizations also encourage their clubbers to volunteer with equine-related concerns. Adult volunteers guide the individual clubs. The training is so thorough that many top adult riders and Olympians have emerged from the ranks of Virginia Pony Clubs, including eventers Stephen Bradley, Phyllis Dawson, and Nina Fout. Its pledge reads, in part: "I stand for the best in sportsmanship as well as in horsemanship."[118]

The 4-H organization also provides training in equestrian fields for children and teenagers. 4-H emerged around 1900 as a midwestern agricultural program, with corn clubs for boys and tomato-canning clubs for girls. It arrived in Virginia in 1908 and took the name 4-H (Head, Heart, Hands, Health) in 1920. It is the youth-development education program of the Virginia Cooperative Extension, run by Virginia Tech and Virginia State, both land-grant universities, along with the U.S. Department of Agriculture and local groups. Members work with horses (as well as other livestock), learning horse care and equitation and competing in all disciplines and with all breeds at shows, including the Virginia State 4-H Championship Horse and Pony Show. One of its most popular equine programs is horse judging. Teams learn minute details of conformation, anatomy, gaits, breeds, and performance before they compete by judging classes alongside official, experienced judges. Afterward, they defend their placings to the real judges, no notes allowed. The program has many sponsors in the Virginia horse community, and the teams of the early twenty-first century did well in national competition.[119]

Like 4-H, the Future Farmers of America (FFA) encourage rural youth in agricultural pursuits. The Future Farmers of Virginia came along in 1928, taking only boys until 1969. By the 1930s, the state had several chapters, and Alexandria hosted the national headquarters from 1959 to 1998. The umbrella organization, now known as the National FFA, sponsors competition in judging horses, another aspect shared with 4-H.[120]

## EDUCATION

Schools around the horse-loving state offered classes in riding and horse science. Hollins University, for one, often won at the national level with its hunter riders. Students rode the thirty school horses and learned at on-campus clinics, conducted horse shows, competed in the Old Domin-

The horse is Susan Flagg and the equestrian is Nancy Mosher, at Mary Washington College in 1951.

ion Athletic Conference (ODAC), joined a riding club, and boarded their horses on campus. In 2005, Hollins received the distinction of "hottest riding school" from a college guide.[121]

Randolph-Macon Woman's College (now Randolph College) also did well in ODAC and IHSA (Intercollegiate Horse Show Association) competition with its hunt-seat riders. Sweet Briar College offered an equine studies certificate as well as training for riders of hunters and jumpers, with dozens of courses about trail riding, dressage, foxhunting, working with young horses, and teaching techniques. Graduates of Sweet Briar and other schools became working students at training barns, wrote about horses for magazines, went on to veterinary school, and pursued other equine-related professions. Virginia Intermont College's curriculum included degrees in equine studies and in pre-veterinary medicine. Its graduates worked for trainers and for breed organizations.[122]

Virginia Tech offered a well-regarded course in equine science, with thorough training in the business of horses, behavior, merchandising, breeding, and related subjects. The university stood stallions and kept broodmares, selling off the resultant foals after the students trained them, an important part of the course. Students, who also worked at internships in various equine-related businesses, rounded off their education by caring for an expectant mare and her foal. As of 2004, Virginia Tech owned three stallions and thirty broodmares, mostly warmbloods (the school is known for its sport horses), with some Arabians, Quarter Horses, and Thoroughbreds. The students worked at the seventy-acre Smithfield Horse Center, in Blacksburg, and the 1,800-acre Kentland Farm nearby. The annual Hokie Harvest sale showcased the students' work by auctioning off the well-trained horses to help fund the program. The university also offered classes in hunt-seat equitation, with the chance to compete on the IHSA circuit with the Tech riding team. An equestrian club coordinated with the other programs and helped youth groups such as 4-H and Pony Club. The horse-judging team learned to evaluate halter and performance horses.[123]

Other Virginia schools with riding or equine programs of one kind or another included Averett University, Bridgewater College, Christopher Newport University, James Madison University, Longwood College, Lord Fairfax Community College, Lynchburg College, Radford University, University of Mary Washington (formerly Mary Washington College), University of Richmond, University of Virginia, Washington and Lee University, and the College of William and Mary. Averett, Vir-

## HISTORICAL VETERINARY CARE

Over the centuries, veterinary practices have usually helped but sometimes hindered equine well-being. In the eighteenth and early nineteenth centuries, for example, fashionable horsemen thought the proper look for horses was an arched tail—best achieved by nicking the muscle. For another stylish look—a short, fly-whisk tail—horsemen docked, or cut off, most of the tail, which the animal uses to rid itself of bothersome biting flies. Some people thought a short tail actually strengthened the animal's back by requiring "less nutriment from the juices of the body." Richard Lawrence, a British expert writing in 1816, thought all it did was leave the horse defenseless against insects. The front end of the horse came in for attention too. When fashion favored small, pert ears, they were produced by foxing—snipping them down to size.

Even into the late nineteenth and early twentieth centuries, some Virginians continued to dock their horses' tails.

Horses sometimes contracted tetanus (lockjaw) after having their tails docked. In the nineteenth century, tetanus was inevitably fatal, as it was to Robert E. Lee's Traveller in 1871. Colic, an intestinal ailment that could kill a horse by shutting down its digestive system, might ease with applications of beef broth, concoctions of gin and pepper, or asafoetida and opium, along with belly rubs, bloodletting, or a dose of Epsom salts. Ginger, brandy, a "physic ball" of turpentine and linseed oil or of turpentine, eggs, and milk also helped. Calomel, anise, treacle, and aloe and ginger rid an animal of internal parasites. Poultices of bran or of sal ammonia and vinegar reduced swelling and lameness of the legs. Wool or tow wrapped around a horse's throat helped burst the abscesses that came with an ailment called strangles. As late as the 1920s, horsemen still kept most of the old remedies on hand, along with cleansers such as iodine and carbolic acid.

When a suffering horse proved beyond help, whether from a broken leg (very difficult to treat in a large, active animal like a horse), a terminal disease, or a battlefield wound, humans could give merciful relief. Some of the usual methods included a bullet to the head; a blow from a humane killer, which shot a retractable bolt into the brain; or inhaled chloroform. (William Carter in the *Richmond Times,* April 6, 1902, notes that a daughter of the racehorse Planet was chloroformed. So was Lucy Long, another horse of Robert E. Lee's.) Today an injected overdose of anesthetic stops the animal's heart for a swift and peaceful end, such as Secretariat's in 1989.

*Sources:* Mason, *Gentleman's New Pocket Farrier,* 52–69, 70–72; Lawrence, *Complete Farrier,* 251–52, 89–92, 46–47, 74–75, 89–92, 109, 181; Brooke, *Way of a Man with a Horse,* 103, 122; Hayes, *Veterinary Notes for Horse Owners,* 521–22.

ginia Intermont, and Virginia Tech all belonged to the Intercollegiate Dressage Association.[124]

As for secondary schools, Chatham Hall prep school offered hunt-seat equitation, foxhunting, and even classes in veterinary science. The Virginia Episcopal School, Lynchburg, had a riding program, and Middleburg's Foxcroft School riding team belonged to the Tri-State Equitation League, heard lectures from prominent horsemen, and traveled to Europe.[125]

IHSA began in 1967 and eventually comprised more than three hundred schools that sent equestrians to compete at varsity levels or as club teams. It welcomed everyone from the greenest student to the show-ring champion. Equitation usually being at the club level, students paid their own way. That may change, however. In 1999, the National Collegiate Athletic Association (NCAA) called equestrian an "emerging sport" that may eventually become official. It required students to refuse payment for teaching or training and to keep up their grades. At the NCAA level, the school paid the riding team's expenses. In 1999, the Virginia horseman Paul Cronin, the riding instructor at Sweet Briar for thirty years, joined the NCAA committee pushing to make equestrian a full-fledged NCAA sport.[126]

It took several years for horses to return to VMI after World War II. In the 1970s, the VMI Greys, a riding team, started up but didn't last long. Horses finally came back in 1999 thanks to the initiative of a few cadets who started the Equestrian Club. Some participants had never ridden, but in best VMI tradition they gave it their all, and in 2001 the Mounted Drill Team and Mounted Color Guard (comprising the same riders and horses) debuted. They rode in parades, appeared at the Virginia Horse Center and horse shows, and demonstrated their abilities at class reunions and other VMI events. They relied on donations of horses and equipment and sometimes hunted with the Rockbridge Hunt. "It's a great feeling to know that an animal as big as a horse will trust you and obey your commands," said Joe Cuthbertson, a member of the class of 2004. Spoken like a true Virginia horseman.[127]

## VIRGINIA VETS

Virginia also educated and housed plenty of veterinarians and other horse-care professionals. Dr. Olive K. Britt, one of the first women large-animal vets in Virginia, treated Secretariat when he was a colt, and worked at Little Hawk Farm. Dr. Tim Ober, of Keswick, worked with the U.S. Equestrian Team and in 2004 served as team vet for the Olympic show-jumping team. The Virginia-Maryland Regional College of Veterinary Medicine was founded in 1978 in partnership with Virginia Tech and the University of Maryland at College Park, both land-grant universities. It has three campuses, two in Virginia: at Virginia Tech in Blacksburg and at the Marion duPont Scott Equine Medical Center in Leesburg.[128]

In northern Virginia, Virginia Tech's Middleburg Agricultural Research and Extension (MARE) Center performed important work. Equine Prosthetics in Charlottesville provided artificial limbs for horses and hosted an Adventure Camp for children who had undergone amputations. The Northern Virginia Animal Swim Center opened in Middleburg in 2001 to provide therapy for injured horses. Alternative forms of health care have nudged close to the mainstream in the twenty-first century, with vets and other caregivers offering massage, acupuncture, chiropractic care, holistic methods, and homeopathy to equines.

## THERAPY FOR HUMANS AND HORSES

Virginia horsemen have always known that the outside of a horse is good for the inside of a human. Therapeutic riding proved that point every day as it helped people of all ages with varying abilities. Riders may be blind, paraplegics or quadriplegics, deaf, or brain injured, may have cerebral palsy, muscular dystrophy, or multiple sclerosis, may be recovering from strokes or have mental disabilities such as autism. Dozens of therapeutic operations all over the state provided these Virginians the physical benefits of riding—stretching, flexing, moving. The rhythmic motion of the horse mimics that of the human walk, helping with balance, control, and strength. And there are the mental bonuses—focus, discipline, being outdoors, enjoying the company of the volunteers and teachers, feeling the soothing movements of a horse, controlling the large animal, participating in a sport, competing, communicating.[129]

Disabled riders are essentially just like riders anywhere. After warming up, they use verbal commands in case their bodies can't do the job. Volunteers help out by walking on either side of the horse and leading it, if necessary. The entire process calls for a calm, stable horse, one that can deal with people all around him and up close, and an often unsteady rider up top.

Kirk Bumstead, of Natural Bridge, rode for several years at Hoofbeats Therapeutic Riding Center. He competed many times and won several prizes, including a gold medal in dressage at the 2001 Virginia Special Olympics, often in partnership with a huge, rock-solid, Percheron–Quarter Horse named Caboose. In addition to riding at the center, Bumstead volunteered there and sat on the board. Most organizations, in fact, rely heavily on volunteers and on donations of time, money, horses, and equipment. The umbrella organization for programs in Virginia and elsewhere is the North American Riding for the Handicapped Association (NARHA), which started in 1969 with Alexander Mackay-Smith as a founder. The Therapeutic Riding Association of Virginia (TRAV) hosts an annual horse show at the Virginia Horse Center.[130]

Hippotherapy, a related field, is practiced by physical and occupational therapists, speech pathologists, and psychiatrists. Equine Facilitated Therapy used the human-horse interaction as a springboard for issues dealing with self-image, emotions, and assertiveness. Miniature horses serve as guide animals for people with visual impairments. At-risk youths also benefit from horses, as Laura Watt Casati, a jumper trainer/rider in Albemarle County, found in 1993 with her I Can We Can program for children and teens. Kenny Harlow, a Virginia horse trainer in Cumberland, put troubled teenagers together with horses to teach them independence and responsibility. Stonelea Farm in Aldie hosted an organization called Life Horse that gave children with chronic and terminal illnesses a chance to be with horses. And in 2007, a partnership between the national Thoroughbred Retirement Foundation and the James River Work Center, in Goochland County, produced a program called Greener Pastures. It provided instruction in horse management to adult inmates. The men gained job skills; the former racehorses, a second chance.[131]

Horses helped humans in a novel way at Louis Wood's Mountainview Ranch, in Waynesboro. Wood, a horse trainer, partnered with John Lord, a human trainer, in using equines to guide employees into more productive relationships in the workplace. Lord conceived of their workshop, Horse Sense for People, after he observed skilled trainers work with his own horse. "These are not new things in leadership," said Lord in 2001. "They're the same basic principles, but we'll give the horse freedom and the benefit of the doubt in a different way than we do people."[132]

Many Virginians formed rescue organizations to care for abused, blind, chronically ill, starved, and abandoned animals. Two examples in southwestern Virginia: the Roanoke Valley Horse Rescue and the

Horse Rehab Sanctuary in Buchanan. Some groups cared for horses until they died; others adopted them out to suitable homes. For example, the Equine Rescue League in Leesburg, founded in 1990, rescued three grandchildren of Secretariat from slaughter and then adopted them out.[133] Like therapeutic riding programs, they are usually nonprofit groups that need volunteers and donations.

## SOME SPECIAL HORSES

From 1924 to 1957, a horse named Lady Wonder held some Virginians spellbound. She didn't win races, jump fences, or pull plows. Lady Wonder predicted the future.

Clarence and Claudia Fonda of Petersburg owned the intriguing horse, the offspring of a Texas mare and a Virginia stallion reportedly descended from the great racehorse Lexington. Lady's dam died when her filly was just two months old, so Mrs. Fonda raised her. Somewhere

Lady Wonder. Some people thought the Petersburg mare could predict the future, spelling out her thoughts on this device.

along the way, Mrs. Fonda decided the horse could see into the future, so Mr. Fonda built a typewriter-like device that the horse would press with her nose, flipping up letters to spell out her answers. In 1927, Lady Wonder predicted that boxer Gene Tunney would beat Jack Dempsey in an upcoming match, and in 1931 she foretold the election of President Franklin Delano Roosevelt. The Fondas charged visitors one dollar for three questions; gamblers sought her out for assistance in playing the numbers. Katherine Lewis Warren, a reporter for the *Richmond News-Leader*, asked a question and held the word "house" in her mind; Lady Wonder, who appeared to go into a trance, indicated "home" on her machine. Some authorities thought Lady Wonder was the real thing, but others believed that she had so imprinted on Mrs. Fonda that they communicated with each other in a nonverbal, unconscious way. In 1952, the psychic horse even appeared in *Life* magazine. Lady Wonder died in 1957.[134]

In 1953, Frank Moser of Giles County called the press's attention to Bill, his Percheron, who "would make Lady Wonder look silly if it ever came to a showdown," he said. Bill aced several tricks—ringing a bell, sweeping the floor, smoking a pipe, and taking Moser's hat off. Math stumped him, however; he pawed the floor eight times when asked the sum of five plus two. "Bill never was what you would call much of a hand at figures," said his owner. Bill, so far as it is known, never appeared in *Life*.[135]

## MISTY OF CHINCOTEAGUE AND THE CHINCOTEAGUE PONIES

Sometime late in the seventeenth century, a British colonist or two or three—perhaps the Blake family, who were among the first settlers on the island of Chincoteague on the Eastern Shore of Virginia—realized that the next-door barrier island of Assateague made a fine pasture for their horses. It also made a good place to hide livestock from the tax collector. The animals were full-grown horses, not ponies, of twelve to fourteen hands, a common size of the time. As the centuries went by, settlers forgot about the horses or deliberately turned them loose, and Assateague Island became home to herds of wild horses. Though they lived on Assateague and carried no ponies in their family tree, the animals became known as Chincoteague ponies.

They also gained a new origin when a romantic story washed up onto

Pony Penning at Chincoteague, the ponies emerging from their swim.

the island. This new history dubbed them the descendants of Spanish horses that had survived a shipwreck off the coast, swum to safety, and populated Assateague. Although no British colonists had reported the presence of any horses before they brought their own, the story stuck and became part of island lore.[136]

The equines thrived on the local cuisine—grass from the salt marsh and beach, twigs, even seaweed—and they stayed on the small side. When the summers grew unbearably hot and the biting insects especially vicious, the horses plunged into the ocean waves for relief. Every year the human residents of Chincoteague would round up the horses, ferry or swim them across the channel from Assateague to Chincoteague, sell off enough to keep the herds viable, and send the rest back home.

In 1925, the necessary chore became a public fund-raiser, dubbed Pony Penning and held the last week in July. The proceeds support the Chincoteague Volunteer Fire Company, which legally owns the ponies. The Chincoteague herds live on the Virginia side of Assateague Island in the Chincoteague National Wildlife Refuge. A fence keeps the rest of the ponies, owned by the National Park Service, confined to the Maryland

Clarence Beebe, known to generations of Marguerite Henry's readers as Grandpa Beebe, roping an animal at Pony Penning.

part of Assateague. At some point, someone introduced actual ponies, perhaps Shetland and Welsh, definitely some with pinto coloring, and they bred with the descendants of the English horses.[137]

The ponies cantered easily along, unknown to a wider audience, until the summer of 1945. One of the guests at a dinner party in Evanston, Illinois, had just attended Pony Penning and entertained his companions with stories about the event—how local horsemen galloped through marshes and forests to round up the ponies on Assateague Island, how the stallions and mares and foals swam across the channel to Chincoteague, how they charged down the streets to the fairgrounds. Another dinner guest, Mary Alice Jones, was a children's book editor at Rand McNally, and the next day she relayed the stories to one of her authors, Marguerite Henry.[138]

Born in 1902 in Wisconsin, Henry had published two books, including *Justin Morgan Had a Horse,* a children's novel about the founding sire of the Morgan breed. She lived with her husband in Wayne, Illinois, and was deep in research for another book, *Album of Horses,* when her editor piqued her interest in the Chincoteague ponies. In 1946, accompanied by Wesley Dennis, an artist from Warrenton, Virginia, who had illustrated *Justin Morgan,* she traveled to Chincoteague for that summer's Pony Penning. The pair took rooms at the Victorian home of Molly Rowley Davis on Main Street while they inhaled the salt air, experienced the exciting whirlwind of the event, and befriended a local family: Clarence and Ida Beebe; their granddaughter, Maureen; and Mau-

A scene from Pony Penning: Chincoteague ponies after their swim across the channel from Assateague Island to Chincoteague Island. As a foal, Marguerite Henry's famous Misty made the same journey alongside her mother.

reen's half-brother, Paul. The elder Beebes were raising the young ones along with ponies at a place on Chincoteague called Pony Ranch.[139]

During her visit, Henry spotted the gold and white, newborn filly of a mare named Phantom. It was love at first sight. "My heart bumped up into my throat until I thought I'd choke. It was a moment to laugh and cry and pray over," she remembered thirty years later. She decided to put aside work on *Album of Horses* in favor of a book about the Chincoteague ponies, and struck a deal with Clarence Beebe. She paid him $150 for the filly, which would stay with her dam for a few months and undergo training by Maureen and Paul before the Beebes shipped her to Illinois. The filly's name: Misty.[140]

A few months later, Misty arrived on a train from Virginia, traveling in a handmade wooden crate that looked "as if each slat had been nailed on with love and sadness," wrote Henry. "Right then I resolved to capture all that love and return it twofold in my book." The only problem was that the newcomer seemed to be the wrong pony—fuzzy where Misty had been sleek, one color all over where the filly had sported a white patch that resembled a map of the United States. With the coming

A young Misty, the inspiration for Marguerite Henry's novel *Misty of Chincoteaque,* with her mother.

of spring, however, the pony shed her winter coat and revealed herself as Misty in all her glory. In 1947, Marguerite Henry published her children's novel: *Misty of Chincoteague*.[141]

The best-selling book interlaced fact and fiction in its pages. Henry's story had Maureen and Paul buying a wild pony named Phantom and her baby, Misty, taming them both, and winning a race with Phantom before they let her return to the wild while leaving Misty behind. Henry painted a vivid portrait of Chincoteague's citizens and culture, both human and equine, and continued the story in two more books that featured the Beebe family. *Sea Star: Orphan of Chincoteague* told the tale of an orphaned foal; *Stormy, Misty's Foal* covered the birth of Misty's first foal and the 1962 hurricane that devastated Chincoteague. Wesley Dennis illustrated both. *Misty's Twilight,* about a descendant of Misty belonging to a different family, came along in 1992. Readers may be forgiven for assuming that the Chincoteague-based stories were entirely true, as Henry described the setting and personalities with all the care she had vowed on Misty's arrival at her home.

In reality, Misty grew up not on Chincoteague but at Henry's place in Illinois. While Henry worked on the first book, she introduced the filly to the neighborhood children and trained her to plant her forelegs on a stepstool and courteously shake hooves and hands. (She also had to teach the animal *not* to hop on her hind legs toward alarmed visitors.) To promote *Misty,* Henry shipped the grown pony to horse shows, schools, and even the American Library Association's national conference. As good-natured and tame as Misty was, Henry still had to play a small music box in Misty's ear to keep the horse from kicking when a crowd of admirers drew too close.[142]

Henry eventually sent Misty back to Virginia after a good-bye party in Illinois with local children as guests. Clarence Beebe bred her to a stallion named Wings; Beebe died before the foal was born. By then Maureen had married and Paul had died in a 1957 car accident, so their uncle and aunt, Ralph and Jeannette Beebe, looked after Misty and her first offspring. (Ida Beebe died in 1960.) Twins Carol and Cheryl Costello, of Wessington Springs, South Dakota, won the contest that Henry's publisher sponsored to name the colt. Their choice: Phantom Wings. A filly, Wisp o' Mist, came along later, and Misty's third foal, the filly Stormy, did indeed make her debut in the aftermath of the 1962 hurricane depicted in the book of the same name.[143]

Hollywood turned *Misty* the book into *Misty* the movie, filmed on location in 1960 and featuring many Virginians. Misty and Marguerite Henry attended the Chincoteague premiere. The real Misty even left a lasting souvenir: her hoofprints in the cement sidewalk in front of the Island Roxy Theater. (Henry helped out by etching the horse's name alongside.) After the hurricane, showings of the movie and personal appearances by Misty and Stormy raised funds to help the islanders. In 1972, Breyer Animal Creations unveiled a toy model of the famous horse.[144]

Misty lived the rest of her life on Chincoteague, dying there on October 16, 1972, at the age of twenty-six. Her chronicler and one-time owner, Marguerite Henry, wrote fifty-nine books in all, most of them about horses. She died in 1997 at age ninety-five in Rancho Santa Fe, California. Maureen Beebe, the last of the human family depicted in the books, spoke of her long friendship with the writer: "People and circumstances have never been allowed to change or influence our private relationship." Marguerite Henry's final resting place was the Pacific Ocean, where her ashes were scattered.[145]

Over on the Atlantic coast, Misty's mortal remains met a different fate. The Beebes had her carcass stuffed (along with that of daughter Stormy after her 1993 death), displayed them at the Misty Museum and Pony Farm (no longer in existence), and leased them to the Misty of Chincoteague Foundation.[146]

Not everyone thought this was a good idea. "I was never interested in getting Misty," said Ruth Calvo, the owner of the Misty Museum and Pony Farm, in 1990. "I think they should bury her." In 1996, Ellen West, a member of the foundation, said: "We don't want a mangy carcass hanging around. It's just something that we'd rather not put out in public."[147]

The nonprofit Misty of Chincoteague Foundation, was formed in 1989 after Elizabeth Sutton, of Albemarle County, struck up a correspondence with Henry. Along with Kendy Allen, a Pennsylvanian who owned some of Misty's descendants, she wanted to see some form of permanent tribute to Misty in Chincoteague. The women raised money by having Maureen Beebe autograph books and toy horses, among other things. The organization tried unsuccessfully to purchase the Beebe property but managed to buy a nearby lot and have another one donated. After discovering the site was not zoned for a museum, the group erected a bronze sculpture of a young, frolicking Misty, by Brian Maughan, of Charlottesville, in 1997—the fiftieth anniversary of the publication of *Misty of Chincoteague*.[148]

"Now Chincoteague has a landmark for the thousands of tourists who travel there from all over the world looking for Misty," said Elizabeth Sutton of the sculpture. "We've put Misty back on Chincoteague." To further mark the occasion, Jeannette Beebe displayed the taxidermic versions of Misty and Stormy at her home. As of 2000, tourists could also visit the Chincoteague Pony Centre, owned by the Richard Conklin family. In addition to displaying items related to Henry and Dennis and selling ponies, the center was the burial place of Misty II, the last grandfoal of Misty. "We wanted her to return to the island of her ancestors," said Kendy Allen, her owner.[149]

Today travelers to Chincoteague at any time of the year can buy copies of the Henry books and other Misty memorabilia, peruse Misty's hoofprints in front of the movie theater, and pay their respects to Paul, Ida, and Clarence Beebe at the cemetery. Each July, Pony Penning draws as many as forty-five thousand visitors. Every rental room on the tiny island is filled, including the bed-and-breakfast occupying the home that hosted Marguerite Henry and Wesley Dennis in 1946. Early birds rise well before dawn to claim the best places to see the ponies swim across the channel. The fire department sells enough foals to keep the herd at a manageable 150 horses. In 2001, the average price was $1,963, but one bidder ponied up $10,500.[150]

Pilgrims in search of Misty may visit Pony Penning, statues, museums, even sidewalks. They just may find her truest spirit, however, by watching a herd of Chincoteague ponies grazing in the piney woods on Assateague, an ocean breeze ruffling their manes.

## WORTH A THOUSAND WORDS: ARTISTS

*Misty of Chincoteague* would not be a classic without the illustrations of Wesley Dennis (1903–1966), a handsome, hard-living, polo-playing artist from Warrenton who devoted his prodigious talent to more than 150 books. A Massachusetts native, Dennis grew up on Cape Cod. As a young man, he studied at the New School of Design in Boston while earning a modest living illustrating newspaper ads for department stores such as Jordan Marsh. In the 1930s, Dennis studied horse anatomy in the butcher shops of Paris with a famed painter of animals, Lowes Dalbiac Luard. Back in the United States, he continued his apprenticeship at racetracks and was soon crafting portraits of racehorses for such patrons as the aristocratic Alfred Gwynn Vanderbilt and the entertainer

Wesley Dennis *(left)* at a fox-hunt, with Liz Whitney *(center)* and an unidentified companion. Dennis was a polo enthusiast in addition to being an artist.

Bing Crosby. He rode with the National Guard and kindled his lifetime passion for polo.

He published his first book, *Flip,* about a playful colt, in 1941. Its appealing illustrations led to his fruitful partnership with Henry. As the author said of the artist, Dennis "saw beyond hide and hair and bone. You could see that he understood and loved animals." They produced fifteen books together, including *King of the Wind, Album of Horses,* and *Justin Morgan Had a Horse.* One of his best-known non-Henry books is John Steinbeck's *The Red Pony,* and he lent his paints and pens to another Virginia author, Margaret Cabell Self, for her *Horsemen's Encyclopedia.* Dennis always called himself an illustrator, not an artist, telling the *Fauquier Democrat* in 1960, "I'll draw anything for money": cartoons, calendars, magazine covers, stationery, even Christmas cards for Filene's department store.

Dennis moved to Warrenton in 1945. He called his farm Oakwood and kept company with horses as well as birds (including a goose named Asthma and an emu named Oikwood), dogs, cats, even a chimpanzee. To maintain a running correspondence with children, his biggest fans, he printed up "Denny Cards" that featured his artwork on the front and a message on the back. Twice married and twice a father, he died at sixty-three. Long afterward, his friend and collaborator Marguerite Henry kept up with his family, writing a thank-you note in 1993 to his son Morgan Dennis and family for a gift of flowers, "with three green leaves framing Lily of the Valley white bells. Wesley Dennis would somehow have made the bells move in a slight breeze." As long as his books are in print, Dennis's artistic gifts will move readers with their beauty.[151]

Jean Bowman (1917–1994) also recorded the Virginia horse world with paint and brush. At age nine, she began to learn her profession from an English artist who was painting her family's dogs and horses. She supplemented the curriculum of art schools in New York City with do-it-herself tutorials in equine anatomy and in the work of George Stubbs, the famed British artist of the eighteenth century. In the 1940s, she began showing at New York and London galleries, moved to northern Virginia, and accepted her first commission for a portrait of a horse, from the Mellon family. Commissions later arrived from such horsemen as Queen Elizabeth II and Robert J. Kleberg, who raised Quarter Horses on the famous King Ranch in Texas. Bowman capped the decade with her 1949 marriage to Alexander Mackay-Smith. They divorced in 1965 but remained friends and collaborators. (See her portrait of him on p. 112.)

Her talents touched many arenas. From 1946 to 1998, for example, Bowman's art appeared on sixty-eight covers for the *Chronicle of the Horse*. She also contributed to other magazines such as *Blood Horse* and *Spur*, and to *The Poster Book of Horses: Paintings of American Equestrian Sport by American Artists and Designers* (1978), which Mackay-Smith edited. In 1980, she, Eve Prime Fout, and other artists turned a suggestion from Mackay-Smith and other boosters into the American Academy of Equine Art (AAEA), modeling it on the British Royal Academy. She helped other artists with advice and encouragement. After her death in 1994, her talents continued to benefit the Virginia equine community through the AAEA's Jean Bowman Trust for Equine Artists. And her detailed portraits of horses—including one of Secretariat—grace many a Virginia home.[152]

Like Bowman, her colleague Eve Prime Fout (1929–2007) shared her energy and talents with the Virginia horse world. Born in New York, Fout grew up in Virginia, riding her horse across the countryside to visit friends and hunting with the Orange County Hunt. As a young woman, she studied at the Three Arts Club in New York and with the famed equestrian artists Paul Brown, Richard Stone Reeves, and Franklin B. Voss. She expressed her artistic sense through oil paintings of wildlife, hounds, and horses and through bronze sculptures. "Most people would rather have their horse or dog painted than their wife," she told the *Chronicle of the Horse* in 2005. Her work can be seen on twenty covers of the *Chronicle* and at the National Sporting Library, where a playful bronze fox greets visitors. Fout also brought her love of Virginia and horses to the founding of the Middleburg–Orange County Pony Club and of the MOC Beagles, a children's version of a full-size hunt. In 1964, she became the first female trainer to win the Virginia Gold Cup, with her horse Moon Rock.

As if her double-barreled career in art and horses wasn't enough, Fout led the Piedmont Environmental Council to conserve open space in the horse country of northern Virginia. A significant victory came in 1994, when the council, along with other individuals and organizations, managed to stop the Walt Disney Corporation from building a sprawling history theme park in the area. "She is directly responsible for . . . preserving a place where people can own, ride, breed and train horses and just enjoy being in the outdoors," the then-president of the council told the *Chronicle* in 2005. Artistic vision can take many forms, as the life of Eve Prime Fout shows.[153]

## A THOUSAND MORE WORDS: WRITERS

In the twentieth century, Alexander Mackay-Smith and Margaret Cabell Self made their marks not only as equestrians but also as scholars and writers. Other authors joined them in studying Virginia horses and horsemen.

William J. Carter (1861–1941) bridged the nineteenth and twentieth centuries. In the 1880s, he befriended the then-owner of the New Market racetrack near Petersburg, O. P. Hare, and became a racing enthusiast and expert. In 1892, he began a regular column, "Horses and Horsemen," for the *Richmond Times,* and wrote for that and other publications for fifty years, sometimes under the byline "Broad Rock" (the name of the early Richmond-area racetrack.) His successor, Walter Craigie, reported on horses for the *Richmond Times-Dispatch* from 1939 to 1972.[154]

Fairfax Harrison (1869–1938) earned his place in the history of Virginia horses with his own pursuit of history. His seven books "without reserve, are considered to be the finest examples of equine research ever printed," wrote Mackay-Smith, who knew a little something himself about the field. The books presented the intricate story of the pre-1830s American racehorse. In pursuit of material, Harrison, the master of

Belvoir in The Plains, and two researchers mined every newspaper and manuscript collection they could find. With his "extraordinary mind," as Mackay-Smith wrote, "the most eminent among all turf historians" left a historical record that many a subsequent researcher (including this one) could not do without.[155]

Jane McIlvaine McClary (1921–1990) turned the horse world of northern Virginia upside down with the 1972 publication of her novel, *A Portion for Foxes.* She composed a colorful story of foxhunting, tradition, and local eccentrics, interweaving it with the African American community's struggle for social equality. She was inspired by the part-time residency in the area of President John F. Kennedy and Jacqueline Kennedy (a foxhunter) and by the Kennedy administration's advocacy of civil rights. Some people viewed the book as a roman à clef of northern Virginia society, but she always scoffed at the notion. McClary, who grew up in Middleburg and rode all her life, also was a writer and a former newspaper publisher who pushed for improved opportunity for her black neighbors. McClary's editor for *A Portion for Foxes,* Michael Korda of Simon and Schuster, long remembered his visit to her home. His hostess genially overestimated his riding experience, plunked him on a horse, and took him for a spin on a steeplechase course. "I simply shut my eyes, held on as hard as I could, and hoped for the best," wrote Korda. "I was glad that Jane couldn't turn her head and see me—she would have seen me grasping the horse's mane for dear life, riding toward each fence with my eyes shut, an expression of abject terror on my face."[156]

Another horsewoman, Katharine Gochnauer "Kitty" Slater (ca. 1913–2000) grew up in northern Virginia and spent her life there. She reported on the many facets of the topic for the *Washington Post* and for equestrian publications, capping her career with a 1967 book, *The Hunt Country of America,* packed with newsy stories about the people and horses of the region.[157]

## A NOAH'S ARK OF BREEDS

The Virginia Pony Breeders Association represented the interests of owners of Welsh ponies, Hackneys, Connemaras, Fells, and other breeds. Virginians rode ponies in all horse sports and showed them, including at breeding classes at national shows.

Morgans had Beryl Herzog, of Green Bay Morgans in Beaverdam, as one of their main cheerleaders. Herzog spent summers growing up

A mixture of Virginia breeds in action at horse shows. *Clockwise from left:* A Morgan stallion, Green Bay Singleton; a team competing at the World Percheron Congress; an Arabian in western tack; and an Arabian ready for a costume class.

152

on Beaverdam's Sunnyside Farm, and in 1968 she bought the farm next door. "If you expect to make money on horses, you're going to be disappointed," she said. "You should never raise horses unless you love them. Even then you have to be a little crazy."[158]

Arabians increased in the 1960s and enjoyed enthusiastic popularity in the next two decades. William Peebles, a Sussex County grocer, starting buying them in the late 1950s because he admired their personality, grace, and intelligence. In the 1960s, James Fielding Lewis Jr. raised them on Lewisfield, his Albemarle County farm. John R. Aldred, a veterinarian in Haymarket, started Rollingwood Farm in 1950 and became a leading breeder, founding the Arabian Horse Association. Riders use Arabians for just about every horse sport; they are especially talented at endurance riding.[159]

Aldred also raised Clydesdales and advocated crossing them with Thoroughbreds to make good hunters. All the draft breeds are represented in Virginia, with owners showing them, crossing them for hunters and other uses, and using them to haul logs out of forests, a practice hailed as ecologically sound by owners such as Jason Rutledge of Rock-

Percherons, traditionally draft horses, also make good saddle horses, such as this one at the Virginia Horse Center. Its rider is performing in saddle-seat style, which differs from the forward seat that riders of hunters and jumpers use.

bridge County, who uses Suffolk Punches named Skidder and Wedge and founded a group called Healing Harvest Forest Foundation. In 2002, the Virginia Foundation for the Humanities named C. Marshall Cofer of Bedford County a master draft horseman in recognition of the history of draft horses and their continued use. That same year, the World Percheron Congress at the Virginia Horse Center drew enthusiasts like Sally and Roddy Moore, Percheron breeders from Ferrum. In Botetourt County, Fred Leonard plowed his substantial vegetable garden with the help of his Belgians, Princess and Lightning. "There's only one thing prettier than a horse," he told the *Roanoke Times,* "and that's a pretty woman."[160]

## HORSE SHOWS

Horse shows sprang up just about every weekend all over the state. Every breed and discipline was represented, and every level of rider was too. Some of them, like Upperville and Warrenton, going strong in their original locations, hosted the highest, most competitive levels of hunters and jumpers. Of Upperville, said show manager Tommy Lee Jones, "We try to maintain the old-fashioned flavor of a horse show." The giant, shady trees in the middle of the main ring, with jumps set up between them, help create that atmosphere.

Other shows took place at local spots and featured classes for beginning and amateur riders and horses, like the Brownsburg Horse Show in Rockbridge County. Draft horses still competed at county fairs, in Rockingham and Rockbridge Counties, for example, and at the State Fair of Virginia. Ferrum College's Blue Ridge Folk Festival had log-skidding and mule-jumping contests, and the Roanoke Valley Horse Show in early summer drew Saddlebreds and show jumpers, some of the best anywhere. The Virginia State Horse Show Association kept everything together.[161]

The town of Buena Vista put on a horse show of a different color. Every December, Horse's Christmas featured horses dressed up as Christmas trees, presents, and any other creation their owners imagined. Horse's Christmas began with the equitation program at the now-defunct Southern Seminary College. Alumni of the junior college and local equestrians maintained the tradition over the years.[162]

Tournaments retained their popularity, with such local organizations as the Eastern Shore Jousting Association, Knights of the Round Table, and the Virginia Jousting Association keeping the tradition going. Jousts took place all over Virginia, including the state and national championships. Natural Chimneys Regional Park, in Mount Solon, Virginia, housed the National Jousting Hall of Fame.[163]

## HORSE FACILITIES

The much-needed Virginia Horse Center opened in Lexington in 1988 after $15 million in construction. It has eight barns, arenas (both outdoor and indoor), hundreds of stalls, camping spots, and a year-round schedule of shows and other horse-related events. It created jobs, added to the tax base, and brought visitors to the area. In 1995 alone, visitors spent $22.8 million in Virginia. Doug Fout (steeplechase expert) and Captain Mark Phillips (a British Olympian, the USET chef d'equipe, and a course designer) advised the center on its cross-country course, and David O'Connor designed it. During Hurricane Isabel in September 2003, the VHC and farms in the area housed horses from the eastern part of the state, which was directly in the path of the hurricane and received a great deal of damage. Even the Budweiser Clydesdales from the Busch Gardens amusement park near Williamsburg took refuge. VHC has hosted everything from local schooling shows, to appearances by the well-known trainer Monty Roberts, to international events like the World Percheron Congress. Other facilities around the state include Great Meadow, with course design by Olympic eventer Torrance Watkins; Morven Park, with its eventing schedule; and Commonwealth Park in Culpeper County.[164]

## THE BIBLES

The *Chronicle of the Horse,* a national weekly magazine about hunting, jumping, dressage, eventing, and related topics, began in 1937 as the *Middleburg Chronicle.* It was the brainchild of Stacy Lloyd Jr., a newspaper reporter and publisher, and Gerald Webb, a newspaper editor. At first the men, both foxhunters, covered all kinds of news about the community in addition to horse-related headlines, but after a while equines starred on every page. Webb died in 1947, and Lloyd sold it in 1952 to George Ohrstrom Sr. Alexander Mackay-Smith took over the editor's pen, relinquishing it at his retirement in 1976. During his tenure, in 1961, the magazine took its current name, and circulation increased nearly sixfold. Peter Winants followed the line of succession in 1976. The horseman and photographer held the post of editor and then publisher until 1991, when it was his turn to retire. (In addition to his magazine work, Winants parlayed his appreciation of steeplechasing and foxhunting into books on the subjects.) Most of its readers owned more than one horse and competed in some kind of equestrian sport. *Spur of Virginia*, *Virginia Breeder*, *Eastern Breeder*, and the *Virginia Horse Journal* round out the list of publications past and present.[165]

## NEW CENTURY, NEW ISSUES

In the early twenty-first century, the equine issues concerning Virginians were things like the existence of open space—places to ride and enjoy horses, a challenge in the face of ongoing development of the countryside. As a possible remedy, the Virginia Gold Cup Association and other organizations promoted horse sports to residents of and newcomers to Loudoun and Fauquier Counties, areas that lost thousands of acres to houses and shopping centers in the late twentieth century. "We're trying to . . . extend our appeal and help people understand the importance of the horse economy," explained Diane Jones, an official with the association, to the *Washington Post*. "People in the horse business are hard-working people, and they're not as elitist as people think. This is a

A farmer and his equine partners, Hampton, ca. 1899.

sport." In 2006, developers began touting equestrian centers situated in communities of luxury homes in Loudoun County.[166]

In 2001, the first year of the twenty-first century, 170,000 horses, ponies, and mules lived in Virginia, making it the fifth-largest horse-loving state, behind Texas, California, Missouri, and Tennessee. The equines were worth an astonishing $1.46 billion, and their owners spent $505 million on them. Some 12,800 horses sold for almost $99.4 million, making them the state's seventh-largest agricultural commodity (based on cash receipts). The top two horse-owning counties were Loudoun (15,800 horses) and Fauquier (13,700). Albemarle County, holding onto its long equine history, was next (7,000), then Augusta (5,000) and Bedford (4,600).

The horse so dear to the heart in the eighteenth century, the Thoroughbred, topped the population three hundred years after its introduction. Right behind it came the made-in-Virginia Quarter Horse. A mixed group of light breeds, crossbreds, warmbloods, racing breeds, draft, and mixed breeds

A young Morgan named Green Bay Heartsong romps in its pasture in Beaverdam.

A Virginian of the 1980s delights in her horse.

A ride through the Virginia countryside, sometime between 1910 and 1930.

## NEW VIRGINIA HORSES

A couple of new types—not quite yet breeds—put in an appearance toward the end of the twentieth century. Virginia Single-Footers (also called Virginia Pocket Horses and Virginia Speed Rackers) came from Saddlebreds and Standardbreds but were much smaller, 15.2 hands at the most. The Virginia Highlander derived from the Arabian, the Tennessee Walking Horse, and the Welsh Pony, along with Morgans, Saddlebreds, and Hackneys. As of 2004, the Virginia Highlander Association had fifty registered animals, and the Virginia American Indian Horse Association formed in 2005.

Melvin Poe, famed foxhunter, was one Virginia horseman who raised miniature horses. Peruvian Pasos, Appaloosas, Icelandic horses, Norwegian Fjords, Hanoverians, Andalusians, Lusitanos, and Galiceños all roamed the late-twentieth-century pastures of Virginia. In 1966, a purebred Caspian stallion named Jehan arrived in Virginia from Iran. The rare horse is prized for its small size of ten to twelve hands (it is considered a horse, not a pony), elegant looks, and jumping ability. Jehan showed in Virginia and left half-Thoroughbred offspring. By 2004, a breeder in Botetourt County owned a few Caspians. Even western mustangs have briefly lived in Virginia, as in 2001, when the U.S. Department of the Interior's Bureau of Land Management brought animals from the West to Lexington for adoption. Between 1973 and 2001, 1,600 Virginians adopted the wild descendants of Spanish horses. Other wild horses, from North Carolina's Outer Banks, occasionally crossed into southeastern Virginia.

A miniature horse competes at the Virginia State Horse Show.

*Sources:* www.thegaitedhorse.com/va_single.htm; gaitedhorses.net/BreedArticles/VAHighlanders.html; *Southeast Equine Monthly,* December 2005, 6; McCormick, "Caspian Pony Is a Rare Breed," 24; Hendricks, *International Encyclopedia,* 112–114; *Roanoke Times,* January 22, 2004; *Richmond Times-Dispatch,* December 27, 1997; October 9, 2001; January 6, 2003.

took third place, and then came Arabians and Anglo-Arabs (half-Thoroughbreds). Plenty of ponies followed. Tennessee Walkers overtook their rivals, Saddlebreds, outnumbering them by nearly 3,000 animals. Bringing up the rear (behind Paints, Appaloosas, mules, donkeys, miniature horses, Standardbreds, Morgans, Belgians, Percherons, and Hanoverians) were 600 Paso Finos, a South American breed.

Owners used nearly half of Virginia's horses, 75,700, for pleasure and trail riding. Next came show and competition horses with 29,100. Broodmares slipped in just under that category at 27,300, followed by horses for "other uses" at 20,300, 12,600 racehorses, and 5,000 breeding stallions.[167]

The business of horses in Virginia encompassed artists; saddlers; sellers of clothing, equipment, and feed; builders of stables; and real estate agents. The field had such promotional and educational organizations as the Virginia Equine Educational Foundation, the Virginia Horse Industry Board, and the Virginia Horse Council, as well as associations and clubs for nearly every breed and sport. All manner of consumers, suppliers, and boosters had an avid interest in Virginia's horses.

## FOUR CENTURIES OF HORSES

Since 1609, the horse has gone from being a necessary part of society—vital to warfare, transportation, and agriculture—to being an objet d'art, an athlete, a friend.

What Virginia has, above all, is a four-hundred-year tradition of horses. Other states do have their equine stars. Kentucky, for example, cornered the market on famous Thoroughbreds based on sheer numbers. Nevada has more herds of mustangs. Idaho can claim the Appaloosa, and Texas refined the Quarter Horse. No other state, however, can boast one of the world's greatest racehorses, Secretariat, or the real-life heroine of a beloved children's book, Misty. The stories of Traveller and Little Sorrel give enduring testimony to the bonds possible between humans and horses. When it comes to Olympic riders, it's hard to believe any other state can claim as many as the Old Dominion. Further, Virginia nurtured the Thoroughbred and birthed the Quarter Horse, two of the most popular breeds in the world. Put it all together, and it's clear that the importance of horses in Virginia reaches far beyond the borders of the state.

It begins and ends, however, in the very core of Virginia's rich history.

ACKNOWLEDGMENTS

Thank you above all to my parents, Don and Shirley Campbell. They gave me everything I ever needed to write this book.

Thank you to these friends who read the entire manuscript: Kristen Muench, Brent Tarter, and Elizabeth R. Varon. The book is so much better because of their discerning eyes.

Kristen volunteered to read it neither as a historian nor a horsewoman but as the painter and sculptor that she is, an outside perspective that I found most useful. During the writing of the book, she offered a lifeline of encouragement and a sympathetic ear—and an occasional kick in the pants.

As every Virginia historian knows, your manuscript isn't done until Brent vouches for its Virginianity. I am proud to call him "Cousin Brent."

Liz, a superb historian and writer, not only made the brilliant suggestion to open the book with George Washington, but she also shared her home and her lovely family, Will, Emma, and Ben Hitchcock.

Thank you to these generous experts who reviewed portions of the manuscript: Dale Harter (Civil War), John Maass (Revolutionary War), Pam Stallsmith (Misty and the Chincoteague ponies), Lucia "Cinder" Stanton (Thomas Jefferson), and Mary Thompson (George Washington).

These good people provided advice, cheerleading, encouragement, a willing ear, consolation, clippings, room and board, technical help, and a thousand other kindnesses that kept me going:

Out west, thank you to Karen Boush, Father Tom Buckley, S.J., Bruce Dinges, Gwen Harvey, Harwood Hinton, Carol Juliani, Karla Buchholz Nystrom, Carol Sonnichsen, Jewel Spangler, Pam Stedman, Joe Waskiewicz, and Jeanne Williams, as well as my aunt and uncle, Gini and George Schneider, and my brother, Doug Campbell.

In Virginia, thanks to Holly and Charlie Bailey; Richard Lee Bland; Jessica Carter; Mary and Steve Clark; Don, Margaret, Ann, and Sarah Gunter; Tracy, Dale, and Lauren

Harter; Calley Goode Jackson; Lynn and Rick Leech; Arthur M. "Laurie" Lipscomb III; Stacy, Tommy, and Callie Moore; Eric Owsley; Emily and John Salmon; Jamie Sims and Errol Somay; Rod Smith; Ben and Barbara Varon; and Lucy and Reggie Wallace.

Thank you to my friends and colleagues in Virginia Press Women, especially Cynthia Price, Pam Stallsmith, Deb Thompson, and Gwen Woolf.

Farther south, thank you, Mary McCall and Steve Cash, for so much.

Up north, thanks to Suzanne Lebsock and Adriana Trigiani, Virginians at heart.

And thanks to these former colleagues at the Library of Virginia, who showed extra interest and helped in all kinds of ways: Jay Gaidmore, John Hopewell, Sarah Huggins, John Kneebone, Chris Kolbe, Don Rhinesmith, Gwynne Tayloe, and Elizabeth Weakley.

Thank you to these Virginians I met in the course of research: Mr. and Mrs. Frederick Fisher, owners of the exquisite Westover plantation on the James River, for inviting me to watch the Princess Anne Hunt in that historic and evocative setting; Carol Miller for sharing her firsthand knowledge of the Virginia horse world; Roddy and Sally Moore for introducing me to their beautiful Percherons; and George Cole Scott III and George Cole Scott McCray for their interest in the project. Sue Cecil, Darlene and Dean Jacobson, and Professor Todd Lowry suggested and provided useful research material. Thanks also to the Richmond Mounted Police Squad, especially Eric Bardon and Rob Lehr.

And thank you to these organizations and professionals for research and illustration assistance: Albert and Shirley Small Special Collections Library, University of Virginia, Edward Gaynor; Charles City County Historical Society, Judith Ledbetter; Colonial Williamsburg Foundation, Marianne Martin; Keeneland Library, Phyllis Rogers; Library of Virginia, Dana Angell Puga in Special Collections, and all the archivists and librarians; Monticello, Jeff Looney, Liesel Nowak, and Lucia "Cinder" Stanton; Mount Vernon Ladies' Association, Dawn Bonner; Museum of the Confederacy, Ann Drury Wellford; National Museum of Racing and Hall of Fame, Beth Sheffer and Kate Stewart; National Sporting Library, Lisa Campbell, Brenna Elliott, Karen Halver, Elizabeth Manierre, Turner Reuter, Liz Tobey, and Robert Weber; Old Guard Museum, Fort Myer, Kirk Heflin; State Fair of Virginia, Sue Mullins; Tazewell County Public Library, Sarah Bowen; Valentine Richmond History Center, Megan Glass Hughes and Beth Petty; Virginia Historical Society, Meg M. Eastman, Frances Pollard, Jeffrey Ruggles, and the library staff; Virginia Horse Center, Kristin C. Waters Wise and Deborah A. Work; Virginia Military Institute Archives, Diane B. Jacob and Mary Laura Kludy; Virginia Museum of Fine Arts, Dennis Halloran, Howell Perkins, and Lee Bagby Viverette; Washington and Lee University, Lisa McCown and Vaughan Stanley of Special Collections, and Elizabeth Teaff of Interlibrary Loan, both in Leyburn Library.

Thank you to Washington and Lee University and Provost June Aprille for supporting some publication costs.

Thank you to everyone at the University of Virginia Press, especially Angie Hogan and Ellen Satrom, and to the freelance copy editor, Susan Murray. They were a pleasure to work with and made the book so much better.

And a very grateful thank you to the three reviewers of the manuscript—Peter Winants, Pegram Johnson, and an anonymous reader—for their useful suggestions and comments. Peter Winants was the epitome of a Virginia gentleman and horseman, and I am so grateful for his courtesy and his careful reading of the manuscript. Pegram Johnson, a proud descendant of William Ransom Johnson, offered kindness and thoughtful advice throughout.

# NOTES

## 1607–1783

1. *Bartlett's Familiar Quotations* (1919), at www.Bartleby.com; Jefferson to Walter Jones, January 2, 1814, Thomas Jefferson Papers, Library of Congress, www.memory.loc.gov.

2. Flexner, *Indispensable Man,* 191; Fitzpatrick, *Writings of George Washington,* 2:321; Prussing, *Estate of George Washington,* 419, 426; Mackay-Smith and Fine, *American Foxhunting Stories,* 4–6; Fusonie and Fusonie, *Pioneer Farmer,* 33.

3. Custis, *Recollections and Private Memoirs of Washington,* 132–34.

4. Twohig, *George Washington's Diaries,* 87–88, 118, 307; Harrison, *Belair Stud,* 92; Fitzpatrick, *Writings of George Washington,* 21:386; 7:301–2; Fusonie and Fusonie, *Pioneer Farmer,* 31.

5. Fitzpatrick, *Writings of George Washington,* 7:121; 8:498; 11:117.

6. Ibid., 12:341; 13:393; 17:267–68; 16:292; Twohig, *George Washington's Diaries,* 296.

7. Flexner, *Indispensable Man,* 192, 362; Twohig, *George Washington's Diaries,* 296, 299, 336; Harrison, *Belair Stud,* 60, 91; W. Robertson, *History of Thoroughbred Racing,* 26–27. The Arabian or Barb stallion named Ranger supposedly broke three legs as a young horse but was nursed back to health and lived to sire Magnolio and many other horses (Denhardt, *Quarter Running Horse,* 37–39).

8. Fusonie and Fusonie, *Pioneer Farmer,* 31–33. For Conestoga horses, a breed that died out in the mid-nineteenth century, see Thompson, *A History of Livestock Raising in the United States,* 51–52. Washington did not record how Jolly was dispatched, but he might have been shot in the head or chloroformed, two methods of killing horses in a quick and merciful fashion.

9. Pogue, "Every Thing Trim, Handsome, and Thriving," 161–64.

10. Twohig, *George Washington's Diaries,* 126, 297–98; Mackay-Smith and Fine, *American Foxhunting Stories,* 4–6; Custis, *Recollections and Private Memoirs of Washington,* 38, 385–87. Custis said Washington's last hunt came in 1785 because he was too busy with the farm and visitors (ibid., 389).

11. Prussing, *Estate of George Washington,* 27, 71, 74, 440–45, 449, 451.

12. Custis, *Recollections and Private Memoirs of Washington,* 386–87; Marquis de Chastellux, *Travels in North America,* 1:111; Rasmussen and Tilton, *The Man Behind the Myths,* 113; Thomas Jefferson to Walter Jones, January 2, 1814, in *Thomas Jefferson Papers,* Library of Congress, www.memory.loc.gov.

13. Salmon and Campbell, *Hornbook of Virginia History,* 3–8 passim; McCary, *Indians in Seventeenth-Century Virginia,* 1–10.

14. Haines, *Horses in America,* 11–12; Edwards, *Encyclopedia of the Horse,* 10–13.

15. Fontana, *Entrada,* 22–24; Haines, *Horses in America,* 35–38.

16. Hendricks, *International Encyclopedia,* 28–33, 50–51, 235–36, 389–93; Edwards, *Encyclopedia of the Horse,* 104–5, 214–17.

17. Denhardt, *Quarter Running Horse,* 4–5; Harrison, *Equine F.F.Vs,* 40 n. 19; Harrison, *Belair Stud,* 24.

18. Harrison, *Equine F.F.Vs.,* 35; Noël Hume, *The Virginia Adventure,* 240, 252, 260; Mackay-Smith, *Colonial Quarter Race Horse,* 5; Straube and Luccketti, *1995 Interim Report,* 39, 53 n. 10; Kelso, *Jamestown,* 20, 92. The sources disagree whether there were six mares and one stallion, or one mare and six stallions. It makes more sense to have six mares for breeding purposes. Modern archaeological digs at Jamestown have found butchered horse bones.

19. Harrison, *Equine F.F.Vs.,* 35; Mackay-Smith, *Colonial Quarter Race Horse,* 6–8; Hendricks, *International Encyclopedia,* 99–100; Anderson, *Creatures of Empire,* 111; Fausz, "Samuel Argall," 197–99.

20. Edwards, *Encyclopedia of the Horse,* 168–71, 178–79; Hendricks, *International Encyclopedia,* 184–85; Denhardt, *Quarter Running Horse,* 7; Mackay-Smith, *Colonial Quarter Race Horse,* 26; Berry, *Standardbreds,* 27–31.

21. Anderson, *Creatures of Empire,* 108–10, 118–19, 122; Mackay-Smith, *Colonial Quarter Race Horse,* 8, 13–14, 27; Harrison, *Equine F.F.Vs.,* 38; Mackay-Smith, *Speed and the Thoroughbred,* 29–31.

22. Mackay-Smith, *Colonial Quarter Race Horse,* 9, 12–13, 38.

23. Harrison, *Equine F.F.Vs.,* 36, 40, 41 n. 19; Mackay-Smith, *Colonial Quarter Race Horse,* 266, 275; Denhardt, *Quarter Running Horse,* 4–6, 11; Hendricks, *International Encyclopedia,* 402–3.

24. Harrison, *Equine F.F.Vs.,* 38; Mackay-Smith, *Colonial Quarter Race Horse,* 3, 58. Bullocke's opponent, Matthew Slader, apparently agreed to throw the race so that both men could bet and win. Slader paid for his part in the illicit arrangement by sitting in the stocks for an hour (Denhardt, *Quarter Running Horse,* 47).

25. Mackay-Smith, *Colonial Quarter Race Horse,* 57–58, 88; Breen, "Horses and Gentlemen," 250–51, 254–56; Denhardt, *Quarter Running Horse,* 14, 16, 50; Fischer, *Albion's Seed,* 360–61. Mackay-Smith and Denhardt had what Mackay-Smith called "a friendly agreement to disagree" about the positive influence of Chickasaws on quarter running horses, with Mackay-Smith saying no, Denhardt saying yes (Mackay-Smith, *Colonial Quarter Race Horse,* 273–76).

26. Breen, "Horses and Gentlemen," 251; Mackay-Smith, *Colonial Quarter Race Horse,* 58, 82. William Robertson says there were five quarter paths around Richmond in the late 1600s (*History of Thoroughbred Racing,* 16).

27. Mackay-Smith, *Colonial Quarter Race Horse,* 11.

28. Fields, *"Worthy Partner,"* 63–74, 174. Custis was the first husband of Martha Dandridge, who survived him and later married George Washington. Her sister died a month after receiving the letter.

29. Rountree, *Pocahontas's People,* 103, 134, 150, 168, 175; Anderson, *Creatures of Empire,* 108, 201.

30. Ausband, *Byrd's Line,* 153–54, 173–74.

31. Harrison, *Equine F.F.Vs.,* 161–63; Withington, *Toward a More Perfect Union,* 209–10.

32. Fischer, *Albion's Seed,* 359, 363–64; Harrison, *Equine F.F.Vs.,* 43.

33. Mackay-Smith, *Foxhunting in North America,* 217–19; Mackay-Smith and Fine, *American Foxhunting Stories,* 2–3; Sands, *This Is the Story of the Deep Run Hunt Club,* 46; Fischer, *Albion's Seed,* 362–63; Mackay-Smith, *Blue Ridge Hunt,* 6; Groome, "The Fox and the Hounds," 10.

34. Edwards, *Encyclopedia of the Horse,* 118, 332; Montgomery, *Thoroughbred,* 35.

35. Edwards, *Encyclopedia of the Horse,* 118–19; Hendricks, *International Encyclopedia,* 173; Mackay-Smith, *Colonial Quarter Race Horse,* 19, 22–23; Mackay-Smith, *Speed and the Thoroughbred,* 7–8.

36. Information in this and the preceding two paragraphs is from Edwards, *Encyclopedia of the Horse,* 118–19; Hendricks, *International Encyclopedia,* 173–74; Henry, *King of the Wind;* Mackay-Smith, *Speed and the Thoroughbred,* 7–8; Peters, "Byerley Turk"; Peters, "Godolphin Arabian."

37. Self, *Horses of Today,* 34.

38. Ibid., 35–37; Edwards, *Encyclopedia of the Horse,* 118. Self says the name "English Thoroughbred" first appeared in the *General Stud Book* in 1793; Edwards says 1821; Harrison, *Equine F.F.Vs.,* 44, 48.

39. Harrison, *The Roanoke Stud,* 15, 204–5. The "spoiling of the Egyptians" refers to Exodus 3:21–22: "And I will give this people favour in the sight of the Egyptians: and it shall come to pass, that, when ye go, ye shall not go empty: But every woman shall borrow of her neighbour, and of her that sojourneth in her house, jewels of silver, and jewels of gold, and raiment: and ye shall put them upon your sons, and upon your daughters; and ye shall spoil the Egyptians."

40. Harrison, *Equine F.F.Vs.,* 43; Culver, *Blooded Horses of Colonial Days,* 111, 113; Mackay-Smith, *Colonial Quarter Race Horse,* 71; Isaac, *Transformation of Virginia,* 60.

41. Isaac, *Transformation of Virginia,* 53, 98–99, 100–101, 119.

42. Harrison, *Roanoke Stud,* 24, 65; Harrison, *Equine F.F.Vs.,* 159.

43. Conn, *Arabian Horse in America,* 10–11; Denhardt, *Quarter Running Horse,* 8; Mackay-Smith, *Colonial Quarter Race Horse,* 23, 72. Another factor in the amble's gradual disappearance was the development of "high-stepping, bold-trotting carriage horses" in England (Berry, *Standardbreds,* 30–31).

44. Harrison, *Roanoke Stud,* 66; Culver, *Blooded Horses of Colonial Days,* 112; Harrison, *Equine F.F.Vs.,* 46; Smyth quoted (page from his book reproduced) in Mackay-Smith, *Colonial Quarter Race Horse,* 226.

45. Harrison, *Equine F.F.Vs.,* 52–54; W. Robertson, *History of Thoroughbred Racing,* 16; Mackay-Smith, *Colonial Quarter Race Horse,* 138, 142; Harrison, *Roanoke Stud,* 113–17.

46. Mackay-Smith gives Jolly Roger's birth and death dates as 1743–1769 (*Colonial Quarter Race Horse,* 142). Denhardt says 1741–1772 (*Quarter Running Horse,* 35).

47. Johnson, "John Baylor," 406–7; Wingfield, *A History of Caroline County, Virginia,* 371–74, 419.

48. Harrison, *Roanoke Stud,* 118–19; Johnson, "John Baylor," 407; Harrison, *Equine F.F.Vs.,* 98–102; Wingfield, *History of Caroline County,* 373; Denhardt, *Quarter Running Horse,* 33; W. Robertson, *History of Thoroughbred Racing,* 17; Mackay-Smith, *Colonial Quarter Race Horse,* 147, 149. In *The Roanoke Stud,* Harrison says Fearnought was a grandson of the Godolphin Barb, but in *Equine F.F.Vs.,* he says he was a great-grandson. Later horsemen of Hicksford included Merritt and Co., horse importers: brothers Dr. A. T. B. Merritt, J. Avery Merritt, and William Townes Merritt. The trio imported at least eighteen stallions between 1832 and 1837 (Mackay-Smith, *Race Horses of America,* 61). Fearnought got a state historical marker in 2006, in Emporia (*Virginia Horse Journal* [hereafter cited as *VHJ*], June 2007, 12–13).

49. Parish, *Journal and Letters of Philip Vickers Fithian,* 126–27. Fithian tutored the children of another prominent planter, Robert Carter III, and his wife, Frances Ann Tasker, of Maryland. They lived at Nomini Hall, which burned in the mid-nineteenth century. The Tayloes still own and live at Mount Airy.

50. Eisenberg, "Off to the Races," 8–12; W. Robertson, *History of Thoroughbred Racing,* 17; Mackay-Smith, *Colonial Quarter Race Horse,* 175; Denhardt, *Quarter Running Horse,* 33, 35–36, 68–71; Harrison, *Belair Stud,* 55, 67, 86; Parish, *Journal and Letters of Philip Vickers Fithian,* 32. Harrison, in *Equine F.F.Vs.,* laments the scarcity of records for the imported mares (136).

51. Denhardt, *Quarter Running Horse,* 65; Mackay-Smith, *Colonial Quarter Race Horse,* 160–62, 165, 167; Bracey, *Life by the Roaring Roanoke,* 144–46; Hutcheson, *What Do You Know About Horses?* 6–8, 13, 14–15, 33.

52. Harrison, *Roanoke Stud,* 21; Harrison, *Equine F.F.Vs.,* 77; Mackay-Smith, *Colonial Quarter Race Horse,* 102, 112, 124–26; 133; W. Robertson, *History of Thoroughbred Racing,* 17.

53. Harrison, *Equine F.F.Vs.,* 76; Mackay-Smith, *Colonial Quarter Race Horse,* 102–3, 106–7.

54. Harrison, *Roanoke Stud,* 107; *Equine F.F.Vs.,* 45, 77; Mackay-Smith, *Colonial Quarter Race Horse,* 105, 109, 112, 122, 124. When Janus mated with Thoroughbred mares, however, the foals' sprinting abilities usually receded (Mackay-Smith, *Colonial Quarter Race Horse,* 122).

55. Harrison, *Roanoke Stud,* 21; Harrison, *Equine F.F.Vs.,* 78–79; Mackay-Smith, *Colonial Quarter Race Horse,* 107–9; Denhardt, *Quarter Running Horse,* 21. Denhardt writes that colonial breeders bred Janus's daughters and granddaughters to him in order to solidify the desired qualities (21).

56. Denhardt, *Quarter Running Horse,* 31, 89–91.

57. Withington, *Toward a More Perfect Union,* 196–200, 215; Isaac, *The Transformation of Virginia,* 247; Harrison, *Equine F.F.Vs.,* 45.

58. Herr and Wallace, *The Story of the U.S. Cavalry,* 3–4, 17–18.

59. Lee, *Memoirs of the War,* 16, 91; Nagel, *The Lees of Virginia,* 161–63. The Revolutionary War was the highlight of Henry Lee's career. He eventually managed to squander his money, family, and reputation, dying alone in 1818 on Cumberland Island, Georgia, far from his wife and children (Nagel, *The Lees of Virginia,* 182–85).

60. Harrison, *Equine F.F.Vs.*, 45–46; Wingfield, *History of Caroline County*, 374; Nelson, "George Baylor," 402.

61. Tyler-McGraw, *At the Falls*, 62–63; Salmon and Campbell, *Hornbook of Virginia History*, 31–33.

62. Maass, "To Disturb the Assembly," 149–52.

63. Ibid., 153–57; Betts, *Jefferson's Farm Book*, 505. Most sources, all secondary, call Jouett's horse a mare named Sallie; the International Museum of the Horse calls the horse Prince Charlie (www.imh.org).

64. Harrison, *Equine F.F.Vs.*, 102, 104; W. Robertson, *History of Thoroughbred Racing*, 17; Denhardt, *Quarter Running Horse*, 63–64; Bracey, *Life by the Roaring Roanoke*, 149–50; Mackay-Smith, *Colonial Quarter Race Horse*, 161.

65. Harrison, *Equine F.F.Vs.*, 165–66; Bracey, *Life by the Roaring Roanoke*, 145.

66. Bear, *Jefferson at Monticello*, 60.

67. Betts, *Jefferson's Farm Book*, 90, 92, 94, 95, 99–101, 103, 108.

68. Randall, *Life of Thomas Jefferson*, 1:6; Bear, *Jefferson at Monticello*, 20.

69. Jefferson to Thomas Jefferson Randolph, November 24, 1808, in Betts and Bear, *Family Letters of Thomas Jefferson*, 363; Brown, *William Plumer's Memorandum*, 194.

70. Bear, *Jefferson at Monticello*, 20; Betts, *Jefferson's Farm Book*, 88–89, 97–98, 103, 105, 109, 110; Bear and Stanton, *Jefferson's Memorandum Books*, 2:1052, 1251.

71. Randall, *Life of Thomas Jefferson*, 1:68; Bear, *Jefferson at Monticello*, 5.

72. "Names of Thomas Jefferson's Horses."

73. Randall, *Life of Thomas Jefferson*, 1:68, 70; Bear, *Jefferson at Monticello*, 74.

74. Bear, *Jefferson at Monticello*, 11, 62; Betts, *Jefferson's Farm Book*, 92, 108; Randall, *Life of Thomas Jefferson*, 1:68–69.

75. Jefferson to Thomas Mann Randolph, August 27, 1786, in *The Papers of Thomas Jefferson*, 10:308; Jefferson to John Barnes, November 11, 1818, Massachusetts Historical Society, copy in "Horses" typescript, Cinder Stanton's Horses folder, Monticello; Betts, *Jefferson's Farm Book*, 87; Jefferson, *Jefferson Cyclopedia*, 411; "Horses: Summary," "Horses" file, Monticello.

76. Jefferson to Thomas Mann Randolph, 21 April 1793, in *Papers of Thomas Jefferson*, 25:581.

## 1784–1865

1. Dederer, "Abraham Buford," 382–83; James, *Border Captain*, 112–14, 118–19; Harrison, *Equine F.F.Vs.*, 168; Mackay-Smith, *Thoroughbred in the Lower Shenandoah Valley*, 39.

2. The four horses pulling Washington's chariot fell into a river while riding a ferry and nearly drowned, but "providentially—indeed miraculously," bystanders on the shore saved them all (Twohig, *George Washington's Diaries*, 378, 381; Harrison, *Roanoke Stud*, 61).

3. Moore, *Albemarle*, 182; Fischer and Kelly, *Away, I'm Bound Away*, 92–93.

4. Harrison, *Roanoke Stud*, 25; Denhardt, *Quarter Running Horse*, 9.

5. Bernard, *Retrospections of America*, 154–55.

6. Harrison, *Roanoke Stud*, 66; Lewis, *Southampton County*, 25; Mackay-Smith, *Colonial Quarter Race Horse*, 159.

7. Betts, *Jefferson's Farm Book,* 103; Dabney, *Richmond,* 86; Click, *The Spirit of the Times,* 60; Mackay-Smith, *Thoroughbred in the Lower Shenandoah Valley,* 30–31; Harrison, *Roanoke Stud,* 16; Moore, *Albemarle,* 155. Alexander L. Botts and David H. Branch owned the New Market racetrack. Mackay-Smith, *Race Horses of America,* 29.

8. J. Robertson, *Stonewall Jackson,* 14.

9. Quoted in Mackay-Smith, *Colonial Quarter Race Horse,* 56.

10. Hotaling, *Great Black Jockeys,* 13, 22, 25, 29–30, 35.

11. Stewart, "My Life as a Slave," 730–38. I standardized the spellings a bit from the dialect spellings that *Harper's* used.

12. Harrison, *Roanoke Stud,* 140–41; Kamoie, *Irons in the Fire,* 135–36. Today the county seat of Caroline County takes its name from Hoomes's house, Bowling Green. A ghost story about the family holds that when Hoomes heard the sound of galloping horses on the racetrack—even though no horses were actually there—one of his sons would soon die. Variations involve Hoomes hearing the nonexistent horses the day before he died; a headless horseman on the track that presaged the death of a Hoomes son; and the appearance of the ghost of Hoomes himself before a death in the family (Wingfield, *History of Caroline County, Virginia,* 357–58; Workers of the Writers' Program, *Virginia: A Guide to the Old Dominion,* 364; Denhardt, *Quarter Running Horse,* 74).

13. Blanchard and Wellman, *Life and Times of Sir Archie,* 15–16; Harrison, *Roanoke Stud,* 141, 147–51; W. Robertson, *History of Thoroughbred Racing,* 37–38; Mackay-Smith, *Thoroughbred in the Lower Shenandoah Valley,* 30–31; Mackay-Smith, *Colonial Quarter Race Horse,* 165, 167; Peters, "Diomed."

14. Denhardt, *Quarter Running Horse,* 71–72; Harrison, *Equine F.F.Vs.,* 70–71; Harrison, *Roanoke Stud,* 208; Kamoie, *Irons in the Fire,* 118–21.

15. Dabney, *Virginia,* 181, 204–5, 216–17; Harrison, *Roanoke Stud,* 13–14, 20, 47, 63; Mackay-Smith, *Colonial Quarter Race Horse,* 96, 113, 115, 118.

16. Mackay-Smith, *Colonial Quarter Race Horse,* 139; Stewart, "My Life as a Slave," 733; Mackay-Smith, *Thoroughbred in the Lower Shenandoah Valley,* 8.

17. Denhardt, *Quarter Running Horse,* 36; Blanchard and Wellman, *Life and Times of Sir Archie,* 15–16. Tree Hill Farm remained agricultural until 2006, when it was sold to Richmond developers (*Richmond Times-Dispatch,* June 8, 2006).

18. Mackay-Smith, *Thoroughbred in the Lower Shenandoah Valley,* 16; Blanchard and Wellman, *Life and Times of Sir Archie,* 16–17, 20–21.

19. Blanchard and Wellman, *Life and Times of Sir Archie,* 26.

20. Ibid., 23, 24; Harrison, *Roanoke Stud,* 169. The name is also spelled "Archie," but "Archy" seems to have been the contemporary preference.

21. Blanchard and Wellman, *Life and Times of Sir Archie,* 25–29; Harrison, *Roanoke Stud,* 170.

22. Stewart, "My Life as a Slave," 733; Blanchard and Wellman, *Life and Times of Sir Archie,* 33, 40, 42, 44, 47, 49; Harrison, *Roanoke Stud,* 171, 172.

23. Blanchard and Wellman, *Life and Times of Sir Archie,* 50, 52; Harrison, *Roanoke Stud,* 173.

24. Blanchard and Wellman, *Life and Times of Sir Archie,* 55, 64, 68, 107; Harrison, *Roanoke Stud,* 175.

25. Blanchard and Wellman, *Life and Times of Sir Archie,* 142.

26. Ibid., 173, 178–79, 193. The hoof story is family lore.

27. Ibid., 192–93; Sands, *This Is the Story of the Deep Run Hunt Club,* 20, 201, 203; *Richmond Times-Dispatch,* November 12, 1970; January 8, 2003, "Your Section"; *Goochland County Historical Society Newsletter,* May 2001; Harrison, *Roanoke Stud,* 179. Harrison calls the Goochland story "pious mythology" and also reports that some people thought Sir Archy was buried at Mount Airy, where he lived for only a few weeks early in his long life. I think he's buried in North Carolina.

28. Blanchard and Wellman, *Life and Times of Sir Archie,* 197; Denhardt, *Quarter Running Horse,* 146.

29. Mackay-Smith, *Thoroughbred in the Lower Shenandoah Valley,* 18–20; Peters, "Sir Charles." Sir Charles's loss to American Eclipse spurred Johnson, John Randolph, and John Tayloe III to organize a rematch with another southern horse. Johnson trained six horses from Virginia, South Carolina, and North Carolina and chose Sir Henry, the North Carolina horse, to compete. The big race took place in May 1843 at the Union Course outside New York City, with Vice President Daniel Tompkins, Aaron Burr, Andrew Jackson, and John Randolph in attendance. (Johnson spent the day in bed at his hotel due to food poisoning.) American Eclipse won in two of three heats. Johnson eventually bought Eclipse and stood him at stud (Eisenberg, *The Great Match Race,* passim).

30. Montgomery, *Thoroughbred,* 147; Peters, "Boston."

31. Peters, "America's Annual Leading Sires."

32. Dabney, *Richmond,* 145; Click, *Spirit of the Times,* 62–65; Mackay-Smith, *Speed and the Thoroughbred,* 116; Harrison, *Roanoke Stud,* 206–7; Erigero, "Planet"; Wright, "The Doswells of Bullfield," 2–4; Mackay-Smith, *Thoroughbred in the Lower Shenandoah Valley,* 29; W. Robertson, *History of Thoroughbred Racing,* 85; *Richmond Times-Dispatch,* October 15, 2000.

33. Montgomery, *Thoroughbred,* 143.

34. Denhardt, *Quarter Running Horse,* 17.

35. Ibid., 8; Mackay-Smith, *Colonial Quarter Race Horse,* 160.

36. Denhardt, *Quarter Running Horse,* xvi, 79.

37. Mackay-Smith, *Race Horses of America,* xxvii, 1, 13, 26, 244, 249, 268.

38. Mackay-Smith, *Colonial Quarter Race Horse,* 234–35.

39. Mackay-Smith, *Race Horses of America,* 60–61, 131–32, 137. The *American Turf Register* sold again around 1837 to Robert Gilmor; in 1839, William T. Porter bought it; in 1842, it sold to John Richards.

40. Winants, *Steeplechasing,* 15–18; Bernard, *Retrospections of America,* 156–57. Bernard wrote that his hunting companions thought he was "a superior rider, which really means a man who believes his skull to be so thick that there can be no danger of cracking it."

41. Sands, *This Is the Story of the Deep Run Hunt Club,* 47–48; Mackay-Smith, *Foxhunting in North America,* 219–20; Mackay-Smith and Fine, *American Foxhunting Stories,* 22.

42. Brady, *George Washington's Beautiful Nelly,* 18, 30, 34, 41.

43. Anderson, *Blood Image,* 35, 36, 37; Thomas, *Bold Dragoon,* 41.

44. Mackay-Smith, *Colonial Quarter Race Horse,* 229–30, 237, 239, 274; Bishko, "A Spanish Stallion for Albemarle," 148–50, 168–80. One British horseman of the time had

quite the opposite opinion of the Spanish horse, calling it "the worst of his [i.e., God's] species in the creation. He has neither strength, speed, nor durability. His form is the very reverse of excellence in every point" (Lawrence, *Complete Farrier,* 20).

45. Bishko, "A Spanish Stallion for Albemarle," 179–80; Jefferson, *Notes on the State of Virginia,* 294; Betts, *Jefferson's Farm Book,* 89.

46. Slater, *Upperville Colt and Horse Show,* 20; Courts and Courts, "Colonel Richard Henry Dulany."

47. Crooks and Crooks, *Ring Tournament in the United States,* 34–40; Anderson, *Blood Image,* 121–24; Wilson and Ferris, *Encyclopedia of Southern Culture,* 1262.

48. Salmon and Campbell, *Hornbook of Virginia History,* 47.

49. Rable, *Fredericksburg! Fredericksburg!* 64–65; Anderson, *Blood Image,* 22; J. Robertson, *Stonewall Jackson,* 230; Ramsdell, "Lee's Horse Supply," 758, 759, 773. A mule named Kate, born in Virginia about 1848, pulled artillery wagons during the war and survived an injury or two. She wound up in California and died in 1893 at age forty-five (*Richmond Times,* November 5, 1893). Oxen were more durable and cheaper, so small farmers with few or no slaves more often used oxen than horses. West of the Blue Ridge, however, farmers preferred draft horses (Brown and Sorrells, *Virginia's Cattle Story,* 70–71).

50. Thomas, *Bold Dragoon,* 74.

51. Anderson, *Blood Image,* 38, 39, 56; Merrill, *Spurs to Glory,* 122; Thomas, *Bold Dragoon,* 257; Ramsdell, "Lee's Horse Supply," 768.

52. Ramsdell, "Lee's Horse Supply," 760, 766, 768, 775.

53. Thomas, *Bold Dragoon,* 248, 285–86; Douglas, *I Rode with Stonewall,* 54.

54. Rable, *Fredericksburg! Fredericksburg!* 199, 200, 202, 415, 528 n. 38; Douglas, *I Rode with Stonewall,* 24.

55. Douglas, *I Rode with Stonewall,* 175.

56. Anderson, *Blood Image,* 216; Thomas, *Bold Dragoon,* 287.

57. Thomas, *Bold Dragoon,* 217–26.

58. Freeman, *R. E. Lee,* 1:615; 2:416–17; Ramage, *Gray Ghost,* 230; Ramsdell, "Lee's Horse Supply," 760, 763, 766, 771, 773.

59. Ramsdell, "Lee's Horse Supply," 761–93.

60. Ibid., 760, 763, 764, 770, 772; Thomas, *Bold Dragoon,* 270–71; Douglas, *I Rode with Stonewall,* 331.

61. Ramsdell, "Lee's Horse Supply," 764, 765, 772–73.

62. Douglas, *I Rode with Stonewall,* 317; Anderson, *Blood Image,* 20. I don't know if George Baylor was related to the Baylors of Caroline County, but chances are good he is.

63. Freeman, *R. E. Lee,* 4:139; *Encyclopedia of Southern Culture,* 25; Perdue and Martin-Perdue, *Talk about Trouble,* 26.

64. Faust, "Equine Relics," 23, 45; L. Campbell, "Origin of the War Horse."

65. Thomas, *Bold Dragoon,* 8, 19, 26, 30.

66. Ibid., 48, 53, 68–69.

67. Freeman, *Lee's Lieutenants,* 1:283; Thomas, *Bold Dragoon,* 84–85, 285–86.

68. Thomas, *Bold Dragoon,* 72, 110–13.

69. Ibid., 113–25, 299.

70. Ibid., 244, 271–72.

71. Ibid., 41, 292–95.

72. Wert, "Turner Ashby," 225–26; Anderson, *Blood Image,* 26–27, 28, 39, 123–24.

73. Freeman, *Lee's Lieutenants,* 1:309; Anderson, *Blood Image,* 18.

74. Douglas, *I Rode with Stonewall,* 82.

75. Anderson, *Blood Image,* 64–65; Douglas, *I Rode with Stonewall,* 41.

76. Anderson, *Blood Image,* 19, 62, 63.

77. Ibid., 67.

78. Ibid., 25, 221.

79. Ramage, *Gray Ghost,* 20; Freeman, *Lee's Lieutenants,* 1:279.

80. Ramage, *Gray Ghost,* 2–3, 9, 10, 81, 102–3.

81. Ibid., 106, 108, 109, 346.

82. Ibid., 159–60.

83. Douglas, *I Rode with Stonewall,* 206–7; J. Robertson, *Stonewall Jackson,* 230.

84. Douglas, *I Rode with Stonewall,* 234; J. Robertson, *Stonewall Jackson,* 300, 470.

85. Douglas, *I Rode with Stonewall,* 115, 206; Pittenger, *Morgan Horses,* 144; J. Robertson, *Stonewall Jackson,* 346.

86. J. Robertson, *Stonewall Jackson,* 597, 628.

87. Ibid., 584, 587–89.

88. Ibid., 730–53, 916 n. 95.

89. Ibid., 922 n. 16; Faust, "Equine Relics," 38–39; *Alexandria Gazette,* June 1, 1887.

90. *Alexandria Gazette,* June 1, 1887.

91. *Richmond Times-Dispatch,* July 21, 1997; *Washington Post,* July 21, 1997; Faust, "Equine Relics," 39. One of the parties involved in the event told me he tried to persuade VMI to bury the hide as well, thus putting *all* of Little Sorrel to rest, but to no avail.

92. Harrison, *Equine F.F.Vs.,* 173; Rhinesmith, "Traveller," 38. At the time of Traveller's birth, the future Confederate president Jefferson Davis had been the secretary of war of the United States and was a senator from Mississippi.

93. Rhinesmith, "Traveller," 39. McCaslin suggests Lee named Traveller after a horse that George Washington had owned (*Lee in the Shadow of Washington,* 91).

94. Thomas, *Robert E. Lee,* 116–17; Freeman, *R. E. Lee,* 4:644–46; Rhinesmith, "Traveller," 39.

95. Freeman, *R. E. Lee,* 4:645, 647; Rhinesmith, "Traveller," 39.

96. Thomas, *Robert E. Lee,* 255, 328–29.

97. Freeman, *R. E. Lee,* 4:143–48.

98. Thomas, *Robert E. Lee,* 383, 402; Flood, *Lee: The Last Years,* 95, 109, 212, 249; Rhinesmith, "Traveller," 40–42. H. Gwynne Tayloe, of Richmond and Mount Airy, confirms that W. H. Tayloe was related to the Virginia family.

99. Freeman, *R. E. Lee,* 1:646; M. Campbell, "Lucy Long," 471–73; Rhinesmith, "Traveller," 40–42.

100. Flood, *Lee: The Last Years,* 253–61; Freeman, *R. E. Lee,* 1:485–92; Thomas, *Robert E. Lee,* 416.

101. Rhinesmith, "Traveller," 44–47.

102. *General Lee's Traveller on the Campus of Washington and Lee.*

## 1866–1945

1. Lay, *Ways of the World,* 132–33. The New York tally also included 1,100 tons of manure per day and 270,000 liters of urine.

2. *Richmond Times,* November 20, 1892; June 4, December 10, 1893; *Rockbridge Advocate,* March 2004, 43–44; *Richmond Times-Dispatch,* January 19, 1908; Perdue and Martin-Perdue, *Talk about Trouble,* 150–51.

3. Perdue and Martin-Perdue, *Talk about Trouble,* 69, 125–26, 214.

4. Dabney, *Richmond,* 286; Dabney, *Virginia,* 442–43; *Encyclopedia of Southern Culture,* 25–26.

5. Dabney, *Richmond,* 287; Harrison, *Equine F.F.Vs.,* 46.

6. Winants, *Foxhunting with Melvin Poe,* 18–19, 22; Perdue and Martin-Perdue, *Talk about Trouble,* 241.

7. W. Robertson, *History of Thoroughbred Racing,* 87–88, 91; Harrison, *Roanoke Stud,* 207; Moore, *Albemarle,* 266–67, 344–45; *Encyclopedia of Southern Culture,* 1224–25; Harrison, *Roanoke Stud,* 207.

8. *Encyclopedia of Southern Culture,* 196; Hotaling, *Great Black Jockeys,* 330; *Richmond News Leader,* October 13, 1924; Wiencek, *The Hairstons,* 36–37.

9. *Richmond Times,* October 16 and 30, 1892, November 20, 1892; *Blood-Horse* (August 10, 1929).

10. *Richmond Times,* April 12, 1896; *Richmond Times-Dispatch,* May 5, 1907; *Charles City County Historical Society Newsletter,* June 1998.

11. Moore, *Albemarle,* 345.

12. Nack, *Secretariat,* 6, 15–16; Montgomery, *Thoroughbred,* 151–52, 157; W. Robertson, *History of Thoroughbred Racing,* 86; Mackay-Smith, *Thoroughbred in the Lower Shenandoah Valley,* 29–30; Moore, *Albemarle,* 252.

13. *Richmond Times,* October 9, 1892, March 19, 1893. Bullfield Stud bought and raced Morello (*Richmond Times,* August 28, 1892).

14. *Virginia Breeder* (hereafter cited as *VB*), August 1939, 15; January 1941, 23–24; Peters, "America's Annual Leading Sires"; www.clabornefarm.com/history1.html. Howard Gentry went on to work for Christopher Chenery at The Meadow.

15. *VB,* August 1940, 12–13; February 1940, n.p.; November 1940, 7–8; W. Robertson, *History of Thoroughbred Racing,* 226–28; *Washington Post,* October 30, 1940.

16. Durden, "Home Ground of Great Thoroughbreds," 19–22; Julie Campbell, "Christopher Tompkins Chenery," 195–97.

17. Harrison, *Equine F.F.Vs.,* 168; Slater, *Hunt Country,* 223–25; *Harrisonburg Daily News Record,* July 20, 1927; Mackay-Smith, *Thoroughbred in the Lower Shenandoah Valley,* 39. Other breeders included Thomas G. Herring and Charles Herring, of Bridgewater; I. Iseman (possibly Iselin) at a Rockingham County farm; Reid Riley, who ran Montana Hall in White Post; and Capt. Phillip M. Walker, who owned Page Brook, near Boyce.

18. *Richmond Times-Dispatch,* undated clipping, in William Joseph Carter Scrapbooks; *Washington Post,* October 28, 1939; Workers of the Writers' Program, *Virginia: A Guide to the Old Dominion,* 528. Harry Payne Whitney apparently owned Audley from 1929 to 1931 (Bowen, *Jockey Club's Illustrated History of Thoroughbred Racing in Amer-*

*ica,* 201). The Joneses sold the farm to James F. Edwards in 1955; Edwards sold it to Hubertus Liebrecht in 1978. His family owned it as of 2005 (www.audleyfarm.com).

19. *Washington Post,* June 18, 1941; www.showjumpinghalloffame.net/inductees/w_stone.shtml; *VB,* August 1939, 15, 24; September 1939, 3; December 1940, 28.

20. *Washington Post,* May 3, 1914; October 31, 1940; June 18, 1941; *VB,* December 1940, 27–28. Perhaps Ernest Ashby was kin to Turner Ashby of Civil War fame.

21. *Washington Post,* July 4, 1941.

22. Ibid., July 2, 1941.

23. *Richmond News Leader,* February 28, 1933; *Washington Post,* June 14, 1941.

24. *Washington Post,* June 20, 1941.

25. Ibid., June 17, 1941.

26. Scott, *Montpelier,* 32, 35–36, 54, 55, 57, 58.

27. Ibid., 39, 63, 74.

28. Ibid., 76, 79, 80, 109–10, 137, 187; Winants, *Steeplechasing,* 94–97, 172; Clancy, "Battleship's Amazing Blast from the Past," 28–31.

29. Scott, *Montpelier,* 96; http://emc.vetmed.vt.edu/index.html. The "Scott" came from her brief marriage in the 1930s to the movie actor Randolph Scott.

30. *Chronicle of the Horse* (hereafter cited as *COH*), August 21, 1998, 62.

31. *Southeast Equine Monthly,* February 2005, 23; www.eventingusa.com/hof; *Washington Post,* August 28, 1998; www.americanhorsepubs.org/communication/communique_archive; "Horseman of the Year," 9–10.

32. "Horseman of the Year," 14.

33. *COH,* July 5, 2002.

34. Winants, "A Life of Burning Interests," 3; "Horseman of the Year," 10.

35. Burke, *Capital Horse Country,* 194, 274–75, 292–93; Mackay-Smith, *Blue Ridge Hunt,* 7, 9; Mackay-Smith, *Foxhunting in North America,* 220.

36. Sands, *This Is the Story of the Deep Run Hunt Club,* 50–53, 59, 60, 64, 66.

37. *Richmond Times-Dispatch,* February 1, 1903; *Washington Post,* September 1, 1910; Burke, *Capital Horse Country,* 282–83. Three years later, Willow King unseated Lee Riddle at the National Capital Horse Show (*Washington Post,* May 3, 1914).

38. Perrin, "Time Out of Mind: A Memoir," 45. Perrin was sister to Christopher Chenery, breeder of Secretariat and owner of The Meadow farm.

39. *Washington Post,* November 12, 1933; Burke, *Capital Horse Country,* 286–87.

40. www.morvenpark.org/huntroom.htm#hsmith; Mackay-Smith, *Foxhunting in North America,* 221; Burke, *Capital Horse Country,* 286–89; Slater, *Hunt Country,* 23, 26; Mackay-Smith and Fine, *American Foxhunting Stories,* 213–16.

41. *Washington Post,* June 18, 1941; Burke, *Capital Horse Country,* 275–76, 284–85; Slater, *Hunt Country,* 33, 74, 76, 87, 90–91; www.middleburghunt.com/history.htm.

42. Burke, *Capital Horse Country,* 279, 285–86, 290; www.farmingtonhunt.org/history.html; personal.cfw.com/~glenmor/; www.middlebrookhounds.org/middlebrook_hounds.001.htm.

43. www.vmi.edu/archives/Alumni/Patton/Patton.html; *Washington Post,* September 18, 1944. The general's grandfather, George Smith Patton, born in Fredericksburg, was a member of the VMI class of 1852 and died at the Civil War battle of Winchester in 1864. Three of that first George's brothers, John Mercer Patton, Waller Tazewell Patton, and

William McFarland Patton, also attended VMI and fought in the Civil War. The general's father, George S. Patton, was born in West Virginia (then Virginia) in 1856 and was a member of the VMI class of 1877. The general himself was born in California and died in Europe in 1945 of injuries he suffered in a car accident.

44. Mackay-Smith, *Foxhunting in North America,* 45.

45. Mackay-Smith and Fine, *American Foxhunting Stories,* 142–43.

46. Winants, *Steeplechasing,* 19; Sands, *This Is the Story of the Deep Run Hunt Club,* 69; *Richmond Times,* February 26, 1893; Burke, *Capital Horse Country,* 69; Ladin and Dementi, *State Fair of Virginia,* 55, 150.

47. *Washington Post,* May 27, 1906.

48. Winants, *Steeplechasing,* 88–89; "A Salute to the Father of the Forward Seat," 43.

49. Winants, *Steeplechasing,* 149–55, 207, 212, 214; Burke, *Capital Horse Country,* 71.

50. Bent, *American Polo,* xvi, xxiii, 1, 10, 119–46, 255–56; *Washington Post,* June 10, August 11, 1897; May 20, 1928; August 1, 1999. In the 1890s, the "Messrs. Crichton" of Virginia put together a match at Berkeley Springs, West Virginia, which was home to a resort popular with many Virginians.

51. *Washington Post,* May 27, 1906.

52. *Polo in Upper Fauquier; VB,* November 1939, 4; August 1940, 15; Burke, *Capital Country,* 147, 155; *Washington Post,* May 26, 1922; February 18, 1923; March 20, 1925. Capt. Samuel White coached the VMI team. The Phipps field passed into the hands of Paul Mellon, then to Senator John Warner (Mellon's one-time son-in-law), and then to Jack Kent Cooke, owner of the Washington Redskins football team (Burke, *Capital Country,* 155).

53. *Washington Post,* November 12, 1933; March 18, 1934; October 14, 1935; July 2, August 6, October 15, 1939; September 29, 1940. Ziegler owned Burrland Stables in Middleburg (*Washington Post,* March 18, 1934). *Eastern Breeder* (hereafter cited as *EB*), May 1942, 3; June 1943, 17. *Eastern Breeder* noted the World War II combat death of Tommy Hitchcock, the star polo player in the United States, calling him the "equivalent of Babe Ruth" (May 1944, 6).

54. Mackay-Smith, *Colonial Quarter Race Horse,* 219–20, 266–67; Hendricks, *International Encyclopedia,* 99–100, 401–5. Hendricks writes, "A gross error is made by those who attribute all of the credit for the American trotters to the horses of England" (100).

55. Hendricks, *International Encyclopedia,* 401–5.

56. Click, *Spirit of the Times,* 69–70; *Richmond Times,* February 17, 1895.

57. *Richmond Times,* November 13, 1892; February 5, 12, 19, March 5, September 17, 1893; *Rockingham Register,* May 25, 1882.

58. *Richmond Times,* March 19, April 9, 23, 1893; *Richmond Times-Dispatch* Sunday magazine, June 23, 1935.

59. *Richmond Times,* April 23, 1893; Trice, *Horse Tales,* 14–15, 19, 23–24, 40, 36.

60. *Shenandoah Herald,* June 5, 1903; Busbey, *Trotting and Pacing Horse,* 329; *Richmond Times,* November 27, December 25, 1892, July 16, 1893; *Lexington News-Gazette Weekender,* July 3, 2004; Trice, *Horse Tales,* 42.

61. *Richmond Times,* May 28, 1893.

62. Ibid., April 1, 1894; *VB,* September 1939, 16–19; *Richmond News Leader,* October 31, 1924.

63. Norman, "Elijah B. White"; *Richmond Times,* December 4, 1892, March 5, 1893; Hendricks, *International Encyclopedia,* 208–11; *Richmond Times,* March 4, 1894.

64. Slater, *Hunt Country,* 220–21; *VB,* February 1940, 25–27; April 1940, 23–24; *EB,* March 1944, 35.

65. *Washington Post,* June 16, July 3, 1941.

66. Burke, *Capital Horse Country,* 195; *Harrisonburg Daily News Record,* July 20, 1927; Slater, *Hunt Country,* 27, 210–17; *VB,* December 1940, 28, 37. European horses had skipped the show due to the war. One of Bonne Nuit's great-grandsons, the famed jumper Gem Twist, won two silver medals in the 1988 Olympics (Jaffer, "There'll Never Be Another Gem Twist," 19).

67. Slater, *Hunt Country,* 139; Self, *Horses of Today,* 112, 116; Winants, *Hunting with Melvin Poe,* 22.

68. *VB,* February 1940, 27; *EB,* March 1944, 35.

69. Leonard, "Remount Depot," 2; *VB,* September 1939, 46–48; January 1940, 60–61; January 1941, 45; *EB,* March 1941, 27.

70. *VB,* December 1939, 11. When horseman George S. Patton Jr. commanded Fort Myer in 1940, he presided over the show.

71. Moore, *Albemarle,* 250–52; *Rockingham Register,* May 30, 1890; Harrison, *Equine F.F.Vs.,* 161; Sanders and Dinsmore, *History of the Percheron Horse,* 460; *State Republican,* March 22, 1888; *VB,* July 1940, 28; November 1939, 15, 43.

72. Norman, "Elijah B. White"; Sanders and Dinsmore, *History of the Percheron Horse,* 460; Mischka, *Percheron Horse in America,* 136–43.

73. *VB,* August 1939, 13; September 1939, 29–31; December 1939, 15; Hendricks, *International Encyclopedia,* 74.

74. *VB,* November 1939, 21; December 1941, 29.

75. Ibid., February 1940, 26–27.

76. Self, *Horses of Today,* 52–54; Hendricks, *International Encyclopedia,* 23–24.

77. Loch, *Dressage,* 123–24; Self, *Horses of Today,* 54–57.

78. *VB,* December 1939, 49.

79. Ibid., October 1939, 31; January 1940, 32; January 1941, 25–26; *EB,* February 1941, 11, 22. Enthusiasts also promoted the breed in Richmond, the Tidewater, and near Charlottesville. They included Mr. and Mrs. John C. Bryant, of Richmond; Murray Coulter, Roanoke; Gwendolyn Davies, a rider at Sullins College in Bristol; Cliffside Farm; Dr. J. P. McDonough, Richmond; and Henry W. Armstrong and Russell L. Law in the Tidewater.

80. *VB,* December 1939, 49.

81. *EB,* January 1942, 3; February 1942, 32; September 1948, 31; Self, *Horses of Today,* 65–68; *VB,* August 1939, 6; clipping, n.d. (ca. 1950–60), in "Equestrian and Racing Scrapbook," National Sporting Library.

82. www.geocities.com/Heartland/Ranch/3479/CMKDAMLines.html; www.bpeah.com/AlKhamsaArticile0916.htm; www.datadubai.com/horse5.htm; telephone conversation with Frederick Fisher, September 24, 2004; *VB,* August 1939, 29; *Richmond News Leader,* July 18, 1938. Mr. Fisher, the great-grandson of Charles Crane, owned and lived at Westover as of this writing. He no longer owned any of the Arabians' descendants.

83. Pittenger, *Morgan Horses,* 123, 206–7; *EB,* May 1942, 5; September 1943, 52; Hen-

dricks, *International Encyclopedia,* 330. To produce more Palominos, Moyer would have enjoyed the best results by crossing his Palominos with chestnuts.

84. Dittrich, "Horses at VMI," 163–65; "Information on VMI Mounted Service."

85. Dittrich, "Horses at VMI," 165–66; Harry W. Easterly Jr., interview by the author, November 2002.

86. Dittrich, "Horses at VMI," 166; Henson, Morgan, and Morrison, *Keydet Grey and Garry Owen,* 56.

87. Dittrich, "Horses at VMI," 165–66; Henson, Morgan, and Morrison, *Keydet Grey and Garry Owen,* 128, 146.

88. *VB,* January 1941, 26–27; *EB,* March 1941, 29.

89. *Washington Post,* May 3, 1914.

90. Crooks and Crooks, *The Ring Tournament,* 42–44, 46, 49–50, 53–55; Winants, *Foxhunting with Melvin Poe,* 24.

91. Courts and Courts, "Colonel Richard Henry Dulany"; Slater, "Upperville Colt and Horse Show," 21.

92. www.warrentonhorseshow.com/history.html; Burke, *Capital Horse Country,* 176; *VHJ,* April 2002, 28; Slater, *Hunt Country,* 143, 144, 149; *Washington Post,* September 1, 1910. Horsemen between the ages of seven and eighteen were still running the show in 2005; *COH* (July 22, 2005), 26. George Patton often competed at Warrenton.

93. Photocopy in "Horses" clipping file, Albemarle County Historical Society; Moore, *Albemarle,* 281, 367.

94. Sands, *This Is the History of the Deep Run Hunt Club,* 91; *Richmond Times,* April 24, May 8, 1898; September 2, 1900; 1904 broadside, Fredericksburg Horse Show Association; prize list, Library of Virginia; Moon, *Sunday Horse,* 92–93; Winants, *Foxhunting with Melvin Poe,* 45–46; *VB,* September 1939, 24–25.

95. *VB,* August 1939, 9–10; May 1940, 14; October 1940, 29–30.

96. www.showjumpinghalloffame.net/inductees/m_w_smith.shtml; *VHJ,* August 2002, 8; *COH,* January 7, 2005, 8–9.

97. *VB,* November 1939, 29; April 1940, 24.

98. Ibid., January 1941, 26; *EB,* January 1942, 3; February 1942, 32.

99. *VB,* January 1940, 31; January 1941, 26; *EB,* February 1941, 11.

100. *EB,* March 1941, 9–10; March 1941, 35; December 1941, 36–37. The attendees came from Leesburg, Newport News, Fredericksburg, White Post, Upperville, Middleburg, Leesburg, Delaplane, Berryville, Richmond, Gordonsville, Mountsville, Warrenton, and Philomont.

101. Ibid., March 1941, 11.

102. Haines, *Horses in America,* 191; Dabney, *Virginia,* 464; *VB,* September 1939, 46–48; December 1939, 11; November 1940, 16; December 1941, 29; *EB,* February 1941, 41; December 1941, 35; January 1942, 33; February 1942, 13, 45; February 1944, 51;

103. *Washington Post,* August 9, 1942.

104. Sands, *This Is the Story of the Deep Run Hunt Club,* 41. Reed would become president of Atlantic Rural Exposition (the State Fair of Virginia) and bring horse shows to the fairgrounds year-round. He also brought the Deep Run steeplechases to the fair (Ladin and Dementi, *State Fair of Virginia,* 55, 117).

105. *EB,* May 1942, 3, 39; June 1943, 17, 19; February 1944, 41; *Washington Post,* March 2, 1943.

106. Pierson, *Dark Horses and Black Beauties,* 13–14; *Encyclopedia of Southern Culture,* 512; *Richmond Times-Dispatch,* August 26, 1951.

107. Brown and Sorrells, *Virginia's Cattle Story,* 123.

108. *EB,* June 1948, 46; October 1948, 27.

## 1946–2001 and Beyond

1. Self, *Horses of Today,* 11–12.

2. *EB,* June 1948, 58; www.vabred.org/history.cfm.

3. vabred.org/history.cfm. Later officials included Tyson Gilpin, Daniel Van Clief, Isabel Dodge Sloan, James L. Wiley, Dr. F. A. O'Keefe, Raymond Guest, John Marsh, Fred Kohler, and Ernie Oare.

4. *Richmond Times-Dispatch,* June 3, 1954; Moore, *Albemarle,* 442; *Spur of Virginia,* February 1968, 48.

5. Scott, *Montpelier,* 96; "Virginia Is Where It All Began!" letter, photocopy, Virginians for Racing, VHS; www.showjumpinghalloffame.net/inductees/w_stone.shtml (Morven Stud).

6. *VHJ,* February 2002, 9.

7. *VHJ,* July 2001, 12; March 2003, 8; February 2005, 8. Other important stables and individuals included the Albemarle Stud, Rose M. Estes, Stoney Lane Farm, Audley Farm, Keswick Stables, and Mr. and Mrs. C. W. McNeely III. Mark Hardin owned Newstead Farm in Upperville and Rockburn Farm in Marshall and restored Meadowville Farm in The Plains. In 2005, the Nydrie Stud went on the market for $8,750,000; *VHJ,* October 2005, 76.

8. *Washington Post,* February 13, 2004.

9. Ibid., February 13, 2004; www.vabred.org/breeding.cfm; www.vabred.org/aboutvta.cfm.

10. *Richmond Times-Dispatch,* April 22, 2003; www.trfinc.org/farms.

11. *Richmond Times-Dispatch,* July 23, 2002.

12. Julie Campbell, "Christopher Tompkins Chenery," 195–97; *National Cyclopedia of American Biography* (hereafter cited as *NCAB*), 58:410–11; Perrin, "Time Out of Mind," 6–7, 15, 83–84, 184. Nack, in *Secretariat* (7), quoting an unpublished family history in the possession of Penny Chenery (Chenery's daughter, Lexington, Kentucky); *Washington and Lee University Alumni Directory, 1749–1970.* Penny Chenery was known by her married name, Penny Tweedy, during Secretariat's glory years. After a divorce, she returned to "Chenery."

13. *NCAB,* 410–11; Penny Chenery, phone interview by the author, March 3, 2004; Nack, *Secretariat,* pp. 9–12; Wright, "The Doswells of Bullfield," 2–4; *W&L: The Alumni Magazine of Washington and Lee University* 48, no. 6 (September 1973): 5.

14. *NCAB,* 58:410–11; W. Robertson, *The History of Thoroughbred Racing,* 432–33, 534; Nack, *Secretariat,* 11, 23–27, 95–96; Durden, "Home Ground of Great Thoroughbreds," 19–22.

15. Nack, *Secretariat,* 40–45.

16. Ibid., 4, 46–48.

17. Ibid., 50–55.

18. Ibid., 56–57.

19. Ibid., 63–65, 199–201, 203.

20. Ibid., 63–72, 74–78.

21. Ibid., 78–82, 83–86, 105–8.

22. Ibid., 103–5.

23. Ibid., 104–5, 132–33.

24. Ibid., 95–99, 135–41.

25. Ibid., 141–83.

26. Secretariat's Racing Record, Appendix B, in Nack, *Secretariat,* 365; abscess story on 222–32, 237–39.

27. Ibid., 254–70, 283–92, 309–25.

28. Ibid., 297–301.

29. Ibid., 336–40, 361–64, 365; Penny Chenery, online forum, New York Racing Association Message Board, June 5, 2003, transcript on www.nyra.com/messageboard.

30. Penny Chenery, online interview, "Secretariat Trivia Page," www.members.aol.com/Me0930/penny.html.

31. Nack, *Secretariat,* 360; *Richmond News Leader,* October 4, 1989; personal visit to Claiborne Farm, September 12, 2004.

32. *Caroline Progress,* July 4, 1990; *Richmond Times-Dispatch,* June 5, 1998; March 7, 10, 2004; *VHJ,* September 2003, 12.

33. *Richmond Times-Dispatch,* June 5, 1998.

34. Nack, *Secretariat,* 334, 343.

35. Mellon, *Reflections in a Silver Spoon,* 38, 85–86, 94, 106, 123–28.

36. Ibid., 106, 152, 183, 187, 188–92, 228, 229, 230.

37. Ibid., 232, 234, 236, 239, 240–41.

38. *Richmond Times-Dispatch,* May 2, 1993; Mellon, *Reflections in a Silver Spoon,* 152, 247–53, 256, 260–62, 265–66, 269.

39. Mellon, *Reflections in a Silver Spoon,* 253, 257, 276–77; Slater, *Hunt Country,* 95–97, 116; Burke, *Capital Horse Country,* 54–55.

40. Burke, *Capital Horse Country,* 31–37; *COH,* January 14, 2005, 4; Winants, *Steeplechasing,* 5, 27, 62–65.

41. *COH,* January 14, 2005, 16–22.

42. *Richmond Times-Dispatch,* April 5, 1975; www.vabred.org/halloffame.cfm; Winants, *Steeplechasing,* 222–29.

43. Winants, *Steeplechasing,* 178–80. Theodora was married to Archibald Randolph.

44. Active breeders of trotters in the area included Turpin Acree, Roger Andrews, Ben Baird, Lynn Charnock, Archie Davis, Wayne Davis, Dr. E. L. W. Ferry and his son Eddie Wright Ferry, Peyton Fidler, H. A. Hinson, Billy Northan, Bob Sanders, Herbert Scott, John Tignor, and Willie Webb (Trice, *Horse Tales,* 16–18, 27–28, 31–32, 71–72).

45. Ibid., 27–28, 31–32; *Richmond Times-Dispatch,* November 16, 1972.

46. Camden ended up as a police officer in Colts Neck, New Jersey (Hoffman, "Leader of the Pack").

47. www.ustrotting.com/trackside/trackfacts; *Richmond Times-Dispatch,* October 27, 2004.

48. Mackay-Smith and Fine, *American Foxhunting Stories,* 242; Mackay-Smith, *Foxhunting in North America,* 225; Yates, "Rita Mae Brown," 11.

49. Winants, *Foxhunting with Melvin Poe,* 33, 41; *Charlottesville Daily Progress,* April

19, 1970. Dr. No belonged to Katherine Berger, of Berryville, a member of the Blue Ridge Hunt (*VHJ*, November 2001, 18).

50. Sands, *This Is the Story of the Deep Run Hunt*, 11.

51. Ibid., 136; Mackay-Smith, *Foxhunting in North America*, 223, 226; *Richmond Times-Dispatch*, March 4, 2001.

52. *Richmond Times-Dispatch*, March 4, 2001; *COH*, November 26, 2004, 4.

53. Mackay-Smith and Fine, *American Foxhunting Stories*, 198.

54. *Washington Post*, November 20, 2000; *COH*, December 8, 2000; Martin, *The Masters of Show Jumping*, 107.

55. Martin, *The Masters of Show Jumping*, 107–11; Moon, *Sunday Horse*, 99–101; Magee, "A Very Precise Gold Medalist," 55–59; Van Clief, "A Champion and a Gentleman," 8–14.

56. www.showjumpinghalloffame.net/inductees/r_jenkins/shtml.

57. www.showjumpinghalloffame.net/inductees/k_kusner.shtml and b_omeara.shtml; www.kathykusner.com; Winants, *Steeplechasing*, 65, 68–69; Stoneridge, *Great Horses of Our Time*, 465–67, 472, 474, 476, 479; "Women at the Top," 40. Kusner's own Web site says she was the *first* licensed female jockey in the United States.

58. Martin, *Masters of Show Jumping*, 123–33.

59. "Women at the Top," 41; www.showjumpinghalloffame.net/inductees/f_rowe .html; *Richmond Times-Dispatch*, January 2, 1985.

60. *Washington Post*, June 17, 1941; "Women at the Top," 41. www.choate.edu/alumniparent/publications/bulletin.

61. *COH*, September 28, 2001; *VHJ*, November 2001, 6; *PH*, December 2001, 15; Moon, *Sunday Horse*, 122–24. As of this writing, the National Horse Show had once again left New York City. Although their careers took place mostly out of the state, two famed jumper riders lived at one time or another in Virginia: Hugh Wiley, rider of Nautical, the Palomino "Horse with the Flying Tail," and Harry deLeyer, who rescued a horse from slaughter and turned him into Snowman, a top competitor ("Horse Country," supplement to *Charlottesville Daily Progress*, May 31, 1988).

62. Friel, "Dreams, Dollars and Devotees," 18; Clayton, *Cross Country Riding*, 145; www.eventingusa.com/about/whatis.htm. The number of stars, one to four (usually denoted with asterisks), after a competition's name denotes its level of difficulty. For example, there are the Morven Park CCI* Three-Day Event and the Rolex Kentucky CCI****. There are only four four-star events in the world, and they represent the very highest, elite level. "CCI" means "cross-country international." For ease of reading, I've omitted the stars from most mentions.

63. Martin, "Eventing in Great Britain," in Clayton, *Cross Country Riding*, 150.

64. www.eventingusa.com.

65. Ibid.; S. O'Connor, "Eventing in North America," 163–69, 170, 184.

66. www.useventing.com/bios/stephen_bradley.htm; *PH*, August 2003, 37.

67. Burke, *Capital Horse Country*, 214.

68. www.teamwindchase.com.

69. www.equestrian.org/olympics/beckydouglas.html.

70. Cooke, "Beanie Baby!" 44; www.oconnoreventteam.com/david.html; "Paul R. Fout," 94. Nina Fout retired 3 Magic Beans in 2006 after ten four-star competitions, two

three-stars, and two two-stars, plus the Olympics; Strassburger, "A Final Run for 3 Magic Beans."

71. K. O'Connor and D. O'Connor, *Life in the Galloping Lane,* 52, 54; www.oconnoreventteam.com.

72. K. O'Connor and D. O'Connor, *Life in the Galloping Lane,* 147; "Tribute to Theodore O'Connor," 38; "Theodore O'Connor, 1995–2008."

73. K. O'Connor and D. O'Connor, *Life in the Galloping Lane,* 110, 111, 112, 118–19, 157; K. O'Connor, "After Sydney, Time for a Family," 152; www.oconnoreventteam.com. The couple had arranged for horse-drawn carriages as part of the wedding festivities. When the truck pulling the horse trailer bearing the carriage horses got a flat tire, Jacqueline Mars substituted her own vehicle and brought the animals to the wedding (K. O'Connor and D. O'Connor, *Life in the Galloping Lane,* 114).

74. K. O'Connor and D. O'Connor, *Life in the Galloping Lane,* 21, 37–38, 42.

75. Ibid., 125, 128.

76. Ibid., 14–15; www.oconnoreventteam.com. (The abbreviation "USCTA" stands for "United States Combined Training Association," which preceded the USEA.)

77. *PH,* September 2003, 20; Friel, "Dreams, Dollars and Devotees," 18.

78. *PH,* February 2002, 34; Rasin, "Overall & Eventing Horse of the Year," 9, 11.

79. Hill, "An Interview with Torrance Watkins."

80. www.equestrian.org/olympics/monitor.html.

81. Eldridge, "Jimmy Wofford Teaches the World"; *Washington Post,* October 17, 2002 (also available at www.culver.org/news/News_Articles/HHOF.Wofford.asp); Cooke, "Beanie Baby!" 44.

82. *VHJ,* July 2004, 7; Jaffer, "Olympics—Athens 2004," 28–39. The U.S. team originally came in fourth but moved up after officials demoted the German rider, Bettina Hoy, from first to fourth place due to an error in show jumping, when she crossed the starting line twice. The re-placing bumped Kim Severson up to silver. The 2004 Olympics also saw the first use of a controversial new format that dropped the roads and tracks and steeplechase portions of the contest, a change hotly debated by the eventing community.

83. Vicki Baker quoted in *VHJ,* September 2001, 16; *VHJ,* May 2003, 78.

84. Harris, *Dressage by the Letter,* 2–3; Edwards, *Encyclopedia of the Horse,* 350–51.

85. Slater, *Hunt Country,* 107–8; Menino, *Forward Motion,* 53–54; *Washington Post,* July 9, 1960; *VHJ,* June 2004, 74.

86. *VHJ,* October 2001, 16–18, 22–24, 30; February 2005, 55; *COH,* February 4, 2005, 68–72.

87. Le, "Horsing Around," 31–35; *Washington Post,* April 18, 1960, April 25, 1963.

88. *Washington Post,* August 31, 1961, April 25, 1963; Grubbs, "Polo in Middleburg at Phipps Field," 66–67; Lees, "Middleburg Polo at Phipps Field," 30–31.

89. Yates, "Great Meadow Takes Aim at Polo," 13; Grubbs, "Polo in Middleburg at Phipps Field," 66–67; Lees, "Middleburg Polo at Phipps Field," 30–31; *Charlottesville Daily Progress,* undated clipping, at Albemarle County Historical Society; Watson, *The World of Polo,* 157; *World Guide to Polo Clubs,* 68–98; *Fredericksburg Free Lance-Star,* October 14, 2002; *VHJ,* September 2003, 24; *Richmond Times-Dispatch,* June 17, 2004; *Washington Post,* September 14, 1997; April 25, 2004.

90. *Washington Post,* August 1, 1999; September 14, 1997. In a controversial trial,

Cummings was convicted of manslaughter amid allegations of abuse and self-defense. She served fifty-one days of a sixty-day sentence and paid a $2,500 fine.

91. Yates, "Rita Mae Brown," 10.

92. *VB,* October 1939; 3, October 1940, 16; *Washington Post,* April 19, 1959; www.olddominionrides.org; Burke, *Capital Horse Country,* 238–39; Smart, *Community of the Horse,* 156. Other organizers of the Old Dominion included Alexander and Ila Bigler of Vienna, Jack Howard and Patricia Horrocks of Leesburg, Wayne Botts, and Jim Werner.

93. Stewart-Spears, "Valerie Kanavy." In 2005, a clone of one of Kanavy's championship horses, the gelding Pieraz, was born at the University of Bologna, Italy (*PH,* July 2005, 72–74).

94. *VHJ,* August 2002, 20; July 2001, 62; October 2001, 54; June 2002, 30; October 2002, 8; Stewart-Spears, "Rogers-Buttram Endures"; *Lexington News-Gazette,* March 26, July 23, 2003.

95. Friel, "Dreams, Dollars and Devotees," 20; *VHJ,* January 2005, 32; *VHJ,* January 2003, 30; July 2004, 57; July 2002, 62; *PH,* March 2000, 47; *Lexington News-Gazette,* April 9, 2003.

96. Slater, *Hunt Country,* 124–25; Harris, "Viola Winmill's Magnificent Legacy," 24; www.morvenpark.org/carriage.htm; V. Armstrong, *"Gone Away" with the Winmills,* 158–59, 192–93, 267–69.

97. *VHJ,* September 2001, 4; Smart, *Community of the Horse,* 411.

98. *VHJ,* September 2000, 28.

99. Burke, *Capital Horse Country,* 228–29; Friel, "Virginia Drivers Take New Direction," 34–40.

100. *VHJ,* December 2003, 54, July 2004, 48; Smart, *Community of the Horse,* 442. Seaton retired the Fleas in 2003 at a public ceremony.

101. *VHJ,* September 2001, 70; September 2002, 24, 32.

102. *Lexington News-Gazette,* May 19, 2004.

103. Hurt, "Full Return of the Quarter Horse," 24, 26; Slater, *Hunt Country,* 220. Adding Thoroughbred genes to Quarter Horses produces a more streamlined animal than the traditional "bulldog" Quarter Horse, with its compact, muscular frame.

104. Friel, "Spirit of America," 24–26.

105. Ibid., 22–23; *VHJ,* May 2001, 60, February 2003, 74.

106. *Richmond News Leader,* August 4, 1986; *Lexington News-Gazette,* July 14, 2004.

107. *Washington Post,* April 20, 2004; *Roanoke Times,* August 7, 2004; *Richmond Times-Dispatch,* October 2, 2000; *Southeast Equine Monthly,* December 2004, 12–13.

108. *VHJ,* April 2001, 44–46; *Richmond Times-Dispatch,* July 15, 2002.

109. *VHJ,* June 2002, 7; November 2002, 66; March 2003, 66.

110. Ibid., June 2002, 66; www.nchacutting.com. Other cutting horse trainers and competitors included Robert Repass, of Bristol; Raymond Mifflin, of Hume; and Greg McDonald, of Goochland County.

111. *Lexington News-Gazette,* February 18, 2004.

112. *Colonial Williamsburg Animal News,* June/July 1989; August/September 1990; "Rare Breeds Program"; Freise, "Carriages of Colonial Williamsburg," 36.

113. Rose, "National Sporting Library," 5–8.

114. www.morvenpark.org/hounds.htm.

115. M. Armstrong, "Saddling Up for the Last Ride," 8–11; *Washington Post,* June 9, 2004; *Richmond Times-Dispatch,* May 28, 1995; *Roanoke Times,* June 10, 2006. In 1957, the seventeen horses that served funerals nearly met their demise due to lack of funding; *Washington Post,* February 10, 1957. Black Jack (named for General John J. "Black Jack" Pershing of World War I fame) also appeared in the funerals of former presidents Hoover and Johnson. He died in 1976 and is interred on the Fort Myer parade ground (White House Horses exhibit, www.whitehousehistory.org/02/subs_horses/08.html).

116. Richmond Mounted Squad, interview by the author, February 2003.

117. *Roanoke Times,* December 20, 2003; *Fredericksburg Free Lance-Star,* October 14, 2002; www.portsmouth.va.us/ppd/mountedpatrol.htm; www.vbgov.com/dept/police; *Charlottesville Daily Progress,* July 14, 1994; Officer Michael D. Hodge, Henrico Mounted Unit, e-mail to the author, July 22, 2004; *VHJ,* January 2003, 14; N. Lee Newman to the author, November 28, 2000.

118. Morris, *United States Pony Clubs,* 26, 28; *VHJ,* June 2004, 7; *Lexington News-Gazette,* February 11, 2004; www.ponyclub.org/about; Sands, *This Is the Story of the Deep Run Hunt Club,* 223–227; Winants, *Foxhunting with Melvin Poe,* 56; Burke, *Capital Horse Country,* 264–65.

119. www.ext.vt.edu/resources/4h/about.html and 4h/horse/vajudgingteam.html; *VHJ,* July 2004, 38.

120. Brown and Sorrells, *Virginia's Cattle Story,* 164.

121. www.hollins.edu/athletics/riding/riding.htm; *Roanoke Times,* August 14, 2004. The bestower of the accolade was the *Kaplan/Newsweek "How to Get Into College" Guide.*

122. *Randolph-Macon Woman's College President's Report 2003,* 23 (the school is now called Randolph College); www.sbc.edu/riding/courses/; Cooke and Rutberg, "Career-Boosting Equine Degrees," 35; *VHJ,* March 2002, 82.

123. *Equine Science at Virginia Tech*; "Virginia Tech 8th Annual Hokie Harvest Sale"; Dr. Rebecca Splan (assistant professor, Virginia Tech), interview by the author, September 6, 2002; *VHJ,* January 2004, 38–40.

124. www.teamdressage.com.

125. www.foxcroft.org/activities/ridingactivities.htm.

126. Cooke and Rutberg, "Career-Boosting Equine Degrees," 31; www.sbcnews.sbc.edu/9907/9907croninsi.html; www.ncaa.org; Iliff, "Playing by the Rules," 47; Cashman and Cooke, "Troubling Trends in NCAA Equestrian Sport," 18–21; http://www.varsityequestrian.com.

127. Hewitt, "Horses Return to Virginia Military Institute," 16; Dooley, "VMI's Mounted Drill Team."

128. *PH,* June 2004, 142; www.vetmed.vt.edu/Organization/Admin/history.asp. Britt died at age eighty-eight in 2006 (*VHJ,* April 2006, 24).

129. *Richmond Style Weekly,* March 25, 1997.

130. *VHJ,* January 2004, 77; December 2004, 60–61. Caboose was named NARHA Region 3 Horse of 2004.

131. *Richmond Style Weekly,* March 25, 1997; *VHJ,* May 2001, 24–26; *PH,* September 2001, 128; *Charlottesville Daily Progress,* August 15, 1999; *VHJ,* November 2002, 30; Beller, "Learning to Breathe Again," 112; Haynie, "Greener Pastures," 48–51.

132. Anne Bromley, "You Can Learn a Lot from a Cowboy," www.virginia.edu./insideuva/2001/07/cowboy.html.

133. *Roanoke Times,* July 30, 2003; *Richmond Times-Dispatch,* December 22, 1996.

134. *Richmond News Leader,* December 7, 1928; March 19, 1957; December 12, 1980; *Richmond Times-Dispatch,* October 18, 1993. Lady Wonder also reportedly led authorities to the bodies of three missing children, but since that item appeared in the *National Enquirer* of October 31, 1978, it is probably best taken with a grain of salt.

135. *Richmond Times-Dispatch,* April 12, 1953.

136. Mariner, *Off 13,* 40–41; Hendricks, *International Encyclopedia,* 48; Edwards, *Encyclopedia of the Horse,* 244.

137. Hendricks, *International Encyclopedia,* 49; Mariner, *Off 13,* 42, 44, 53; Edwards, *Encyclopedia of the Horse,* 244–45.

138. Henry, *Dear Marguerite Henry,* 1–23.

139. Mariner, *Off 13,* 44; Henry, *Dear Marguerite Henry,* 23, 32; Henry, *Pictorial Life Story of Misty,* 10.

140. Henry, *Pictorial Life Story of Misty,* 7, 12.

141. Ibid., 22–23, 34, 45.

142. Ibid., 45, 58, 71.

143. Ibid., 77, 87, 89, 90, 92, 94, 97, 100, 116, 136; Mariner, *Off 13,* 46; *Richmond News Leader,* March 12, 1962.

144. Henry, *Pictorial Life Story of Misty,* 104, 107, 110, 127; Sutton, "When Hollywood Made Chincoteague a Star," 37–38; Stallsmith, "Chincoteague to Celebrate Debut of 'Misty.'"

145. Henry, *Pictorial Life Story of Misty,* 131; Stallsmith, "Saluting a Legend."

146. Henry, *Pictorial Life Story of Misty,* 132–33; *Richmond Times-Dispatch,* April 19, 1990; November 25, 1993.

147. *Richmond Times-Dispatch,* April 19, 1990; *Washington Post,* July 25, 1996.

148. *Charlottesville Daily Progress,* June 29, 1997; Stallsmith, "Chincoteague to Celebrate Debut of 'Misty.'"

149. Stallsmith, "Chincoteague to Celebrate Debut of 'Misty'"; Stallsmith, "Return to Chincoteague."

150. Mariner, *Off 13,* 44; Stallsmith, "You Can Lead a Horse to Water."

151. Typescript obituary, Wesley Dennis scrapbooks, National Sporting Library; obituary, *Richmond Times-Dispatch,* September 5, 1966; *Falmouth Enterprise,* August 17, 1956; L. Campbell, "Inspired Animations," 7–8; *Fauquier Democrat,* October 13, 1960; Marguerite Henry to Sue, Morgan, and Devon Dennis, February 22, 1993, Wesley Dennis scrapbooks, NSL. Some newspaper articles, such as one in the *Akron Beacon Journal,* on October 5, 1959, refer to a John Singer Sargent painting propped up against the wall of Dennis's studio.

152. Julie Campbell, "Jean Bowman," 151–52. Bowman died in a small-plane crash. The trust provides the AAEA's Jean Bowman Memorial Award for Painting. Her family also divided her library between the AAEA and the National Sporting Library.

153. L. Campbell, "Eve Fout Is Fortifying Hunting's Future," 20–27. The equestrian careers of Fout's husband, Paul (who died in 2005), and of her children Nina, Doug, and Virginia are discussed elsewhere in the book.

154. *Richmond News Leader,* October 24, 1941.

155. Mackay-Smith, "Fairfax Harrison."

156. *Washington Post,* October 30, 1966; April 2, 1972; February 1, 1990; Korda, *Horse People,* 34.

157. *Washington Post,* October 6, 2000; *Richmond Times-Dispatch,* October 6, 2000.

158. *Richmond News Leader,* November 7, 1979.

159. *Richmond Times-Dispatch,* December 11, 1961; Archer, *Arabian Horse,* 71; *Charlottesville Daily Progress,* June 29, 1969; *Washington Post,* November 6, 2002.

160. *Richmond Times-Dispatch,* January 14, 1952; *VHJ,* September 2002, 44; conversation with Roddy Moore, 2002; *Roanoke Times,* April 22, 2005.

161. Program, Rockingham County Fair, August 12–17, 2002; Program, Rockbridge Regional Fair, 2004; Oldham, "Behind the Scenes at the Upperville Horse Show," 51; *Lexington News-Gazette,* July 14, 2004; *Roanoke Times,* June 25, 2004.

162. *Lexington News-Gazette,* November 24, 2004.

163. www.nationaljousting.com/fame.htm.

164. *Richmond Times-Dispatch,* November 30, 1997; Friel, "Dreams, Dollars and Devotees," 18, 20; *Lexington News-Gazette,* September 24, 2003; *VHJ,* April 2003, 32–34. Phillips was once married to Britain's Princess Anne, herself an Olympic eventer; their daughter, Zara, is also a skilled competitor.

165. Scott Shenk, "Hunt Country Bible," www.citizenet.com, May 30, 2002. Webb was a descendant of Jefferson Davis, the president of the Confederacy (Slater, *Hunt Country,* 85).

166. *Washington Post,* August 9, 2002; November 20, 2006. An example of the flip-flop that occurred in the twentieth century: In 1900, with a human population in Virginia of 1.8 million, 82 percent lived in the country. By 1990, with 6.1 million people, 80 percent lived in towns and cities. Growth also affected the cattle market of northern Virginia, as developers subdivided farms into small lots more suited to keeping horses. In a strange way, this may have benefited the horse industry, as the Fauquier Livestock Exchange handled fewer cattle and more horses for old-timers and newcomers alike (ibid., April 20, 2004).

167. All figures in this and the preceding two paragraphs come from *Virginia 2001 Equine Survey Report,* Virginia Agricultural Statistics Service. In 2005, the *Chronicle of the Horse* reported that the American Horse Council counted 9.2 million horses in the United States, with between 200,000 and 281,000 in Virginia (July 8, 2005, 40).

# BIBLIOGRAPHY

Anderson, Paul Christopher. *Blood Image: Turner Ashby in the Civil War and the Southern Mind.* Baton Rouge: Louisiana State University Press, 2002.

Anderson, Virginia DeJohn. *Creatures of Empire: How Domestic Animals Transformed Early America.* New York: Oxford University Press, 2004.

Archer, Rosemary. *The Arabian Horse.* London: J. A. Allen, 1992.

Armstrong, Marcia. "Saddling Up for the Last Ride." *Town & County* (weekend supplement of Fredericksburg *Free Lance-Star*), June 29, 2002, 8–11.

Armstrong, Virginia Winmill Livingstone. *"Gone Away" with the Winmills: A Biography of Robert Campbell Winmill and Viola Townsend Winmill of Warrenton, Virginia, Covering the Period from 1884 to 1975.* Warwickshire, England: Tomes of Leamington, 1977.

Ausband, Stephen Conrad. *Byrd's Line: A Natural History.* Charlottesville: University of Virginia Press, 2002.

Bear, James A., Jr., ed. *Jefferson at Monticello: Recollections of a Monticello Slave and of a Monticello Overseer.* Charlottesville: University Press of Virginia, 1967.

——, and Lucia C. Stanton, eds. *Jefferson's Memorandum Books: Accounts, with Legal Records and Miscellany, 1767–1826.* 2 vols. Princeton: Princeton University Press, 1997.

Beller, Elizabeth. "Learning to Breathe Again." *Practical Horseman,* November 2001, 112.

Bromley, Anne. "You Can Learn a Lot from a Cowboy." www.virginia.edu/insideuva/2001/07/cowboy.html.

Bent, Newell. *American Polo.* New York: Macmillan, 1929.

Bernard, John. *Retrospections of America, 1797–1811.* Edited by Mrs. Bayle Bernard. New York: Harper, 1887.

Berry, Barbara J. *The Standardbreds.* South Brunswick and New York: A. S. Barnes, 1979.

Betts, Edwin Morris, ed. *Thomas Jefferson's Farm Book*. Charlottesville: University Press of Virginia, 1976.

Betts, Edwin Morris, and James Adam Bear Jr., eds. *The Family Letters of Thomas Jefferson*. Columbia: University of Missouri Press, 1966.

Bishko, Lucretia Ramsey. "A Spanish Stallion for Albemarle." *Virginia Magazine of History and Biography* (April 1968): 146–80.

Blanchard, Elizabeth Amis Cameron, and Manly Wade Wellman. *The Life and Times of Sir Archie: The Story of America's Greatest Thoroughbred, 1805–1833*. Chapel Hill: University of North Carolina Press, 1958.

Boatner, Mark M., III. *The Civil War Dictionary*. New York: David McKay, 1959.

Bowen, Edward L. *The Jockey Club's Illustrated History of Thoroughbred Racing in America*. Boston, New York, Toronto, London: Little, Brown, 1994.

Bracey, Susan L. *Life by the Roaring Roanoke: A History of Mecklenburg County, Virginia*. Boydton, Va.: Mecklenburg County Bicentennial Commission, 1977.

Brady, Patricia, ed. *George Washington's Beautiful Nelly: The Letters of Eleanor Parke Custis Lewis to Elizabeth Bordley Gibson, 1794–1851*. Columbia: University of South Carolina Press, 1991.

Breen, T. H. "Horses and Gentlemen: The Cultural Significance of Gambling among the Gentry of Virginia." *William and Mary Quarterly*. 3rd ser., 34, no. 2 (April 1977): 239–57.

Brooke, Geoffrey. *The Way of a Man with a Horse*. London: Seeley, Service, 1929.

Brown, Everett Somerville, ed. *William Plumer's Memorandum of Proceedings in the United States Senate, 1803–1807*. New York: Macmillan, 1923.

Brown, Katharine L., and Nancy T. Sorrells. *Virginia's Cattle Story: The First Four Centuries*. Staunton, Va.: Lot's Wife, 2004.

Burke, Jackie C. *Capital Horse Country: A Rider's and Spectator's Guide*. McLean, Va.: EPM, 1994.

Busbey, Hamilton. *The Trotting and the Pacing Horse in America*. New York: Macmillan, 1904.

Campbell, Judith. *Police Horses*. New York: A. S. Barnes, 1968.

Campbell, Julie A. "Christopher Tompkins Chenery." *Dictionary of Virginia Biography*, 3:196–97. Richmond: Library of Virginia, 2006.

———. "Jean Bowman." *Dictionary of Virginia Biography*, 2:151–52. Richmond: Library of Virginia, 2001.

Campbell, Lisa. "Eve Fout Is Fortifying Hunting's Future." *Chronicle of the Horse*, September 23, 2005, 20–27.

———. "Inspired Animations: The Art of Wesley Dennis." *Middleburg Life*, September 2001, 7–8.

———. "The Origin of the War Horse." *National Sporting Library Newsletter*, Summer 2002.

Campbell, Mary. "Lucy Long." *William & Mary Quarterly*, ser. 2, 19 (1939): 471–73.

Campbell, T. E. *Colonial Caroline: A History of Caroline County, Virginia*. Richmond: Dietz Press, 1954.

Carter, William Joseph. Scrapbooks, 1881–1941. Library of Virginia, Richmond.

Cashman, Peter, and Sandra Cooke. "Troubling Trends in NCAA Equestrian Sport." *Practical Horseman,* December 2004, 18–21.

*Charles City County Historical Society Newsletter,* June 1998.

Chastellux, Marquis de. *Travels in North America in the Years 1780, 1781 and 1782.* Edited by Howard C. Rice Jr. 2 vols. Chapel Hill: University of North Carolina Press for Institute of Early American History and Culture, 1963.

Clancy, Joe. "Battleship's Amazing Blast from the Past." *Mid-Atlantic Thoroughbred,* June 2008, 28–31.

Clayton, Michael, ed. *Cross Country Riding.* New York: Dutton, 1977.

Click, Patricia C. *The Spirit of the Times: Amusements in Nineteenth-Century Baltimore, Norfolk, and Richmond.* Charlottesville: University Press of Virginia, 1989.

Cohen, Kenneth. "Well Calculated for the Farmer: Thoroughbreds in the Early National Chesapeake, 1790–1850." *Virginia Magazine of History and Biography* 115, no. 3 (2007): 370–411.

*Colonial Williamsburg Animal News* 2, no. 2 (June-July 1989); and 2, no. 7 (August-September 1990).

Conn, George H. *The Arabian Horse in America.* Woodstock, Vt.: Countryman Press, 1957.

Cooke, Sandra. "Beanie Baby!" *Practical Horseman,* May 2001, 44.

Cooke, Sandra, and Shara Rutberg. "Career-Boosting Equine Degrees." *Practical Horseman,* December 2003, 35.

Courts, John Dulany, and Frank J. Courts. "Colonel Richard Henry Dulany: A Founder's Legacy, Part I." *Upperville Sesquicentenary Newsletter,* August 2002, electronic publication.

Cronin, Paul D. *Schooling and Riding the Sport Horse: A Modern American Hunter/Jumper System.* Charlottesville: University of Virginia Press, 2004.

Crooks, Esther J., and Ruth W. Crooks. *The Ring Tournament in the United States.* Richmond: Garrett and Massie, 1936.

Culver, Francis Barnum. *Blooded Horses of Colonial Days: Classic Horse Matches in America before the Revolution.* Baltimore: Privately printed, 1922.

Custis, George Washington Parke. *Recollections and Private Memoirs of Washington, by his Adopted Son, George Washington Parke Custis.* New York: Derby and Jackson, 1860.

Dabney, Virginius. *Richmond: The Story of a City.* Charlottesville: University Press of Virginia, 1990.

———. *Virginia: The New Dominion.* Garden City, N.Y.: Doubleday, 1971.

Davis, Thomas W. *A Crowd of Honorable Youths: Historical Essays on the First 150 Years of the Virginia Military Institute.* Lexington: VMI Sesquicentennial Committee, 1988.

Dederer, John Morgan. "Abraham Buford." *Dictionary of Virginia Biography,* 2:382–83. Richmond: Library of Virginia, 2001.

Denhardt, Robert Moorman. *The Quarter Running Horse: America's Oldest Breed.* Norman: University of Oklahoma Press, 1979.

Dennis, Wesley. Scrapbooks. National Sporting Library, Middleburg, Va.

*Dictionary of Virginia Biography.* Vols. 1–3. Richmond: Library of Virginia, 1998, 2001, 2006.

Dittrich, James F. "Horses at VMI." In *A Crowd of Honorable Youths: Historical Essays on the First 150 Years of the Virginia Military Institute,* ed. Thomas W. Davis, 163–65. Lexington: VMI Sesquicentennial Committee, 1988.

Dillon, Jane Marshall. *Form over Fences: A Pictorial Critique of Jumping for the Junior Rider.* New York: Arco, 1972.

———. *School for Young Riders.* New York: Arco, 1958.

Dooley, Louise K. "VMI's Mounted Drill Team: Horses Are Welcomed Back to VMI's Parade Ground." *Virginia Military Institute Alumni Review,* Spring 2002, 131–32.

Douglas, Henry Kyd. *I Rode with Stonewall.* Chapel Hill: University of North Carolina Press, 1940.

Durden, Chauncey. "Home Ground of Great Thoroughbreds: Virginia's Meadow Farm." *Commonwealth,* August 1962, 19–22.

Easterly, Harry W. Jr. Interview by the author. November 2002.

Edgar, Patrick Nisbett. Extracts concerning Virginia racehorses from "The American Turf Register, Sportsman's Herald and General Stud Book." Typescript. Library of Virginia, Richmond.

Edwards, Elwyn Hartley. *The Encyclopedia of the Horse.* New York: Dorling Kindersley, 1994.

Eisenberg, John. *The Great Match Race: When North Met South in America's First Sports Spectacle.* Boston and New York: Houghton Mifflin, 2006.

———. "Off to the Races." *Smithsonian,* August 2004, 8–12.

Eldridge, Annie. "Jimmy Wofford Teaches the World." *Chronicle of the Horse,* May 19, 1995. Available at www.jimwofford.com.

Ensminger, M. E. *Horses and Horsemanship.* Danville, Ill.: Interstate, 1977.

Equestrian and Racing Scrapbook. National Sporting Library, Middleburg, Va.

*Equine Science at Virginia Tech.* Brochure.

Erigero, Patricia. "Planet." www.tbheritage.com/portraits/Planet.html.

"Famous War Horses of Confederate Leaders." Typescript. Copied from United Daughters of the Confederacy Filing and Lending Department, Library of Virginia, Richmond.

Faust, Drew Gilpin. "Equine Relics of the Civil War." *Southern Cultures* (Spring 2000): 23–49.

Fausz, J. Frederick. "Samuel Argall." *Dictionary of Virginia Biography,* 1:197–99. Richmond: Library of Virginia, 1998.

Fields, Joseph E., comp. *"Worthy Partner": The Papers of Martha Washington.* Westport, Ct.: Greenwood Press, 1994.

Fischer, David Hackett. *Albion's Seed: Four British Folkways in America.* New York: Oxford University Press, 1989.

Fischer, David Hackett, and James C. Kelly. *Away, I'm Bound Away: Virginia and the Westward Movement.* Richmond: Virginia Historical Society, 1993.

Fitzpatrick, John C., ed. *The Writings of George Washington from the Original Manuscript Sources, 1745–1799.* Washington, D.C.: U.S. Government Printing Office, 1931–44.

Flexner, James Thomas. *Washington: The Indispensable Man.* Boston: Back Bay Books, Little, Brown, 1969.
Flood, Charles Bracelen. *Lee: The Last Years.* Boston: Houghton Mifflin, 1981.
Fontana, Bernard L. *Entrada: The Legacy of Spain and Mexico in the United States.* Tucson: Southwest Parks and Monuments Association, 1994.
Fox, Tyler J., and John L. Knapp. *Economic Impact of the Virginia Horse Center.* Charlottesville: Center for Public Service, University of Virginia, 1991.
Freeman, Douglas Southall. *Lee's Lieutenants: A Study in Command.* 3 vols. New York: Charles Scribner's Sons, 1949.
———. *R. E. Lee: A Biography.* 4 vols. New York: Charles Scribner's Sons, 1935.
Freise, Kathy. "The Carriages of Colonial Williamsburg." *Virginia Horse Journal,* September 2007, 36.
Friel, Lisa B. "Dreams, Dollars and Devotees Make Virginia Tops for Eventing." *Virginia Horse Journal,* June 2001, 18.
———. "Spirit of America: Virginia Quarter Horses Past and Present." *Virginia Horse Journal,* November 2001, 22–26.
———. "Virginia Drivers Take New Direction." *Virginia Horse Journal,* September 2001, 34–40.
Fusonie, Alan, and Donna Jean Fusonie. *George Washington: Pioneer Farmer.* Mount Vernon, Va.: Mount Vernon Ladies' Association, 1998.
*General Lee's Traveller on the Campus of Washington and Lee.* Brochure at Lee Chapel Museum at Washington and Lee University.
Groome, H. C. "The Fox and the Hounds." *Commonwealth,* October 1934, 10, 32.
Grubbs, Don. "Polo in Middleburg at Phipps Field: Unique Spectacle on Sunday Afternoon." *Spur of Virginia,* July 1967, 66–67.
Haines, Francis. *Horses in America.* New York: Thomas Y. Crowell, 1971.
Harris, Moira C. *Dressage by the Letter: A Guide for the Novice.* New York: Howell Book House, 1997.
Harrison, Fairfax. *The Background of the American Stud Book.* Richmond: Old Dominion Press, 1933.
———. *The Belair Stud, 1747–1761.* Richmond: Old Dominion Press, 1929.
———. *Early American Turf-Stock, 1730–1830.* Richmond: Old Dominion Press, 1934–35.
———. *The Equine F.F.Vs.: A Study of the Evidence for the English Horses Imported into Virginia before the Revolution.* Richmond: Old Dominion Press, 1928.
———. *The Roanoke Stud, 1795–1833.* Richmond: Old Dominion Press, 1930.
Hayes, M. Horace. *Veterinary Notes for Horse Owners: A Manual of Horse Medicine & Surgery.* 14th ed. New York: Charles Scribner's Sons, 1949.
Haynie, Terri. "Greener Pastures." *Virginia Horse Journal,* July 2008, 48–51.
Hendricks, Bonnie L. *International Encyclopedia of Horse Breeds.* Norman: University of Oklahoma Press, 1995.
Henry, Marguerite. *Dear Marguerite Henry,.* Chicago: Rand McNally, 1978.
———. *King of the Wind: The Story of the Godolphin Arabian.* Chicago: Rand McNally, 1948.
———. *Misty of Chincoteague.* Chicago: Rand McNally, 1947.
———. *A Pictorial Life Story of Misty.* Chicago: Rand McNally, 1976.

——. *Stormy: Misty's Foal.* Chicago: Rand McNally, 1963.

Henson, Edward L., Jr., James M. Morgan Jr., and James L. Morrison Jr. *Keydet Grey and Garry Owen: The Horse at VMI.* Lexington: Virginia Military Institute, 2006.

Herr, John K., and Edward S. Wallace. *The Story of the U.S. Cavalry, 1775–1942.* Boston: Little, Brown, 1953.

Hervey, John. *Racing in America, 1665–1865.* 2 vols. New York: Scribner Press for the Jockey Club, 1944.

Hewitt, Lynn. "Horses Return to Virginia Military Institute." *Virginia Horse Journal,* May 2002, 16.

Hill, Dawn. "An Interview with Torrance Watkins." www.flyingchanges.com.

Hinsdale, Harriet. *Confederate Gray: The Story of Traveller, General Robert E. Lee's Favorite Horse.* Peterborough, N.H.: R. R. Smith, 1963.

Hoffman, Dean A. "Leader of the Pack." *Hoof Beats.* www.ustrotting.com.

"Horse Country." *Charlottesville Daily Progress,* May 31, 1988, supplement.

"Horseman of the Year: Alexander Mackay-Smith." *Chronicle of the Horse,* February 5, 1999, 9–14.

"Horses: Summary." In "Horses" file, Monticello.

Hotaling, Edward. *The Great Black Jockeys: The Lives and Times of the Men Who Dominated America's First National Sport.* Rocklin, Calif.: Prima, 1999.

Hunt, Frazier, and Robert Hunt. *Horses and Heroes: The Story of the Horse in America for 450 Years.* New York: Charles Scribner's Sons, 1949.

Hurt, Frances Hallam. "The Full Return of the Quarter Horse." *Commonwealth,* August 1963, 24–26.

Hutcheson, Nathaniel Goode. *What Do You Know About Horses? Mecklenburg County and the Aristocratic Thoroughbreds.* Clarksville, Va.: Clarksville Printing, 1958.

Iliff, Elizabeth. "Playing by the Rules." *Practical Horseman,* December 2000, 47.

"Information on VMI Mounted Service." Typescript, n.d. VMI Archives.

Isaac, Rhys. *The Transformation of Virginia, 1740–1790.* Chapel Hill: University of North Carolina Press for the Omohundro Institute of Early American History and Culture, 1999.

Jaffer, Nancy. "Olympics—Athens 2004: From Surprise to Predictable." *Practical Horseman,* November 2004, 28–39.

——. "There'll Never Be Another Gem Twist . . ." *Practical Horseman,* June 2006, 19.

James, Marquis. *The Border Captain: Andrew Jackson.* New York: Garden City Publishing, 1940.

Jefferson, Thomas. *The Jefferson Cyclopedia.* New York: Funk and Wagnalls, 1900.

——. *Notes on the State of Virginia.* Electronic Text Center, University of Virginia Library. http://etext.lib.virginia.edu/modeng/modengJ.browse.html.

Johnson, Pegram, III. "John Baylor." *Dictionary of Virginia Biography,* 1:406–7. Richmond: Library of Virginia, 1998.

Kamoie, Laura Croghan. *Irons in the Fire: The Business History of the Tayloe Family and Virginia's Gentry, 1700–1860.* Charlottesville: University of Virginia Press, 2007.

Kelso, William M. *Jamestown: The Buried Truth.* Charlottesville: University of Virginia Press, 2006.

Korda, Michael. *Horse People: Scenes from the Riding Life.* New York: HarperCollins, 2003.

Ladin, Lou Ann Meadows, and Wayne Dementi. *State Fair of Virginia since 1854: More Than a Midway.* Manakin-Sabot, Va.: Dementi Milestone, 2006.

Larrabee, Sterling. "The Horse in Virginia." *Commonwealth,* October 1934, 11–12.

Lawrence, Richard. *The Complete Farrier and British Sportsman.* London: Thomas Kelly, 1816.

Lay, M. G. *Ways of the World: A History of the World's Roads and of the Vehicles That Used Them.* New Brunswick, N.J.: Rutgers University Press, 1992.

Le, Sam. "Horsing Around: Virginia Polo Gets Down and Dirty." *Virginia: The University of Virginia Alumni News,* Summer 2002, 31–35.

Lee, Henry. *Memoirs of the War in the Southern Department of the United States.* New York: University Publishing, 1869.

Lees, Douglas. "Middleburg Polo at Phipps Field." *Spur of Virginia,* August 1968, 30–31.

Leonard, Thomas C. "Remount Depot." *Richmond Times-Dispatch,* December 4, 1939, Sunday magazine, 2.

Lewis, Henry W. "Nineteenth Century Horses and Horsemen in Southampton County, Virginia." *Southampton County Historical Society Bulletin,* March 1983, 23–27.

Linford, Lloyd J. "The Horses of George Washington." *Horses for Juniors! The Magazine for Young Horse Lovers,* January/February 1982, 12.

Loch, Sylvia. *Dressage: The Art of Classical Riding.* North Pomfret, Vt.: Trafalgar Square, 1990.

Longrigg, Roger. *The History of Horse Racing.* New York: Stein and Day, 1972.

Maass, John. "To Disturb the Assembly: Tarleton's Charlottesville Raid and the British Invasion of Virginia, 1781." *Virginia Cavalcade* 49, no. 4 (Autumn 2000): 148–57.

Mackay-Smith, Alexander. *Blue Ridge Hunt: The First Hundred Years.* Berryville, Va.: Blue Ridge Press, 1988.

———. *The Colonial Quarter Race Horse: America's First Breed of Horses, America's Native Breed of Running Horses, the World's Oldest Breed of Race-horses, Prime Source of Short Speed.* Richmond: Whittet and Shepperson, 1983.

———. "Fairfax Harrison: Genius of the Turf." *National Sporting Library Newsletter,* n.d. Copy in *Dictionary of Virginia Biography* file, Library of Virginia, Richmond.

———. *Foxhunting in North America: A Comprehensive Guide to Organized Foxhunting in the United States and Canada.* Millwood, Va.: American Foxhound Club, 1985.

———. *The Race Horses of America, 1832–1872: Portraits and Other Paintings by Edward Troye.* Saratoga Springs, N.Y.: National Museum of Racing, 1981.

———. *Speed and the Thoroughbred: The Complete History.* Lanham, Md.: Derrydale Press, 2000.

———. *The Thoroughbred in the Lower Shenandoah Valley, 1785–1842.* Winchester: Pifer Printing, 1948.

Mackay-Smith, Alexander, Jean R. Druesedow, and Thomas Ryder. *Man and the Horse: An Illustrated History of Equestrian Apparel.* New York: Metropolitan Museum of Art and Simon and Schuster, 1984.

Mackay-Smith, Alexander, and Norman M. Fine, eds. *American Foxhunting Stories.* Millwood, Va.: Millwood House, 1996.

Magee, John. "A Very Precise Gold Medalist and a Kiss from Touch of Class." *Virginia Country,* January/February 1985, 55–59.

Mariner, Kirk. *Off 13: The Eastern Shore of Virginia Guidebook*. New Church, Va.: Miona, 1997.

Martin, Ann. *The Masters of Show Jumping*. New York: Howell Book House, 1991.

Mason, Richard. *The Gentleman's New Pocket Farrier*. Richmond, Va.: Peter Cottom, 1820.

McCary, Ben C. *Indians in Seventeenth-Century Virginia*. 1957. Reprint, Charlottesville: University Press of Virginia, 1992.

McCaslin, Richard B. *Lee in the Shadow of Washington*. Baton Rouge: Louisiana State University Press, 2001.

McClary, Jane McIlvaine. *A Portion for Foxes*. New York: Simon and Schuster, 1972.

McCormick, Kathleen. "Caspian Pony Is a Rare Breed but Excels in Many Disciplines." *Southeast Equine Monthly*, September 2004.

Mellon, Paul, with John Baskett. *Reflections in a Silver Spoon: A Memoir*. New York: Morrow, 1992.

Menino, Holly. *Forward Motion: World-Class Riders and the Horses Who Carry Them*. New York: Lyons Press, 1996.

Mischka, Joseph. *The Percheron Horse in America*. Whitewater, Wisc.: Heart Prairie Press, 1991.

Montgomery, E. S. *The Thoroughbred*. New York: Arco, 1971.

Moon, Vicky. *The Private Passion of Jackie Kennedy Onassis: Portrait of a Rider*. New York: HarperCollins, 2005.

———. *A Sunday Horse: Inside the Grand Prix Show Jumping Circuit*. Sterling, Va.: Capital Books, 2004.

Moore, John Hammond. *Albemarle: Jefferson's County, 1727–1976*. Charlottesville: Albemarle County Historical Society, 1976.

Morris, Robert R. *The United States Pony Clubs, Inc.—1954–2004*. Virginia Beach, Va.: Donning, 2004.

Nack, William. *Secretariat: The Making of a Champion*. Cambridge, Mass.: Da Capo Press, 2002.

Nagel, Paul C. *The Lees of Virginia: Seven Generations of an American Family*. New York: Oxford University Press, 1990.

"Names of Thomas Jefferson's Horses." Typescript. In "Horses" file, Cinder Stanton, Monticello.

*National Cyclopedia of American Biography*. Clifton, N.J.: James T. White, 1984.

Nelson, Paul David. "George Baylor." *Dictionary of Virginia Biography*, 1:402. Richmond: Library of Virginia, 1998.

Noël Hume, Ivor. *The Virginia Adventure, Roanoke to James Towne: An Archaeological and Historical Odyssey*. Charlottesville: University Press of Virginia, 1997.

Norman, Lillian. "Elijah B. White (1864–1926)." In WPA Box 215; photocopy in *Dictionary of Virginia Biography* files, Library of Virginia, Richmond.

O'Connor, Karen. "After Sydney, Time for a Family." *Practical Horseman*, January 2001, 152.

O'Connor, Karen, and David O'Connor, with Nancy Jaffer. *Life in the Galloping Lane*. Gaithersburg, Md.: Primedia Equine Network, 2004.

O'Connor, Sally. "Eventing in North America." In *Cross Country Riding*, ed. Michael Clayton, 163–69, 170, 184. New York: Dutton, 1977.

Oldham, Pamela. "Behind the Scenes at the Upperville Horse Show." *Virginia Living,* June 2004, 50–51.

*Papers of Thomas Jefferson, The.* Princeton: Princeton University Press, 1954–.

Parish, Hunter Dickinson. *Journal and Letters of Philip Vickers Fithian, 1773–1774: A Plantation Tutor of the Old Dominion.* Williamsburg: Colonial Williamsburg Inc., 1943.

"Paul R. Fout." Obituary. *Chronicle of the Horse,* August 26, 2005, 94.

Perdue, Charles L., Jr., and Nancy J. Martin-Perdue. *Talk about Trouble: A New Deal Portrait of Virginians in the Great Depression.* Chapel Hill: University of North Carolina Press, 1996.

Perrin, Blanche Chenery. "Time Out of Mind: A Memoir." Manuscript. Special Collections, Alderman Library, University of Virginia.

Peters, Anne. "America's Annual Leading Sires, 1700s-2002." www.tbheritage.com/HistoricSires/AmLeadSires.html.

———. "Boston." www.tbheritage.com/portraits/Boston.html.

———. "Byerley Turk." www.tbheritage.com/Portraits/Byerley Turk.html.

———. "Diomed." www.tbheritage.com/portraits/Diomed.html.

———. "Godolphin Arabian." www.tbheritage.com/Portraits/GodolphinArabian.html.

———. "Sir Charles." www.tbheritage.com/portraits/SirCharles.html.

Pierson, Melissa Holbrook. *Dark Horses and Black Beauties: Animals, Women, a Passion.* New York: Norton, 2000.

Pittenger, Peggy Jett. *Morgan Horses.* South Brunswick: A. S. Barnes, 1967.

Pogue, Dennis J. "Every Thing Trim, Handsome, and Thriving: Re-creating George Washington's Visionary Farm." *Virginia Cavalcade* 48, no. 4 (Autumn 1999): 158–67.

*Polo in Upper Fauquier.* Pamphlet. 1920. Special Collections, University of Virginia Alderman Library.

Prussing, Eugene E. *The Estate of George Washington, Deceased.* Boston: Little, Brown, 1927.

Rable, George C. *Fredericksburg! Fredericksburg!* Chapel Hill: University of North Carolina Press, 2002.

Randall, Henry Stephens. *The Life of Thomas Jefferson.* 3 vols. New York: Derby and Jackson, 1858.

Ramage, James A. *Gray Ghost: The Life of Col. John Singleton Mosby.* Lexington: University Press of Kentucky, 1999.

Ramsdell, Charles W. "General Robert E. Lee's Horse Supply, 1862–1865." *American Historical Review* 25, no. 4 (July 1930): 758–77.

*Randolph-Macon Woman's College President's Report 2003.*

"Rare Breeds Program." Colonial Williamsburg.

Rasin, Beth. "Overall & Eventing Horse of the Year: Winsome Adante." *Chronicle of the Horse,* February 4, 2005, 9–11.

Rasmussen, William M. S., and Robert S. Tilton. *George Washington: The Man behind the Myths.* Charlottesville: University Press of Virginia, 1999.

Rhinesmith, W. Donald. "Traveller: 'Just the Horse for General Lee,'" *Virginia Cavalcade* 33, no. 1 (Summer 1983): 38–47.

Robertson, James I., Jr. *Stonewall Jackson: The Man, the Soldier, the Legend.* New York: Macmillan USA, 1997.

Robertson, William H. P. *The History of Thoroughbred Racing in America.* Englewood Cliffs, N.J.: Prentice-Hall, 1964.

Rose, Laura. "The National Sporting Library: Horses from A–Z." *Virginia Librarian* (October–December 1995): 5–8.

Rountree, Helen C. *Pocahontas's People: The Powhatan Indians of Virginia through Four Centuries.* Norman: University of Oklahoma Press, 1990.

Rutland, Robert Allen. "Virginians & Their Horses." *Iron Worker,* Winter 1979, 2–15.

Salmon, Emily J., and Edward D. C. Campbell Jr. *The Hornbook of Virginia History: A Ready-Reference Guide to the Old Dominion's People, Places, and Past.* Richmond: Library of Virginia, 1994.

"Salute to the Father of the Forward Seat, A." *Practical Horseman,* January 2000, 43.

Salvator. "Great American Breeders of Early Days." *Turf and Sport Digest,* April 1936, 36–37, 85–87.

Sands, Oliver Jackson, Jr. *This Is the Story of the Deep Run Hunt Club.* Richmond: Sands, 1977.

Sanders, Alvin Howard, and Wayne Dinsmore, comps. *A History of the Percheron Horse.* Chicago: Breeders Gazette Print/Sanders Publishing, 1917.

Scott, Marion duPont. *Montpelier: The Recollections of Marion duPont Scott.* As told to Gerald Strine. New York: Charles Scribner's Sons, 1976.

Self, Margaret Cabell. *Horses of Today: Arabian, Thoroughbred, Saddle Horse, Standardbred, Western, Pony.* New York: Duell, Sloan and Pearce, 1964.

———. *Horses: Their Selection, Care and Handling.* New York: A. S. Barnes, 1943.

"Sir Archy, 1805–1833." *Goochland County Historical Society Newsletter,* May 2001.

Slater, Kitty. *The Hunt Country of America.* South Brunswick and New York: A. S. Barnes, 1967.

———. *Upperville Colt and Horse Show.* Show program, 1999.

Slatta, Richard W., ed. *The Cowboy Encyclopedia.* New York: Norton, 1994.

Smart, Bruce. *A Community of the Horse: Partnerships.* Middleburg, Va.: Lost Mountain Graphics, 2003.

Splan, Rebecca (assistant professor, Virginia Tech). Telephone interview by the author, September 6, 2002.

*Spur of Virginia,* February 1968, 48.

Stallsmith, Pamela. "Chincoteague to Celebrate Debut of 'Misty.'" *Richmond Times-Dispatch,* July 27, 1997.

———. "Return to Chincoteague." *Richmond Times-Dispatch,* September 18, 2000.

———. "Saluting a Legend: Family, Others Will Honor 'Misty' Author Henry." *Richmond Times-Dispatch,* December 7, 1997.

———. "You Can Lead a Horse to Water." *Richmond Times-Dispatch,* July 25, 2002.

Stewart, Charles. "My Life as a Slave." *Harper's Magazine* 69 (1884): 730–38.

Stewart-Spears, Genie. "Rogers-Buttram Endures for Biltmore Victory." *Chronicle of the Horse,* June 9, 2006, 32–33.

———. "Valerie Kanavy." www.aerc.org.

Stoneridge, M. A. *Great Horses of Our Time.* Garden City, N.Y.: Doubleday, 1972.

Stong, Philip Duffield. *Horses and Americans.* New York: Frederick A. Stokes, 1939.

Strassburger, John. "A Final Run for 3 Magic Beans." *Chronicle of the Horse,* May 12, 2006, 18.

Straube, Beverly, and Nicholas Luccketti. *1995 Interim Report*. Jamestown Discovery, 1996.
Sutton, Elizabeth. "When Hollywood Made Chincoteague a Star." *Virginia Living*, June 2003, 37–38.
"Theodore O'Connor, 1995–2008." *Virginia Horse Journal*, July 2008, 12.
Thomas, Emory M. *Bold Dragoon: The Life of J.E.B. Stuart*. New York: Harper and Row, 1986.
——. *Robert E. Lee: A Biography*. New York: Norton, 1995.
Thompson, James Westfall. *A History of Livestock Raising in the United States, 1607–1860*. U.S. Dept of Agriculture, 1942. Reprint, Wilmington, Del.: Scholarly Resources, 1973.
Travis, Lorraine. *The Mule*. London: J. A. Allen, 1990.
"Tribute to Theodore O'Connor, A." *Chronicle of the Horse*, June 13, 2008, 38–39.
Trice, Lewis Latane. *Horse Tales, Oh, doo-dah-day! The Standardbred Trotters and Pacers: A Brief Historical Narrative about the Standardbred Trotters and Pacers and Harness Racing in Virginia's Northern Neck and Middle Peninsula Areas and the People Who Made It Possible*. Privately printed, 1999.
Twohig, Dorothy, ed. *George Washington's Diaries: An Abridgement*. Charlottesville: University Press of Virginia, 1999.
Tyler-McGraw, Marie. *At the Falls: Richmond, Virginia, & Its People*. Chapel Hill: University of North Carolina Press for the Valentine Museum, Richmond, 1994.
Van Clief, Court. "A Champion and a Gentleman." *Virginia Sportsman*, March/April 2004, 8–14.
Vineyard, Ron. *Horses and Vehicles in Virginia, 1788–1800, from Personal Property Tax Records*. Research Report Series 354. Colonial Williamsburg Foundation Library, 1996. In Special Collections, John D. Rockefeller Library, Williamsburg.
*Virginia Tech 8th Annual Hokie Harvest Sale*. Booklet. 2002.
Watson, J.N.P. *The World of Polo, Past and Present*. Sportsman's Press, 1986.
Wert, Jeffry D. "Turner Ashby." *Dictionary of Virginia Biography*, 1:225–26. Richmond: Library of Virginia, 1998.
Wiencek, Henry. *The Hairstons: An American Family in Black and White*. New York: St. Martin's Press, 1999.
Wilson, Charles Reagan, and William Ferris, eds. *Encyclopedia of Southern Culture*. Chapel Hill: University of North Carolina Press, 1989.
Winants, Peter. *Foxhunting with Melvin Poe*. Lanham and New York: Derrydale Press in association with the National Sporting Library, 2002.
——. "A Life of Burning Interests: Remembering Alexander Mackay-Smith." *National Sporting Library Newsletter*, Fall 1998, 3.
——. *Steeplechasing: A Complete History of the Sport in North America*. Lanham, Md.: Derrydale Press, 2000.
Wingfield, Marshall. *A History of Caroline County, Virginia*. Baltimore: Regional Publishing, 1969.
Withington, Ann Fairfax. *Toward a More Perfect Union: Virtue and the Formation of American Republics*. New York: Oxford University Press, 1991.
Wofford, James C. *Take a Good Look Around*. Lanham, Md.: Hamilton Books, 2007.
"Women at the Top." *Practical Horseman*, January 2000, 40.

Workers of the Writers' Program of the Work Projects Administration in the State of Virginia, comps. *Virginia: A Guide to the Old Dominion.* Oxford University Press, 1940. Rev. ed., Richmond: Virginia State Library and Archives, 1992.

*World Guide to Polo Clubs.* Rolex, n.d.

Wright, Sarah J. "The Doswells of Bullfield." *Hanover Historical Society Bulletin,* November 1975, 2–4.

Yates, Bill. "Great Meadow Takes Aim at Polo." *In & Around Horse Country,* June/July 1994, 13.

———. "Rita Mae Brown: 'Never Play Polo with Makeup On!'" *In & Around Horse Country,* June/July 1994, 10–11.

Young, James L. *The World of Marshall P. Hawkins: A Field of Horses.* Dallas: Taylor Publishing, 1988.

# INDEX

*Italicized page numbers refer to illustrations.*

# ILLUSTRATION CREDITS

Photo by Howard Allen, courtesy of Matthew Mackay-Smith: 112
Architect of the Capitol: 6–7
Photo by Sue Byford: 180, 181 top left
Charles City County Center for Local History: 102
Charles Cook Collection, Keeneland Library: 110
Photo by Asim Choudhri: 37 top
The Colonial Williamsburg Foundation: 213 top and bottom
Bob Coglianese and Secretariat.com: 164, 171
Corbis: 168–69
Photo by Hayley Cox: 181 top right
Photo by Brant Gamma: 190
Peter Fischer, Westphalia Ranch, Port Royal, Virginia: 207
Green Bay Morgans, Beaverdam, Virginia: 240 top, 246
Chris Harrison: vi-vii
Photo by Marshall P. Hawkins, distributed by Robert McClanahan, print courtesy of the National Sporting Library: 131, 166, 173, 175, 176 top, 179, 182, 183, 185, 200
Hollins University: 146 bottom
Holsinger Studio Collection, Special Collections, University of Virginia Library: 99 top, 100 top left, 125, 132, 133
Photo by Denise Levy, courtesy of the Florida Cracker Horse Association: 18
Library of Congress. Copy print courtesy of the Museum of the Confederacy, Richmond, Virginia: 76 top; FSA-OWI Collection: 99 bottom left (LC-USF33-002191-M5); Prints and Photographs Division: 10 (LC-USZ62-1310, LC-USZ62-8272), 33 (LC-USZ62-37913), 65 bottom (LC-USZ62-108279), 68 (LC-B811-2381), 70 (LC-USZC4-5989), 71 (LC-B8184-604), 88 bottom (LC-USZ62-14182), 134 left (LC-F81-44411), 146 top (LC-USZ62-61073), 180 top (LC-USF34-057465-E, photo by Marion Post Wolcott), 245 (LC-USZ62-94281), 247 bottom (LC-USZ62-113034)
Library of Virginia: 27, 31, 46, 54, 121, 140, 143, 148 bottom, 152 left, 152 right, 212, 220, 226, 228; Harry C. Mann Photograph Collection: 98 top left and bottom
Photo by Robert Llewellyn: ii-iii, 40, 118–19, 158, 198–99
Mount Vernon Ladies' Association: 2, 9
The Museum of the Confederacy, Richmond, Virginia: 76 bottom, 79, 80–81 (photo by Katherine Wetzel), 88 top
National Gallery of Art, Washington, D.C. 62: Gift of Edgar William and Bernice Chrysler Garbisch, image courtesy of the Board of Trustees
National Museum of Racing and Hall of Fame: 48, 56, 57
National Sporting Library: 29; Gerald Webb Collection: 115, 116, 147, 229; Life Estate of Jacqueline L. Ohrstrom, from bequest of George L. Ohrstrom Jr.: 49; Lucy Linn Collection: 108, 204; Peter Winants Collection: 176 bottom; Sterling Larrabee Papers: 134 right; Wesley Dennis Album: 232, 236
The Old Guard Museum, Fort Myer, Virginia: 215
Photographic Archive, Fairfax County Public Library: 99 bottom right
Portsmouth Public Library: 94
Photo by Kevin Remington: 86 bottom
Richmond Police Mounted Squad: 216 bottom
Photo by Claire Rossiter: 15 middle
Photo by Kay Schlumpf: 181 bottom right
scotsshots.ca: 15 top
Special Collections, John D. Rockefeller, Jr., Library, the Colonial Williamsburg Foundation: 16
State Fair of Virginia: 15 bottom, 209, 211, 248
Photo by Genie Stewart-Spears: 202
Tazewell County Public Library: 96, 100 top right and bottom, 128, 150 bottom
Thomas Jefferson Foundation/Monticello: 37 bottom
Valentine Richmond History Center: 65 top left, 97 top left and bottom, 157, 160, 216 top, 247 top; Beveridge Collection: 137 top; Cook Collection: 64, 101, 105, 126, 127, 129, 136, 138, 148 top, 154, 222
Virginia Historical Society, Richmond: 14, 42, 44, 47, 59, 61, 65 top right, 74, 90, 97 top right, 141
Virginia Horse Center, Lexington: 130, 137 bottom, 142, 181 bottom left, 191, 193, 196, 206, 208, 210, 218, 219, 240 bottom, 241 top and bottom, 242
Virginia Military Institute Archives: 85, 86 top, 123, 145 top, 145 bottom (photo by A. Aubrey Bodine)
Virginia Museum of Fine Arts, Richmond. 23: Oil on canvas, 35 x 48 inches, Paul Mellon Collection, photo by Katherine Wetzel. 28: Engraving on heavy laid paper, 7⅜ inches x 11¼ inches, Paul Mellon Collection, photo by Travis Fullerton. 52–53: Oil on canvas, 25¼ x 35½ inches, gift of Mr. T. Kenneth Ellis, photo by Travis Fullerton. 60: Oil on canvas, 24¾ x 29½ inches, Paul Mellon Collection, photo by Ron Jennings. All photos © Virginia Museum of the Fine Arts.
Washington and Lee University: 92 (photo by Patrick Hinely)
Waynesboro Public Library: 98 top right
Photo by Mary S. Woodson: 217